The Politics of Prose

The Politics of Prose
Essay on Sartre

Denis Hollier

Translation by Jeffrey Mehlman

Foreword by Jean-François Lyotard

Theory and History of Literature, Volume 35

University of Minnesota Press, Minneapolis

The University of Minnesota Press gratefully acknowledges translation assistance provided for this book by the French Ministry of Culture.

Published by the University of Minnesota Press
2037 University Avenue Southeast, Minneapolis MN 55414.
Published simultaneously in Canada
by Fitzhenry & Whiteside Limited, Markham.
Printed in the United States of America.

Library of Congress Cataloging-in-Publication Data

Hollier, Denis.
    The politics of prose.
    (Theory and history of literature ; v. 35)
    Translation of: Politique de la prose.
    Includes index.
    1. Sartre, Jean Paul, 1905-   —Criticism and
interpretation.   I. Title.   II. Series.
PQ2637.A82Z73613   1986   848'.91409   86-11208
ISBN 0-8166-1509-8
ISBN 0-8166-1510-1 (pbk.)

For Tzvetan,
more than entitled.

Theory and History of Literature
Edited by Wlad Godzich and Jochen Schulte-Sasse

The character in this book having been cleansed of the sin of existing in the course of its composition, any resemblance with a (still) real person, whether living or not, would have to be verified and would not be any the less contingent for that.

Queneau

It should be remembered that most critics are men who have not had much luck and who, at the moment when they were about to lose hope, found a quiet little place as guardian of a cemetery. The dead are there; they did nothing but write; they have long been cleansed of the sin of living, and moreover, their lives are known only through other books that still other dead men have written about them. The critic tends to live poorly; his wife does not properly appreciate him; his children are ingrates; he has trouble paying his bills. But it is always possible for him to enter his library, take a book off the shelf, and open it.

Sartre

Contents

Acknowledgments

The completion of this book took place during time granted me by the John Simon Guggenheim Foundation. For its inception, however, I am indebted to the University of California at Berkeley, where Leo Bersani invited me to teach, thereby originating the book's transatlantic *translatio*, that is, the persistent jetlag in which my estrangement with (rather than from) Sartre took root. But I owe the real *translatio*, of course, to Jeffrey Mehlman, who even managed to erase my French accent every time Sartre himself (and Sophie Tucker) had prompted me into a decidedly nonnative English.

Somewhere, I mention the fact that Sartre never lent his reader the helping hand of an index. In this sense, thanks to Robert Harvey, there is now something frankly non-Sartrean, at least in the very last pages of this volume.

Foreword
A Success of Sartre's
Jean-François Lyotard

Translated by Jeffrey Mehlman

I confess that he was neither my favorite novelist nor my favorite philosopher, playwright, or political thinker. To put it bluntly, I did not like the air of *capability* his writings exuded. Hollier alludes to the crisis Sartre went through in the early fifties and to which *Les Mots* bears witness. A doubt began to undermine the redemptive role he had accorded to the writer ever since the revelation that befell him in his captivity. Yet he did not elaborate that doubt, but rather rid himself of it by shifting from the writer's vocation to the "intellectual" 's an identical responsibility for curing the world of alienation. That bit of acting out resulted in a number of unworthy texts (in both tenor and tone), such as the "Réponse à Claude Lefort" and "Les Communistes et la paix." In reading them, the militant I then was (alongside Lefort and several others) experienced the same vague, menacing feeling I had felt ten years earlier as a student of philosophy on reading *L'Etre et le néant.*

In each case, negativity was annexed without any ado by human freedom, and dialectic by project. The latter dimension availed itself of the former in order to set forth its claim to universality. In the face of which, passivity was banal, shameful, and as tempting as a sin. Of their own accord, Being and the world, merging, collapsed into an abject viscosity. The summary diagnostic bearing on the In-Itself (said to be nonsense) found its rhyme in the clear verdict in favor of the unitary Party (capital *P*) against the spontaneous inconsistency of the working "class." Left to itself, the latter fell to (nauseating) pieces, "molecular

Jean-François Lyotard, "Un Succès de Sartre," *Critique* 432 (Feb. 1983).

eddies, a multiplicity of infinitesimal reactions either reinforcing one another or canceling one another out, whose net result is a force that is more physical than human. Namely: the mass(es). The mass(es), which is precisely the negation of the class'' (*Situations* VI). *La Transcendance de l'ego*, read later on, completed the picture: I am nothing, therefore I can do everything.

And the plays? In the age of Artaud, Brecht, and Beckett, of the meditation on signs, representation, and events, his plays were as edifying as those of Diderot, with the single difference that in Sartre's case, sentimental domestic tragedy had yielded the stage to sarcastic political comedy: *Les Mains sales, Les Séquestrés d'Altona*. The theater of the bourgeoisie continues to exist, he thought, but in a moribund state. But how does one know that a class is dying? That he was passionately bent on it is all that is certain, and that desire was itself the mainspring of his politics. But it was not clear that that excellent sentiment would yield decent results on the stage.

As for the novels, the generation that was mine discovered Dos Passos and Faulkner, to be sure, but also Thomas Mann, Joyce, Beckett, and Proust. But what was *Les Chemins de la liberté* compared with them, I wondered. Where did it lead that one had not already been taken by *La Condition humaine, Terre des hommes*, and *Les Misérables*? In what way did his novelistic prose reveal itself to be commensurate with the ''Mallarméan'' crisis? Sartre later declared that he had wanted it Einsteinian, as opposed to the Newtonian universe of the classical novel. But what was at stake in the novel from the time of Joyce and Gertrude Stein was no longer best conceived under the sign of the relativity equations but of the uncertainty principle. The *nouveau roman* set its clock according to Heisenberg and the pagan Danes rather than the pious Einstein.

Later there was a love for *Les Mots*, which gaily confessed the extravagant pretension of its subject to save the world, in the guise of Pardaillan. Sartre seemed to be realizing that something was toying with him. But he quickly couched the matter in the past: ''I have changed. I will recount later on. . . . The retrospective illusion is shattered. . . . I see clearly, I am disabused. . . . I am a man who is awakening, cured of a long, bitter-sweet delirium'' (*Les Mots*). He was dreaming, to be sure, while writing that, and believed nothing (or almost nothing) of it. All the same, he believed just enough of it for *Les Mots* to be possible, had just enough self-deprecating irony and just enough indulgence toward that irony to make of the book a splendid introduction to his Confessions. Writing is a sweet delirium, I agree, but I write as much. It is not Philoctetes, as he believes, but Epimenides, in the version of the liar's paradox quoted by Aristotle: I declare myself on oath to be a perjurer, which in the case of Sartre becomes: I am a traitor, but a self-confessed one. On the last page of *Les Mots*: ''I sometimes wonder whether I am not playing a game of loser wins.'' Indeed, with the sole reservation that it was not *I* who was playing, but writing, and that to believe it was *I* was already to leave the sweet delirium beyond cure at the very moment it was diagnosed.

Without the slightest conversion, the heroism of fiction was transferred to that of action, from *La Mort dans l'âme* in 1949 to "Les Communistes et la paix" in 1952. Sartre's writing once again spared itself an analytic phase, and enlisted an excellent reason — modesty — in justification: "My madness has protected me from the seduction of elitism." As in the case of many others, "politics" enters into play in order to blind the time and place of analysis. That blindness is called lucidity. Under the names of almost random adversaries, praxis is always opposed to the same enemy: Being In-Itself. In *Les Mots*, Sartre polemicizes against another Sartre, the childhood one, and it is in order to shut him definitively up, as may be heard in the very disposition of many a sentence: a brief description of a fact, a short pause, and the (absurd) meaning Poulou attributed to it. There is a repression of anxiety in that demonstrative syntax and in such lapidary "cautionary" tales. Childhood, the figure of disquiet, is vigorously put in its place. It is a matter of affixing, stapling meanings to things in order to be done as quickly as possible with that ultimately unessential phase, which is to be bypassed since it is past, and is of necessity laughable.

Now the arrogance of the polemic is of the same vein as the stylistic regimen administered to Poulou. Allow me to insist on this, somewhat more than Hollier: the discord was painful. Lefort was treated as though he were suffering from the same fantasy that haunted Karl Schweitzer's grandson: escaping from his "situation," "to be missing, like water, bread, or air, to all other men in all other places" (*Les Mots*). Lefort wants to know nothing of his situation — to know neither who he is nor where and whence he is. It frightens him. And that is because "your situation would teach you what you are not (You are not Hegel. You are not Marx. Nor a worker. Nor absolute Mind) and what you are (You are a remarkably intelligent young intellectual who has thoughts on the subject of Marx the way one had thoughts on the subject of women in 1890)" (*Situations* VII). In parentheses, Lefort's situation declares what it is and isn't, thanks to Sartre's pen. Sartre can write what is missing. And it is not Lefort (but water and bread?). Lefort is but a minor elitist or thinking situation, as antiquated as that of the feminists of the end of the century, having nothing to do with the movement of history, with its crude masculine hands. "Woman," a subject for intelligent ideas, like "Marx": the parallel seems ripe for exploitation by Hollier.

If the young man was to be shut up for good, it was because the immanentist notion of history and its struggles that Lefort was in the process of elaborating deprived the Sartrean stage of its principal protagonist, the Absent One, crucial to the sublation of the viscosity of the particular to universality and of the dispersion and contingency of experience to the status of a single drama. In the new Sartrean cast, the Absent One (who, before the crisis of the 1950s, was the writer) is called the Party. If I don't intervene to plead the role of the Party, Lefort will pounce on history, refusing it that lack which the mediator is called on to fulfill. A hole is needed in every lock because a key is needed in order for it to work. "What you refuse on principle I accept without discomfort; and I admit that there are in the workers's collective memory partially or provisionally undecipherable episodes whose key is to be found in the hands of the comintern or of another proletariat." One is not very demanding when it comes to opening the lock. The passkey can be called Stalin, Togliatti, or Mao, as one prefers. What is important is the hole. The situation may be deciphered "by means of a mediation." A mere possibility? No, the liberality continues, this time with reference to modality in addition to name. "It is possible if not necessary to request aid." The comintern or, if you prefer, Togliatti. Mediation as possible or, if you prefer, necessary. In addition, there is no question of "a party imposing its keys: it tries them out, that is all" (*Situations* VII). That was in 1953. The Stalinist apparatus had been trying out its keys for almost thirty years in the locks of the workers' movement, that was all. No forced entry anywhere. Rest assured.

The attempts, in the last analysis, were even fruitful in proportion to their failure, since they left the "request for aid" emanating from the working class still gaping and, consequently, the need for a supreme locksmith unsatisfied. With "Lefortism" in politics (as with Merleau-Pontyism in philosophy), with the opposition between nothingness and being neglected in favor of more local distinctions and that gaping hole receding, who then would forge man? If the Party were no longer missed by the masses or felt to lack amid contingencies, Lefort's proletariat would remain inert like a woman unaware that it was hers to await fulfillment, a "frigid woman." Which is why, "if I were a young employer, I would be a Lefortist" (*Situations* VII).

I am not recalling these oddities of diction in order to relaunch the polemic. Not that Sartre ever made honorable amends. In 1975 he would still not yield an inch. Contat told him: *Socialisme et barbarie*, in the 1950s, was right in its opposition to you, and the libertarian socialism that you discovered in '68 had been promoted by that group for twenty years. Had he not "taken advantage of the passage of time"? Didn't Cohn-Bendit "offer proof of it"? And Sartre responded: first of all, it was "really a two-bit nothing." (To which Contat: and aren't your Maoists today in the minority? Pretending thereby to overlook the fact that the central issue was the role of the Party, in which — since the Maoists were Stalinists — Sartre could be a Maoist.) Second, the group is right today but was wrong then. It was imperative to defend the U.S.S.R. "Truths have 'become,' and what counts is the path leading to them, the work one does on oneself and with others in order to get there" (*Situations* X). The path of my freedom at the time passed through Moscow; today in '75 it passes through Peking, and if you tell me that Peking is no better than Moscow, you will be wrong, even if you are right, because you are moving against the flow of my praxis. How did the exorbitant privilege attached to Sartre's praxis — which made him deaf to everything — achieve legitimation? It was the praxis, he thought, of the most unfavored individuals, the little men, of the everyday sort. The responsibility to everyman is set up against the imperative of truth. A humanist ethic or an intellectual cynicism? In any event, the response sheds light on another problem, that of notoriety: if Sartre was popular, it was because he was a populist.

There can thus be no question of reviving the polemic; Sartre is dead, "he succeeded in depriving us of himself," as Hollier puts it, and this is no time for disputation. I am less sure than Hollier is that he deprived us of himself. At one and the same time, it was always the case from the beginning and it will never be so. Which is what he wanted. He must be having a hearty laugh at the sight of me trying to come to terms today with his immortality. A circumstance he will have owed to Hollier's book. I'm coming to it, but one more preliminary in order not to conceal anything of my prejudices. What was at stake in the polemics (of which the one with Lefort was exemplary) was neither the proletariat, nor Communism, nor the direction of history, but the metaphysics of the subject of will. Sartre was the name of that subject. Even as the autobiography of *Les Mots* was a polemic, the polemics were always an autobiography of that subject. Beneath the adversary's mask was concealed a face from Sartre's Inferno. Other people are hell because they are those faces of identity, of the past, of the inert, passions that the temporality of will deposits: being, degenerated into itself, that the nothingness of the future never stops transcending.

The polemics were negativization in action, the sleight of hand allowing pure lack to hold off the viscosity of all that does no more than be. Sartre himself observed that he had no "debate of ideas" with Lévi-Strauss, Aron, or even Merleau-Ponty, who all the same argued with the intent of refuting him. It was not a matter of being true, convincing, or even persuasive, but exemplary in one's transcendence of the situation. It is not through debate that freedom is defended and expressed, but in running an adversary through. Bourgeois is the name of that which is to be pierced, the secular name of Being In-Itself. And how does one know that one is exemplary in transcending situations when one does not have at one's disposal, as do the Germans, a dialectical logic and a labor of the concept? Through the "work done on oneself and with others," through the suffering felt when one thinks "against oneself" (against viscosity), through the popularity that welcomes you and that is the sign that the common run of humanity recognizes its freedom in your gesture.

Hollier plainly did not have to overcome such prejudices to approach Sartre. He does not debate "in depth" the affairs concerning which the prosecutor has argued. He does not seem to believe in depth. He attempts rather to outspeed the prosecutor. He follows the thread of denials, occasionally right to a series of minute unperceived nodes, but without either love or hatred. He is gay, alert, without disdain, without demagogy, at times amused to the point of disrespect, always guided by a meticulous consideration of the surfaces of the text and the life, with a touch of the rake in his delicacy. I write these notes solely in order to understand how or why, aside from his talent, Hollier succeeded in having his curiosity shared by the worst reader of Sartre that Sartre could conceivably dream of. Might it be that he related to the work in the same way as he related to Bataille's, so diametrically opposed to it? *Politique de la prose* is not a biography or a psychoanalysis of the man or his work; it is neither a study of literature nor a history of ideas nor an erudite essay in textualist criticism. It is an attempt at a portrait of commitment [*engagement*], or rather of its impossibility.

Hollier does not analyze commitment as a philosopher; he rather composes its portrait in small strokes. And the face that emerges from his sketches is then exposed to a devastating light; its grain reveals unexpected asperities; a different face begins to surface within the one we knew. In the triptych entitled *Mirrorical Return*, which Ruth Francken designed from Sartre's face as an old man and which furnished the special issues of *Obliques* with their unforgettable cover, the active and rather good-old-boyish gesture of negativization finds itself similarly infiltrated by an I-don't-know, worse yet, by an I-can't that both anguishes and delivers, like a caress. The writing of commitment is accompanied by its own imposssibility. Such is the "collapse" that Hollier pursues throughout Sartre's text, exposing it to a light that comes from Blanchot in its essential aspect, but he is not conscientious in the manner of so many epigones. More feminine. In the manner of Paulhan, perhaps.

Commitment does not take place. It presupposes a present, a situation construable as a presence, a future end, beneficiaries, a concerted action. But there is no presence at the outset, if the formula be permitted. Roquentin writes: "I am in the Café Mably; I am eating a sandwich, everything is more or less normal." And Hollier: "More or less, he says. The sandwich in one hand, the pen in the other? But which in which? With which hand is he eating and with which hand is he thinking? Try it." (It is as though one were reading Guyotat.) The beginning of *L'Imagination*: "I look at this blank sheet placed on my table." How might one write that without looking at the sheet on which one is writing? Sartre thus begins with perception, by what he believes (as a good phenomenologist) to be reality. Second sentence: "But now, here I am turning my head away. I no longer see the blank sheet." This worries Hollier: the "I" that doesn't see the sheet of paper cannot be the "I" writing that he doesn't see it, since in order to write as much, he is obliged to see it; or perhaps there are two sheets, the one on which I write and the one I no longer see but imagine. (This slippage, which governs every phenomenology, replaces the referential — deictic — value of the term *I* with its autonymical value, *the I*.) Hollier dubs the episode "allegorical." Sartre perpetually believes that he is starting with reality, in the phenomenological sense, and later in the Marxist sense. He begins with "a brief story," a "fable" forged to demonstrate that reality must not be confused with imagination. But the story designated to present reality is itself imaginary. The subsequent political texts, submitted to the same analysis, reveal the same sort of fictioning of the real through writing, the same type of uncontrolled sophism.

And, second, there is no present. "Committed fiction," writes Hollier, quoting Sartre, "should present the present, become 'the reflexive self-presence of a classless society,' 'the world become present to itself.'" But "the present is not up to presenting itself." The "enormous presence" of existence is unpresentable: Roquentin observes that nothing escaped presence, except for itself. "A viscous temporality, a temporality of the absence of temporality," as Hollier concludes. The present is gnawed at by the future and the past, by the nothingness of freedom and the massive inertia of the already accomplished. And yet the idea persists that it is here and now that praxis has its place and time. The presentation of *Les Temps modernes*: the future that interests us is only "the future of *our* era," "a restricted future barely distinguishable from it" [that is, from the future of our era]. The ex-tasis of temporal instances within time has been a matter of course at least since Saint Augustine. Sartre's "sweet delirium" does not lie therein but in the denial of the temporality of writing. Holler clocks the time of the narration of the lunch with the Self-Taught Man, which is in the present. Thirty pages to describe the two hours of the meal. But since they are theoretically written in the present tense of absolute simultaneity (the persistence of the imaginary deictic), Roquention would have had to spend no more than two hours to write the thirty pages (while eating). "Atopical and without extension, the narrative is also instantaneous: it takes neither time nor place. Costs nothing. Its writing, utterly gratuitous, claims not to enter into account." The narrator forgets himself and has himself forgotten. When he writes in the past, he is free to take all the time he wants, and even sustain losses in relation to actual time, like Tristram Shandy or Marsel. But writing in an absolute present entails that writing does not take any time, that the story is directly inscribed in the narrative. As in the principle of the tape recorder, or oral history: "the direct free style," as Hollier dubs it rather nicely. That style obeys a wish: I the writer do not write because I have no being; I merely exist. As an aspect of negativity or negativization, writing is the phase of the For-Itself, and if it is to be, it has neither body, duration, nor place.

And, third, there is no end. Hollier underscores that all of Sartre's books end with a "to be continued," present themselves as unfinished. They are merely, he writes, the serialized installments of a future work. He sees a correlation between that incompletion, the genre of the novel, and the Sartrean problematic of the series. The serialized world — of separation, of idiocy or schizophrenia, of non-sense — which is also the American space deployed by the novelistic technique borrowed from Dos Passos, Faulkner, and Hemingway for *Les Chemins de la liberté*, is opposed to the fusionary world, the being-together of the group reconciled with itself and with meaning, of a free and socialist humanity. Sartre responded to a militant imploring him to write a truly popular work (instead of the Flaubert): "A popular and revolutionary work ought not to be read by each individual in his corner: one would have to be able to read it *together*." But reading cannot be done together, Hollier observes; what can be done together is attending a play or a movie. In the dark, one escapes from the other's gaze, from serialization. Once socialized, the addressee becomes obscure. There is no end for writing because it fails in the presentation of presence; onto the text are grafted other texts, as many texts as there are readers, and diverging in every direction; that proliferation consecrates in Sartre's eyes the regime of seriality. Socialism would be the end of that writing, whose terrian, temporality, and audience are bourgeois. Sartre writes for the bourgeoisie, which instituted seriality, and against the bourgeoisie, in order to effect its undoing. The crisis of 1940 reveals to Roquentin the existence of the group in fusion, the prison-audience of *Bariona*. The crisis of '52 is tensed around the question. "How might one emerge from the idiocy of separation by means of writing, which entails that very idiocy?" To which the abbreviated fiction of the "people," and those most unfortunate, offers a response: write in the dark, think like the majority, be affected like the most wretched. From there comes political writing not in the service of the Communist party, but rather having as its horizon that community for which, in Sartre's eyes, it bears responsibility. What Sartre wanted was epic and an audience that was also his hero, the masses. Which he always confused with the proletariat, which he in turn confused with its leaders.

Fourth: was there at least action? But how might what is pure negativity transform inertia, the past, the passive? Where might be the point of application of what is not on what is? Hollier devotes two chapters, "A Study of Hands" and "Insinuations," to that question. The only body that the For-Itself can stand is that of the striated muscles. Those organs which are not under cerebral control are a defiance to freedom, its very failure, and are rejected in a spasm of nausea. Things are instruments for the pure project; they must not touch it; it can touch them, but at a distance. They are outside, as objects, at the end of intentionality's focus. In Berlin Sartre read Husserl, and was jubilant to learn from him that consciousness is not inhabited by impressions or sensations, as the English claimed, but that it manipulates at a distance and even constitutes eidetic objects. When a thing touches, penetrates, or inhabits you, the result is nausea: the striated muscle, like an intestine, escapes control. In a caress, a hand is touched at the same time that it touches. It is animated by involuntary mmovements, mired in the viscous. Similarly, an act is opposed to a gesture: the latter is an "act become an object"; it "has already been done," is not freedom, but archaic tradition, seductive nature, dangerous for freedom, magic, as is said of emotion in *Théorie des émotions*.

The caressing-caressed hand undergoes the fate of a sexual organ; it acts only insofar as it is affected and, consequently, passive. Hollier composes a bouquet of philosophical, political, novelistic, and critical texts in which that schema is repeated; they come from every phase of his work. The anxiety linked to the feminine (as we shall thus term an "impure" negativity) is constant, the horror of "pursuing in the moistness of one's bed the sad dream of absolute immanence" (*Saint Genet*). After '68, Sartre's texts, for the most part, stem not from his hand, but from his mouth. From tape recorder to megaphone: the immediate phonation of intentionality without flesh. There are equivalences here — which should be pondered — between, on the one hand, time, passivity, immanence, the feminine, and writing and, on the other, the act, transcendence, the virile, and voice. I admire the delicacy and elegance with which Hollier plucks these flowers and assembles them — I was about to say, without touching them.

What is at stake in all these impasses is not sex, but writing. And at this point, at the cost of an additional step I was obliged to take six years ago by Michel Enaudeau, it will be discovered that the politics of prose, perhaps even in its failure, reveals poetry's success. Sartre's theory of language, wrote in a 1979 issue of *Obliques*, is "the most conventional variant of the theory of the sign." According to Sartre in *Saint Genet*, meaning is "a certain conventional relation that makes of a present object the substitute for an absent object." The present "object," be it word or sentence, is a sign; its true value is the object it signifies. Thus "if you attend to meaning, the word disappears, and you move beyond it in order to fuse 'meaning' with the thing being signified." Such is the norm assigned to writing by Sartre after the "crisis of language" of 1948. As may be recalled: "The writer's function is to call a spade a spade. If words are sick, it is up to us to effect their cure. Instead of this, many are currently living off the illness itself. Modern literature in many cases is verbal cancer. . . . Specifically, nothing is more nefarious than the literary exercise called, I believe, poetic prose, which consists in using words for the obscure harmonics resonating around them and which are composed of vague meanings opposed to the clear sense" (*Situations* II). That latter dimension "is conferred on the object from without by a signifying intention." I intend to say such and such a thing, and in order to do so, I employ such and such a word or sentence, "for I consider myself to be the signifier" (*Situations* IX). From there, an entire philosophy of language can be derived — a politics of prose. "The art of prose is interdependent with the sole regime in which prose retains a meaning: democracy. When one is threatened, the other is, as well." Individual subjects communicate meanings through language, that is: intended objects. Names of objects give way to the transcendence that names objects. In prose, freedoms communicate. But in prose insofar as it is an art.

Hollier reminds us that at the time Bataille was publishing *Haine de la poésie* and Caillois *Les impostures de la poésie*, Sartre, at the beginning of *Qu'est-ce que la littérature?* was analyzing poetry as a language become natural, turned back on its own words and turned away from meaningful objects — perverted speech, "language in reverse." Like many others, Hollier understands this analysis as an appeal to committed literature to rid itself of its poetic narcissism. Poetry would be an aristocratic practice of language: it would not use words toward the end of the freedom of its speakers, but would rather make of words in themselves their own ends. Meschonnic sees in that self-reference the origin of the litanies of "enclosure," of the "rhetoric of limits, of the play of madness," of the "literature of noncommunication" denounced by Sartre.

But matters are not that simple. In capitalism (and this is one of the issues at stake in the Flaubert study) prose has ceased being, for Sartre, the medium within which transcendences communicate. It has become the accumulation of established meanings. We no longer speak within it, but are rather spoken. The rule is no longer free usage, but the constraint of commonplaces and received ideas. It is within that collapse that the crisis of democracy and the decline of the bourgeoisie are to be situated: meaning, become immanent, is escaping signifying subjects. And it was in vain that the poetic withdrawal into language games tried to pass itself off, with Mallarmé, as a literary revolution; from Sartre's point of view, it was but the flip side of the opaqueness to which prose had fallen victim, an all too simple manner of overthrowing the literature of consumption and amusement, an acceptance of language's neurosis. Meschonnic concludes from that analuysis that Sartre, all things considered, with his refusal of the cult of writing, is perhaps more lucid than the philosophers of writing's self-enclosure and the politics of the revolution of poetic language. At least, he writes, Sartre is not like them "deficient in historicity." I wonder if in order to save the thesis attributed to Sartre it is worth paying the price of abandoning the entire critique of subjectivity! Which is not, as Meschonnic seems inclined to believe, a vagary of philosophers and writers. The politics of prose runs smack against the impasses enumerated by Holloer — presence, the present, the reader, and so forth. But its failure reveals at the core of language an essence that is more than — or different from — a function of signification, and which Sartre did not fail to perceive.

In *Saint Genet* he opposes meaning [*sens*] to signification [*signification*] in these terms: "By meaning, I understand participation in a present reality, in its being, in the being of other realities, be they present or absent, visible or invisible, and thus, little by little, in the universe itself. . . . meaning is a natural quality of things." Signification "is a transcendent relation from one object to another; meaning is a transcendence fallen into immanence." The question is the following: is this fall no more than that accompanying the growing inertia of linguistic praxis, the fact that once the word has lost its arbitrary character in relation to the thing itself, we traffic in words as though they were the things they designate? That would amount to the alienation of language in the already spoken, its ideologization. That meaning of meaning would be the opaqueness within which the spark of freedom is extinguished. But meaning is also its total opposite: the compost of signification.

Verstraeten asked Sartre in 1966: do you devalue poetry? Sartre, astonished, clarified his thought: In prose, words are exchanged between interlocutors, between author and reader; such is the democracy of prose. In poetry, the author reconquers "what is for all of us a moment of solitude, . . . the moment, precisely, in which words refer us back to the solitary monster that we are" (*Situations* IX). It is a different communication than that effected through prose: in a movement of a narcissistic identification, the reader enters into resonance with the sentence. A frequent phenomenon, declares Sartre, and a regrettable one, if the resonance is not "contained within certain limits" (ibid.) (We should not lose sight of the subject's rights over the associations to which the devil prompts him.) Already in 1948, Sartre had given Leiris as an example of a "search for lost time" by way of words charged with affective implications. The moment of solitude may indeed be constantly transcended, but one is constantly "obliged to come back to it again." And why is that? Because even in prose "there is a perpetual exceeding of simple signification. It might even be said that everything exceeds signification, and it is that everything which founds communication, or, better put, deep communication" (*ibid*). Already in '48, an excess within poetry itself: "the word, the sentence-thing, as inexhaustible as things, exceed in every direction the sentiment which gave rise to them" (*Situations* II). Perfect communication, the republic of freedoms, would require that interlocutors exchange the entirety of their respective situations, one whole world for an other. In theory that takes place only in the writing of prose, in its art-form at least, if not in commonplace prose. And in literary prose, it is precisely the "indispensable" — "absolutely indispensable" — poetic moment which gives to prosaic communication its depth. Prose is the transmission of significations outside the self; in prose, poetry is "the moment of respiration in which one returns to oneself," in which resonances are attended to and liberated (within certain limits); it is a stasis in which Desire (capital *D*) or History (capital *H*) is acknowledged. History or desire slips into the articulations of the language of signification in order to give voice to the "inarticulable."

Those specifications come much later than 1940, the year that interests Hollier; they are from the sixties, and the echo of Lacan's thought can be heard in them. The instrumentalist thesis by then had lost something of its contours, and the transcendentalist critique lodged in 1944 against Ponge's materialism at the end of "L'Homme et les choses," for example, could not be maintained. When one calls a spade, one is not calling a spade, but a world, a "micrososm." The arrogance of the For-Itself is given rather harsh treatment. An aesthetic that is more ontological than humanist begins to surface. By which I mean that poetry may be a failure (Ponge, Baudelaire, and all of modern poetry as a conflict with the religion of success), but it is such from the perspective of man. Fromm the perspective of being, it remains a success. That aesthetic had already brought with it into the 1948 text expressions such as "the fleshly face" of the word, its "physiognomy," "its affinities with earth, sky, water, and all things created," with the result that if there were indeed "misuse of language" (*Saint Genet*) in poetry, it is not to be understood as an abuse or aberration, but as a different situation, a different project than those called into play in the politics of prose. And even as a different style of commitment, if one likes: the modern poet is "man committing himself to lose"; he doesn't contest modernity any less than the writer of prose, but through differnt means: "Prose's act of defiance is achieved in the name of a greater success, and poetry's in the name of the hidden defeat concealed by every victim" (*Situations* II). It is consequently imperative to observe "an absolute difference" between prose and poetry, as Hollier says; Sartre maintained that it was a matter of "clearly delimited structures," but it is no less the case that each is, he added, "complex and impure."

If I insist on what is a constant in Sartre's commentary on poetry (the failures of Baudelaire, Mallarmé, Ponge), it is because the diagnosis ends up spreading, via the *prosateur* par excellence named Flaubert, to Sartre himself. Immediately after 1940, he became aware that there was no way to win, that words could not be dissipated in the transparency of a signifying intention, that capitalist modernity, but perhaps also the being of language itself, was part and parcel of pure communication and freedom. But if the performance principle requires speech to attain expression in a wooden language, triumphalism is doomed to aggravate that alienation, for one can triumph in such language alone. The proper strategy, instead of choosing to ignore the thickness of words, would be to explore it, since history and desire are embedded therein. And that one become the witness not of constitutive freedom, but of the intermediary realm, of combinations of being and nothingness, of viscosities, of the entire transitional region which is the business of poets. A politics of poetry? That would be saying too much, and saying it poorly. But does not the work of Sartre as a writer — in its incompletion, in the very impasses revealed by Hollier, and even in the secret dissonances that he "insinuates" — bear witness to a success carried off by language against him who wanted to turn it to his own use? At the foot of the popular, populist, political Sartre, massive in his printings and in the notoriety he excited, the shadow of a different Sartre — withdrawn into himself, secret, captivated by failure, unknown and never managing to recognize himself in the words that came to him or, rather, failed to. The shadow wins out over the hero toward the end, when the committed writer lays down his pen, renounces in favor of his comrades, advances in the wilderness of the Paris suburbs with a megaphone in his useless hands, only to realize at the end that his prose has no audience at all, and that the poetry in his work would have won out over his life's work. It would be a marvelous story, to which I am prompted by Enaudeau, behind Hollier, in which the subject is defeated by words.

First Theme

(to miss, to lose, to fail:
rater, manquer, échouer, faillir, abandonner,
perdre, égarer, omettre, se tromper, regretter)

"Some of These Days" is one thing more I owe to Mollie. I was riding
high in Chicago, palling around with a fast crowd, too full of myself to
pay attention to a lot that was happening around me. Many song writers
used to bring me their work, beg me to try the songs in my act and plug
them. Every performer is besieged with that sort of thing. At first you hear
them all, you're so fearful of missing a good thing. But after a few years
of it you get careless. I guess it was that way with me.

One day Mollie came and stood in front of me, hands on hips, and a
look in her eye that I knew meant she had her mad up.

"See here, young lady," said she, "since when are you so important
you can't hear a song by a colored writer? Here's this boy Shelton Brooks
hanging around, waiting, like a dog with his tongue hanging out, for you
to hear his song. And you running around, flapping your wings like a
chicken with its head chopped off. That's no way for you to be going on,
giving a nice boy like that the run-around."

"All right. I'll hear his song," I promised. "You tell him."

"You can tell him yourself," said Mollie. And she brought him in.

The minute I heard "Some of These Days" I could have kicked myself
for almost losing it. A song like that. It had everything. Hasn't it proved
it? I've been singing it for thirty years, made it my theme song. I've turned

it inside out, singing it every way imaginable, as a dramatic song, as a novelty number, as a sentimental ballad, and always audiences have loved it and asked for it. "Some of These Days" is one of the great songs that will be remembered and sung for years and years to come.

> — Sophie Tucker, *Some of These Days*. According to the author, in 1945, she had already been singing the song for thirty years — that is, since about the beginning of the First World War.

Second Theme

VARIATION: *s.f.* . . . 2. A change in doctrine, in ideas. . . . *The Variations*, title of a work by Bossuet on the changes occurring in Protestant confessions. "It is those variations [of the Protestant churches] whose history I am attempting to compose" — Bossuet. *Var. Pref.* . . . 8. *pl.* Musical term. Changes made in a tune through the addition of ornaments which nevertheless allow the basic melody and movement to be maintained. . . .

— SYN. VARIATION, CHANGE: Variation consists in being sometimes one way, sometimes another; change consists only in ceasing to be the same. A change can be complete; variation allows much similarity to remain.

Littré, *Dictionnaire de la langue française, Q–Z.*

The Politics of Prose

Chapter 1
Portrait of the Artist in an Auto

Glide gently, mortals. Don't apply any pressure.

Lyotard, in an occasional piece, somewhere evokes "the pleasure one might experience in starting up an automobile by activating a rhetoric." This is, to be sure, only a manner of speaking, a metaphor, a particularly opportune example, but only an example, of those figures of rhetoric of which it can be said that they move crowds but concerning which it is known that none, in reality, has ever started up a single car. And yet who would be able to say, precisely, concerning a metaphor, where and when it *starts* — or stops. Who, for instance, could determine the precise moment when an automobile becomes a metaphor? Each is, in its way, a means of transport, a certain kind of instrument used in order to effect a displacement. And if it is objected that metaphor (since it does not transport a real object from one point to another in real space) is such, insofar as *it* is concerned, only metaphorically, the economy of that restriction immediately imposes its conversion into a generalization: all the more reason. I continue: What happens when a metaphorical vehicle is borrowed in order to take a spin in reality? What kind of transference is called into play by that *acting out*? What, moreover, might one make of a band of nomads who, in order to transport themselves, would make use only of metaphorical translators? And how, then, prevent those nomads (Deleuze's "nomads in place"?) from being immediately tapped in order to restore currency to the deplorable expression *literary movement*? In place does not mean without surprise.

It will perhaps not be out of place to recall at this juncture that Lyotard inserts

3

his metaphor of the rhetorical starter in the dismantling of a narrative machination, the story put out by Renault after the murder of Pierre Overney, 26 February 1972, at the gates of its factory in Billancourt. The event will be recalled, perhaps; it happened just eight years ago. Many things have moved since then, many a displacement has been effected; surprised or in place, who has not taken the trip? It was at the gates of Renault, but Lyotard does not give the make of the car that would oblige the rhetorician by starting up at his word. February 1972: the date, as well, of Sartre's decision to confide himself to another machine, the motion picture camera of Astruc and Contat, for the filmed autobiography that would be shot mostly during that month. The film begins with a lecture delivered by Sartre on the eve of Overney's murder. It ends with images showing him inquiring at the gates of Renault, a few days after the killing.

We shall be following here, through several rather crowded intersections of Sartre's text, the trace of a desire which might be formulated by reversing Lyotard's metaphor: the desire to start up, or activate, a rhetoric by driving an automobile, to submit, more exactly, the entirety of what has been subsumed under the category of the rhetorical, including literature, to the general model of a technology — to ask, that is, a meditation on tools and machines to teach us what a sign is.

Committed literature (which is doctrinally what Sartrean rhetoric can be reduced to) demands of the writer that through his texts he act within and upon his time. But it simultaneously condemns any modality of such action that might resort to means smacking of what could be called symbolic effectiveness. The writer addresses the reader's freedom, and that suffices for the writer to rule out any will to trouble him, plunge him into excessively violent feelings, or overwhelm him. He must not call the magic of words into play. For the great Sartrean dream, as we shall see, is that one might be able, even while writing, to leave words in peace, that one not lose one's time (and a lot more) sounding them in order to make them say what they don't mean, that one allow them to accomplish the task for which they were conceived, as one would allow any other tool. It is in the vicinity of that dream that the first version of the class struggle in Sartre will take shape. If, in order to complete any of his projects, a proletarian needs a tool and his strength (since he stands in contact with things and with matter), a bourgeois, on the contrary, needs nothing more than signs, the money he pays or the orders he gives, for it is not over things but men that he exercises his power. "He has," writes Sartre, "a relation with natural forces only through an intermediary; his task consists in manipulating abstract symbols, words, figures, diagrams." From which it will ensue, among a number of consequences fatal to the future of the bourgeoisie, that this class will remain in total ignorance of the reality principle; however senile it may be, it has not yet been weaned from that infantile world in which it is enough to express a wish for someone to satisfy it for you without delay. We shall retain from this brief and archaic reference to the class struggle simply the notion that rhetorical figures start up automobiles only if those automobiles are driven by workers willing to lend an ear to the boss's tropes.

In 1938, a vehicle is sketched in the margins of Sartre's text. Significantly, it appears at the precise time that Sartre begins retreating from what he will later call, concerning Mallarmé and Flaubert, his literary "engagement," or commitment: the idea that it is possible for man to effect his salvation but that the only means at his disposal for doing so consists of the production of a work of art. Literary commitment is, in sum, a recasting in aesthetic terms of what theologians call salvation through works. Beauty, which is not of this world, will cleanse us of the sin of existing. Salvation lies only in one's own hands. Artists? Redeemable. The last pages of Roquentin's diary will be recalled. When he began *La Nausée*, Sartre, for his part, believed in it. But we also know that in the course of writing the novel his conviction began to crumble and that it eventually disappeared, according to him, at the time of the book's publication. In 1938, he no longer believed that literary commitment was in any way adequate. To be sure, he did not stop writing, but writing was no longer for his own personal salvation but, rather, to assist in that of others. A new kind of commitment was instituted, in relation to which literary commitment would no longer be an end but a means. It was at first a "worldly" commitment, in Husserl's sense of the word, but one that was quickly, with the war, to take on the social and political cast which the phrase *committed literature* is presently hard put not to connote. One begins by discovering that consciousness is consciousness of something other than itself. A few additional turns, and one concludes that literature does not have its end in itself. It is precisely as a vehicle of that revision of the ends of writing that the aforementioned automobile emerges. A sign, a sentence, or a text transcends itself toward the reality from which its meaning comes back to it. The car is charged with an analogous mission: it is to establish the connection between words and things, to bridge their difference or, more precisely, establish a kind of extratextual bridgehead in reality. Its mission is to go beyond the text that engendered it. In a word, it is charged with rendering itself real, with crossing the bridge beyond which it will cease being a metaphor. For real, to be sure. Since it *should* do so, it will have to be able to.

A few months after the publication of *La Nausée*, Claudine Chonez interviewed Sartre about his projects. He gave her a few insights concerning the novel he had in mind: "*La Nausée* has been accused of being too pessimistic. But wait for the end. In my next novel, which will be its continuation, the hero will set aright the machine [*redresser la machine*]. Existence will be found rehabilitated and my hero acting, having a taste for action." Perhaps it would be preferable to glide over this passage, as Mamie puts it in *Les Mots*, not to insist too ponderously, and to shut our eyes to this machine which has plainly eluded its author. Sartre, without a doubt, meant to say *redresser* — and *la machine* followed. That is true. I shall nevertheless make an observation.

Once *La Nausée* had appeared, Sartre decided — or discovered — in any event, announced that the book was not finished. He had, however, not inscribed in his novel any intentional or unambiguous sign of its incompleteness. A disconcerting duplicity (or duplication) of the ending is invoked, in an improvised defense, to counter any precipitous accusers. *La Nausée* has two endings, and I'm keeping one for myself. A first ending, in effect, concludes the novel from within. It consists of the last pages of Roquentin's diary and is available to everyone. But Sartre announces that this ending, left behind for his readers to ruminate about, is only temporary. One should not stop there, for there is another one in reserve: "The hero — but since when does Roquentin deserve that characterization? — will set aright the machine." That second ending, which we shall call its external ending — as opposed to the preceding one, which closed *La Nausée* in on itself, as it were, from within — is first defined in topical terms, by the fact that it does not figure within the book whose ending it nevertheless constitutes.

Its mention by Sartre in the course of the interview is quite congruent with the heterotelic doctrine to which his theory of the ends of writing was at the time committed: the very structure of literary intentionality, insofar as it is governed by the transcendence of meaning, forbids a book from ever having ("bearing") its end within itself. To which can be added that that "heterotelia" of the work of art, and most particularly of the literary work of art, is elaborated very precisely on the model of instrumental finality: a tool, a weapon, or a machine does not have its ends within itself. A revolver is never its own target. There is thus sketched a synonymous space in which "waiting for the end" would consist in nothing other than "setting aright the machine" and vice versa. As we shall see, setting aright the machine is the Sartrean manner of designating perception. That synonymy inaugurates the interminable orthopractic series (mobilizing the French terms *redressement, dressage, correction, relève, direction, érection, soulèvement*, and so on) around which will be elaborated a technology of perception, which is not so much (in Mauss's phrase) a technique of the body proper as a technique of appropriating the body.

Two questions:

1. In what way does this "setting aright of the machine," which constitutes the external ending of the novel, differ — from a point of view that would no

longer be topological but thematic — from its internal ending, whose message, it may be recalled, duplicates and comments on its own position with maximal literality, affirming that the work of art is its own end, that it "bears" its end within itself? Every time he hears "Some of These Days," Roquentin, in his way, which is not a hero's but almost an artist's, sets aright something in the order of a machine. The voice that rises, he says, "thin and firm" above the brutalized contents of existence awakens in whomever it calls the desire to "purify" himself, even, he says, to "harden" himself. And he says it more than once: "When the voice rose, amid the silence, I felt my whole body hardening. It was almost painful to become entirely hard like that, all aglow." There can be no doubt that something is already being set aright (or erect) even within *La Nausée*, which consequently cannot be construed purely and simply as the realm of soft machines and poorly raised tools. "*La Nausée* has been accused of being too pessimistic." But is it against pessimism or out of pessimism that one sets a machine aright? Valéry said that Sisyphus was building his muscles, a circumstance undoubtedly to be accounted for by Medusa's head. In a much later interview, accorded to Jacqueline Piatier at the time of the publication of *Les Mots*, at the same time as he would accuse *La Nausée* of lacking the requisite weight in the face of a dying child, Sartre would manifest signs of an enduring indecision on the subject. He begins regretfully: "I have always been an optimist. I have even been too much of one." But he does so to contrast himself, shortly thereafter, with Beckett: "My own pessimism has never been of the soft variety." Might there be no difference between excessive optimism and hard pessimism? Which of the two would give more weight to *La Nausée*? How are they distributed: hard pessimism within? excessive optimism without?

2. Recall the very last page of *La Nausée*. We leave Roquentin on the platform of the station at Bouville awaiting not the end (which he already has) but a train, that is, a machine, which is to take him to Paris. One does not leave Bouville — or *La Nausée* — by foot. But is it enough to board a train? What relation is there between boarding a train and setting aright a machine? Sartre would almost immediately renounce that sequel to and conclusion of *La Nausée*, announced in the 1938 interview, in order to feed its elements into a new novelistic project, which was totally independent of the previous novel and was to become *Les Chemins de la liberté*. "Revolutions," said Lenin, "are the locomotives of history." The question posed at this juncture of Sartre's text thus bears precisely on the potential relations between railroads and the roads of freedom. More generally, between the roads of freedom and public transportation. For Lenin speaks of the locomotives and not the automobiles of history. Just how far should we take the real distinction between conductor and passengers?

On that rainy evening of 29 February 1932, on the platform in Bouville, Roquentin was not yet in a position to set any machines aright or to savor any action. It was as a passive passenger that he prepared to get onto the train. He was, however, on the right track: for three years, he had been an assiduous *habitué* of the café Rendez-vous des Cheminots.

> For me, flying and writing are the same thing. The aviator and the writer merge in the same growing awareness.
>
> Saint-Exupéry

What is a date? What effects does it produce in a text? Can anything other than a text give a date? What meaning should be given to those numbers borne by the world in its course? Claudine Chonez's interview is dated: December 1938. Two months earlier was the Munich crisis. France, for the first time since 1919, had mobilized (or, rather, had been mobilized). The interview comments on its date: "Roquentin, in the next novel, will discover his freedom, but in order to do so, he will need a major upheaval in the world. Making use, like the good novelist he is, of what lies before him, Jean-Paul Sartre has his hero live the recent events which had us believing that everything would be swept away in the war; he imagines him mobilized, etc." That mobilization, which allows Roquentin to discover his freedom, is part of the process of setting aright the machine.

It was also the period in which Sartre, in his writings on psychology, developed a theory of behavior or conduct [*conduite*] according to which consciousness, in order to act freely, takes charge of and assimilates as its own the motifs (the *data*) given it by the world; in which case they become its motives [*mobiles*]. Consciousness is a form of behavior which does nothing but motivate, or mobilize, itself.

Just after the mobilization of 1938, Sartre began *Les Chemins de la liberté*, whose second volume, *Le Sursis*, was to describe that mobilization which would have brought to an end, beyond the novel's publication, *La Nausée*. It was also the period in which he began the elaboration of a theory of commitment, as a theoretical double of *Les Chemins de la liberté*; it might be defined — in all senses of the word, as will be seen — as a theory of the mobilization of the narrator. Or, more exactly, of his automobilization: he commits himself to no longer allowing himself to be mobilized from without, by surprise, by and for a cause that would not be his own.

In 1947, Sartre published in *Les Temps modernes* the theoretical serial entitled *Qu'est-ce que la littérature?* Coming just after the publication of the first two volumes of *Les Chemins*, *L'Age de raison* and *Le Sursis*, but also in the expectation of resuming that long-term novelistic project, in a sequel and conclusion, it is something in the order of a theoretical pause, a moment both for regaining energy and for reflection. More substantially, that manifesto in favor of committed literature commits literature, to begin with, to rid itself of poetry. It sends an appeal to responsible writers to maintain as discrete as possible the difference between prose and poetry. One does not choose one's era. A short time before, Bataille had published *Haine de la poesie*, and Caillois, *Les Impostures de la poésie*. After the poets of the Resistance, the Liberation was initiating a resistance to poetry.

One must choose between a revolution in language and a revolution through language. Because words have been so tampered with, they are no longer good for anything. What is needed, instead of destroying linguistic tools, is to gain control of the means of expression. Words, to be sure, but all the technology linked with them and, notably, what "the Americans have already decorated with the name of mass media: newspapers, radio, and the movies." Poetry is the infantile stage of the aristocracy. There will be a revolution only on condition that it not be of poetic language. "The art of prose is in solidarity with the sole regime in which prose retains a meaning: democracy. When one is threatened, the other is also."

There is but one politics, the politics of prose. The poet "commits himself to losing." Granted. That does not constitute sufficient grounds for making of lyrical misfortune the platform for a political program. One is not born a child; one becomes one. Baudelaire is free to choose to play the child; he can opt to spend his life in tutelage. It merely proves that there are a thousand ways for a poet to be minor. On the eve of the war, Leiris's *L'Age d'homme* had drawn up the balance sheet of the cost to poetry entailed by attaining maturity. *L'Age de raison*, which opens *Les Chemins de la liberté*, will suggest in related terms that virility is infanticidal: it is not by thinking of his descendants that Mathieu would rectify Roquentin's machine. *Les Mots*, moreover, would also be more relentless than necessary in its attacks on the imaginary child Sartre did not quite succeed in being.

I return to poetry, to the failure of Baudelaire. "There is emotion when the world of instruments abruptly vanishes," ran the conclusion of *Esquisse d'une théorie des émotions* (1939). *Qu'est-ce que la littérature?* condemns poetry for a similar disappearance: the poet does not have technique and does not want to have it; he refuses work, condemning himself to perpetual leisure, willed un-employment; he has decided that words will not be used as means. Consciousness is moved when it does not achieve its ends; the poet affirms that he had no end. What I succeed in achieving, he says, is *not* achieving my ends. All I know is how not to use words instrumentally. I have succeeded in losing. In the *Esquisse*, Sartre quotes the fox of the fable who ends up rejecting as sour the grapes he has not been able to reach. It is said that before going to sleep, Saint-Pol Roux would hang a sign on his door: The Poet Is Working. The world of tools is thus not alone in disappearing; the poet contributes his own swoon to the process.

There follows in *Qu'est-ce que la littérature?* a brief discussion of what the poet *wanted to say*. No doubt, had Saint-Pol Roux wanted to, he would have said it. But, precisely, he no longer meant or wanted to say anything, since he was asleep, stretched out on the other side of words. Theorem: the poet never wants to say, never means; he absents himself.

For Saint-Exupéry, technology and the activity of consciousness were one. For Sartre, the disappearance of the world of utensils is a loss of consciousness. Poetry must be repudiated as the literary ally of those hypnagogic spans in which consciousness degenerates. In which consciousness, as the *Esquisse* and *L'Imaginaire* put it, captivates itself: I am the trap and the victim, the Bastille and the prisoner. Sartre's discourse on emotions, the imaginary, and poetry can be assembled under a single title: The Paths of Captivity [*Les Chemins de la captivité*. If the French were never more free than under the German Occupation, it is above all, in Sartrean logic, because for the first time they were not captives of themselves.

Who said that to think, to ponder [*penser*], is to weigh [*peser*]? On both sides of the class struggle, nineteenth-century man has heavy shoulders. Rodin's thinker may not have a dockworker's manners, but he certainly has his silhouette. Nor does Ingres's *Oedipus* seem particularly light-headed. Exhaustion appears to thrive in this century of *leaning* men. One follows one's inclinations. Sartre: "Baudelaire's original attitude is that of a man bent. Bent over himself, like Narcissus." The primal attitude of the novelists, his contemporaries, would also be that of men leaning — over their era. Thought loses something of its rigor when indivisible substance inclines to stretch out. Bed or couch, no difference: Sartre would reproach psychoanalysis with spreading the belief that a cure can be effected horizontally. "But wait for the ending. In a future novel, which will be a continuation, the hero will set the machine aright (or erect)." The poet did not respond; he had shifted out of gear. The prose text begins by engaging the narrative shifter: Sartre might be unsparing in his sarcasm concerning what he would call escapist literature; the function of the novelistic vehicle will nonetheless be to allow us to leave the paths of captivity. Whence our deliverance from Proust, to be sure, but also from poetry, Baudelaire, and several others in that family of idiots traveling by sleeping car.

Derrida, in *Glas*, decorates Sartre with an unaffectionate title: "the philosopher of [the] liberation." I no longer recall if he writes it upper or lower case. It would be difficult, in fact, to mention a single liberation movement after 1944 — that is, after the Liberation — with which Sartre's signature has not been associated. In the interviews of *On a raison de se révolter* (whose publication was to help finance the launching of the newspaper *Libération*), one of the last chapters, with its anti-Proustian title "La Liberté retrouvée," gives the maxim informing that course of action: "We know only one goal, which is the liberation of men."

Of *Les Chemins de la liberté*, the paths of freedom, it can be said that they will get bogged down in the semantic difference that separates, and will separate every day a little more, liberation as a proper noun and as a common noun, (the) Liberation as a date, a given, that occurring in 1944, and liberation as an aim, an end, a future, awaited by humanity. "I wanted," we read in the blurb Sartre appended to the first two volumes, "to retrace the path trodden by several individuals and several social groups between 1938 and 1944. That path will take them up to the liberation of Paris, perhaps not at all to their own." The "perhaps" takes into account the possible reticences of the characters regarding the author's ends. For the sole convincing act of freedom issuing from a novelistic character would no doubt consist not (as one too often hears said) in managing to have his voice heard but, rather, in arranging to cut short the author's speech, to interrupt him and prevent him from bringing his novel to completion. Whatever the novelist's intentions concerning them, his characters will be all the more real to the extent that they know how not to comply with them: their liberation, after all, is their own business. But the "perhaps not at all" points to a more serious hitch, which is less available to the indulgences of theory. Formulated as early as 1945, it can be read as an anticipation of the decision Sartre would take some five years later upon abandoning the last volume before completion: not to conduct, or drive [*conduire*], or follow, or accompany, as you like, his characters, this time not even until their own liberation but, contrary to the announcement, until that of Paris. In 1952, everything stops in 1942. Mathieu, Brunet, Boris, none of the characters of *Les Chemins de la liberté*, will attain either liberation, upper or lower case. Simone de Beauvoir tells how Sartre planned coldly to liquidate them in a novelistic purge of the best Stalinist vintage: "Not redeemable."

"Do you want your characters to live? Then make them free." The first liberation movement on which Sartre bestowed his signature was that of the novelistic character. He did more, even going so far as to compose the charter that would appear in the *N.R.F.* in February 1939, entitled "M. François Mauriac et la liberté." He called there for a novel whose hero would manage to escape the surveillance of his creator, to demystify his alleged omniscience by taking off, scaling the wall. But at the same time that the hero would escape, the novelist would be obliged in an inverse movement, to penetrate within: he must not remain outside. It is then that the novelistic vehicle appears for the first time. "Is it really possible to confuse those jerky starts, that violent slamming down on the brakes, those painful accelerations, those breakdowns, with the majestic flow of novelistic time?" A vehicle which, to all appearances, M. François Mauriac does not know how to drive. And Sartre (M. Jean-Paul Sartre?) consequently refuses him his license. Flunked. And properly so, once one realizes that M. François Mauriac refuses to enter into the novels he drives (conducts [*conduit*]).

The same ideas would resurface, with a less specific, less idiotic target, in *Qu'est-ce que la littérature?* "In the stable world of the prewar French novel, the author, located at a point *gamma* representing absolute rest, disposed of points of reference for determining the movements of his characters." The narrative axiomatic could not be simpler: "a local change in a system at rest." The last word accrues to the principle of inertia, and the function of the narrator is limited to sublimating movement, gradually attenuating it: a few affective transports have taken hold of a character moved by them; stabilize them, analyze them, condemn them. Sartre saved Aristotle for Giraudoux. And yet Mauriac as well, with his novels teleguided by an immobile engine, deserves the accusation of Aristotelianism. Immobile or exhausted, it is not clear which, the repose of the bourgeois novelist shares more than one trait with the slumbers of the Surrealist poet. Yet it is not Aristotle's physics but Newton's that Sartre attacks: as much as Bachelard's "new scientific spirit," the new novelistic spirit should take into account the gains of the theory of relativity, which he specifies, in fact, "applies in its entirety to the novelistic universe." "No more in a true novel than in Einstein's world is there any place for a privileged observer." In *Qu'est-ce que la littérature?* the same reference concludes the onslaught against bourgeois narrative statics: "As of 1940, if we wanted to account for our time, we had to move novelistic technique from Newtonian mechanics to general relativity." Is the bourgeois world, in fact, as stable as Sartre has it? We shall leave the question pending. As for the novel, we now know that it is not conducted, driven (*conduit*) from without. The pilot and the engine (Sartre is not always sensitive to their eventual distinction) are part of the trip just as the characters are. The reader will not budge if the novelist begins to remove himself from the narration.

The motif of interiority and exteriority is at the heart of Sartre's writings around the time of the war. It is through that motif, in particular, that the concept of commitment will be able to ensure the articulation between an aesthetic meditation bearing on the structures of novelistic discourse and the discovery of the political insofar as it is that within which one is always already engaged, or embarked. The critique of the extraterritoriality of the subject, as it emerges simultaneously from the descriptions of phenomenological (or existential) psychology and the rudiments of relativity theory it calls to its assistance, is prolonged in a more specific critique of the extraterritoriality of the writing subject.

1. The most frequent form of the motif attacks what might be called narrative weaning, or separation. The novelist should be a native, not a foreigner. Sartre always condemned (without the slightest nuance) the position of the narrator maintaining a detachment from what he relates. He did so concerning Mauriac, but also in the case of Camus. The entire

argument sustaining the famous "Explication de *L'Etranger*" (1943) consists in showing that Meursault's "strangeness" is but the effect of a narrative gimmick. As in a film for which the sound track has been disconnected, the characters are presented through a window that suspends the meaning of their acts, reducing their behavior to an absurd agitation. The stranger, in that sense, is less Meursault than Camus himself — for which Sartre would reproach him nine years after that article, in 1952, in a letter breaking off relations after the publication of *L'Homme révolté*. "Like the little girl who feels the water with her toe, asking 'Is it warm?' " he writes him, "you look at History with suspicion, stick one finger in, withdraw it immediately, and ask: 'Does it have a meaning?' " Camus's error, as a novelist and thinker, will have been to believe that he was not inside, that it was up to him and his free will whether to be "engaged."

Significantly, at the very time he was publishing "Explication de *L'Etranger*," Sartre was having a play of his own performed that took the opposite position from the one he attributed to Camus. *Les Mouches* is a kind of anti-*Etranger*. Its principal character, Orestes, refuses exile and returns home because he wants to have a country, a place that is his own; he wants to stop being a stranger amid the men with whom he is to live. One can understand how reticent Sartre would later be on the subject of the Brechtian *Verfremdungseffekt*. The novelistic or theatrical work of art should *territorialize*, rather than distance. Sartre's aesthetic is not one of "estrangement," (to quote Lacan's translation of Freud's *Unheimlichkeit*). In the very first lines of *La Nausée*, moreover, Roquentin notes in his diary: "One should not introduce strangeness where there is nothing."

Sartre reproaches Camus with resorting to procedures used by Voltaire in *L'Ingénu* or *Micromégas*, by Swift in *Gulliver's Travels*: "The eighteenth century also had its strangers." In the twentieth century, those procedures smack of what he calls "the American technique." The reference is to Hemingway. But it was concerning Dos Passos that he had analyzed and judged the technique a few years earlier. Curiously enough, though, he spoke of it in extremely favorable terms. The shift in position is a function of the difference between sociology and metaphysics, between America and man. Camus's error is to want to show allegorically that man is a stranger to his fellow creatures, Dos Passos's greatness is to describe an inhuman society, American capitalism, in which men, bereft of interiority, can thus be presented "as simple external surfaces."

A distinction should be made between two neighboring motifs that frequently overlap in Sartre: that of foreignness *to* and that of foreignness *within* (the "alien" and the "resident alien"). The critique of the first is simple: nothing that is human is foreign (or strange) to man. But the second motif cannot be so easily reduced: no doubt it is untrue that a man can be outside of humanity, pass beyond the boundaries of humanity; but it remains possible that within humanity he might refuse to allow himself to be reduced and function like an alien internal entity. Not foreign to humanity, but foreign within it. That fantasy of the alien internal entity will be the theme in Sartre of very powerful movements of repulsion and nausea that will not be without effects on his theoretical efforts. His first important publication, "La Transcendance de l'ego," thus refuses for consciousness to be "inhabited" by an Ego that would be a heterogeneous core of opacity and heaviness. It is the same movement of expelling, or repressing, the stranger beyond the border that inspires (from the works on imagination up to the Flaubert study) the critique of Anglo-Saxon associationism and what he also calls American neo-realism — that is, above all, the critique of the illusion of immanence, of the real inclusion of the contents of consciousness and of the mental image in particular. "Having an idea of a chair is not having a chair in one's consciousness."

The power of that repulsive scheme is sufficient to have Sartre make comments whose xenophobic resonances are, to say the least, unexpected. In 1939, he published a harsh critique of Nabokov's novel *Despair*, whose final argument evokes the author's emigrant status: this novel is without interest, because the author is a foreigner in the country where he wrote it. I should not write to you from a distant land. Literature, for whoever writes in a country not his own (for whoever does not write in the language of the country in which he is writing) can be no more than a timid form of a gratuitous act. When one is a *"déraciné"* (and Sartre uses Barrès's word), one keeps quiet. After the war, Sartre would reuse the argument in the course of an interview with Bernard Dort in which, concerning popular theater, he would be led to criticize the insistence with which Beckett and Ionesco indulge in the description of moments of solitude and incommunicability. "All these writers," he notes, "are people who have been excluded. Of foreign origin, they are strangers to our language and our society. Consequently they look at it from without." If one had to suggest a prototype for those foreign agents, one would undoubtedly have to go back to his grandfather Karl (who asked that he be called Charles), a German speaker in Paris who chose France only, it turned out, in order to receive Prussian money.

Sartre's text is haunted by the Trojan horse. He is obsessed by what might be called the containment of the strange — or the foreign. Who contains whom? A vase will always be betrayed by its contents. From which it follows that to be in shape is to be empty. "Les Communistes et la paix" would thus show the bourgeoisie being submerged by the proletariat it was intent on containing. When Haussmann chased the workers who had survived the massacres of the Second Empire to the suburbs, the bourgeoisie was besieged, encircled. Significantly, Malthusianism would be a way for it to control what now, in terms of social morphology, formed its demographic context, a way of containing what was encircling it. Not far from those zones (since it is a question of birth control), lies one of the most frequent Sartrean (and perhaps existentialist) formulations of sexual difference: contents never allow themselves to be contained; by definition, they attack their enclosure. From which it follows that the female body, precisely because of what English calls "pregnancy," is but a "pregnant" shape in the sense that *Gestalttheorie* gives the word. To be in shape is to be empty. But women are always full, or at least occupied.

2. The preface to Stéphane's *Portrait de l'aventurier* again returns to this motif by opposing the militant, who belongs to the community in which he acts, and the adventurer, who (like T. E. Lawrence and Malraux) is always "a *stranger* in the land in which he fights." And yet that preface is not a condemnation pure and simple of the adventurer and his foreignness. Already Roquentin, faced with the Self-Taught Man's humanism, wanted to vomit: "I don't want to be integrated." And if it is true that Orestes, in *Les Mouches*, decides at the beginning of the play that he ought no longer to be "a stranger in his own land," he nonetheless leaves that land which he has made his own at the play's end, a stranger still — if not to other men, at least "to himself," as he tells Jupiter: the most intimate foreignness. Similarly, the preface to *Portrait de l'aventurier* oscillates until the end between the militant's integration and the adventurer's foreignness. To be sure, one ought not to remain outside. But the inside is hardly any better.

At about the same time that he was reproaching Camus with believing he was outside, Sartre in an article on *Aminadab* reproached Blanchot with remaining at the threshold of his own narrative; neither within nor without but each simultaneously. Sartre, in effect, accuses him of opening and closing "like a box" the souls of his heroes, whom the reader at times observes from without like bizarre insects and with whom he at times identifies in intimate empathy. The back-and-forth motion of that oscillation — "without ceasing to be inside, I can see myself from outside" — strains Sartre's patience, and he calls on the narrator to choose the locus of his discourse and to stay there: "One has to be either inside or outside." It will be recalled that "Explication de *L'Etranger*" had reproached Camus with precisely what Sartre had given Dos Passos credit for a few years earlier. The same situation holds for the article on Blanchot. The most well-defined characteristics are perhaps delineated with an eye to the pleasure of taking one's distance from them. And if Sartre reproaches his compatriot with being neither within nor without, he had bestowed on the foreigner Dos Passos the far from negligible title of "the greatest writer of our time" for having been able to describe in his novels a man who is in his entirety outside and in his entirety inside. "Dos Passos' man," he wrote in his enthusiasm, "is a hybrid internal-external creature."

In *Qu'est-ce que la littérature?* the same ambiguity would define the position of the intellectual, seen as the consciousness of a class to which he does not belong. "A class," Sartre began by writing, "can acquire its consciousness only if it sees itself simultaneously from within and from without." Class consciousness thus shuttles back and forth between the inside and the outside of the class that it defines. And the intellectual, as a result, can not be included, comprehended in — or by — the class he is in a position to comprehend. The production of class consciousness would be impossible without what Sartre calls "outside assistance." "That is the function of intellectuals, those perpetual *déclassés*," he adds. Class consciousness, in the last analysis, is thus ultimately always consigned to the hands of class-less bastards. It is, for that reason, always already marked by a propensity to betrayal. It is through its consciousness that a class is betrayed. It betrays itself precisely where it leaves its mark, in those margins where it inscribes itself (betraying itself as it expresses itself), at those borders giving it its definition — in just that limbo.

3. A last remark. Sartre rejects any exteriority within, the introduction into consciousness of an entity alien by definition. Consciousness, on the other hand, will be defined as an interiority without, to the extent that (1) it is at home in the external world and (2) it consists precisely in the inverse insertion of a void at the heart of a plenum, a zone of nonbeing at the heart of presence. The exterior (the inert) should rest outside. If it infiltrates consciousness, it must be expelled. But nothing must replace it inside consciousness, which is but an absolute evacuation, an allergic rejection of all contents. According to the Husserlian concept of intentionality, it "is nothing but the outside of itself" and has no "inside." Existential ekstasis excludes by definition any valorization of intimacy. There is thus sketched out a first synthesis of exteriority and interiority: man is not exterior to the outside; to the contrary, outside is where he is at home, and exteriority is infinitely more familiar, closer to him than any instance of intimacy. The retreat to intimacy in Sartre will always be a gesture of alienation and depersonalization. One loses oneself by approaching oneself too closely, by turning back on oneself. A second synthesis would transcend the opposition by temporalizing it. Beyond the inside and the outside there is the prior, considered as a future which is at once outside the present (foreign to it) but also internal to it to the extent that it is the present's future, contained by it, if only as what it is lacking: contained by what it overflows.

I cut short these marginal observations, themselves internal-external, whose inclusion might otherwise also begin to overflow.

Three months later, in an article on Faulkner, the artist finally enters the novelistic vehicle launched in the piece on Mauriac. The portrait of the artist in an auto is sketched, concerning *The Sound and the Fury*, in "La Temporalité chez Faulkner." In an auto and not a train. An American auto, to be sure, front-wheel drive and, no doubt, a coupé.

A coupé: that is, a coach whose interior has been cut, or divided, near the front so that (1) everybody, passengers and driver, is seated in the direction of travel and (2) the driver's seat is situated at once in front and above the passengers' seat, at once within and without: inside in relation to the coach but outside in relation to the compartment in which the passengers are seated.

Sartre, as is proper, even as he depicts it, is thinking of only one thing: how to [sur]pass it. This article, most often cited as a literary discovery of America, is, in fact, a condemnation of American novelistic technique. Faulkner is accused of cheating. Einstein had been thrown in Mauriac's path, and Heidegger will fulfill the same role for Faulkner. If the novelist must of necessity enter the vehicle he is driving — and, according to Sartre, Faulkner does — that condition is not sufficient. He must, precisely, drive it and must not err as to seat or direction, not confuse front and rear. For one can always continue (even inside a moving auto) not knowing either how to drive [*conduire*] or how to behave [*se conduire*]. That is, to play the child. To behave — why not? — like an idiot, of the family or not, who, for example, instead of looking forward would tell a story and — why not? — a story full of sound and fury signifying nothing. A story running backward, against common sense. He would continue, even within the novelistic vehicle, to behave like a poet and refuse to open his eyes and direct them forward. The poet, according to Sartre, "considers language backward." Sartre diagnoses an identical inversion in Faulkner: "It appears that Faulkner's vision of the world can be compared to that of a man seated in a convertible car and looking out the back. At every instant, shapeless shadows spring up on his right, on his left — flickerings, filtered tremors, confetti of light, etc." A few years later, Baudelaire is accused by Sartre in identical terms: he chose "to advance in reverse, facing the past, crouched in the rear of the car carrying him away and staring at the road as it flees." In Egyptian mythology the ferryman [*passeur*] who brought the dead to the other world looked toward the rear of his craft. Sartre's ferryman, the intellectual, belongs to the world of the front. The reference to Baudelaire, who does not see that "the arrow indicates the direction of the road," allows us to localize precisely Sartre's grievance against Faulkner. He is guilty of a poetic misappropriation [*détournement*] of the tools of prose. A few paragraphs after that quotation, his *Baudelaire* will name Faulkner, who "similarly turned away [*s'est détourné*] from the future." Merleau-Ponty defines schizophrenia as "the pulverization of time and the loss of the future." It should be left to poetry, which is, after all, only a specific type of depersonalization crisis. The Sartrean theory of the novel is subtended by presuppositions taken from psychopathology. A good novel should reinforce the synthesis of the subject. Against escapist literature, Sartre posited that a novel is not a refuge. Nor is it an asylum, for such is the argument invoked to condemn Giraudoux ("Might M. Giraudoux be amusing himself by playing a schizophrenic?") as well as Faulkner ("Why is it that the first window opening onto this novelistic world is the consciousness of an idiot?").

Sartre, in *Les Mots*, declares himself as old as motion pictures. From Mauriac to Faulkner, the distance is of the same order as that separating Niepce or Nadar from the brothers Lumière. The narrative technique of the French novelist bears the imprint of the dominant stability. For the bourgeoisie, during an entire century, stipulated: nobody move. And it complied. Facing an objective they identified with the absolute, the *salauds* took themselves for statues. Faulkner and the Americans invent a narrative cinematics that relegates to the attic of family albums the statics of Mauriac.

But the movement they discover will condemn them and sweep them away. For from Mauriac to Faulkner the distance is homologous as well to that separating the Third Republic and the crisis of 1929, the European bourgeoisie and American capitalism. Having denounced the bourgeois tendency to immobility, Sartre launches an attack in *Qu'est-ce que la littérature?* against America: "The richer it is, the heavier it gets; overcome with fat and pride, it lets itself roll, with closed eyes, toward war." Capitalism is a movement without direction. To perceive is to think ahead. The bourgeoisie, which doesn't, is left dreamy eyed. And since an object is always a project, it will make do with images. They don't commit one to anything, or object to anything. On the rear seat of the class struggle, the bourgeoisie stretches out as though on the couch that would earn for it the name of analytic class. Saint-Exupéry compared the aviator and novelist, each of them activists of consciousness. In the Sartrean theory of the novel, the Faulknerian vehicle figures rather as the instrument of a loss of consciousness, the means of production of that degraded structure of consciousness to which, historically, the bourgeoisie is condemned and that might be called its unsurpassable class unconsciousness.

Around 1950, Sartre begins to lose his way in *Les Chemins de la liberté*, no longer quite sure where its "paths" are leading. He begins to doubt whether literature, even when committed, can ever be anything more than nourishment for his writer's neurosis. The novelistic option and, still more radically, the option of literature itself lead to nothing in the order of an end. Whereupon he begins writing a book entitled, significantly; *La Reine Albemarle et le dernier touriste*. The book is unfinished, its manuscript, save for a few fragments, lost. It was to be, it is said, a kind of antitourist guidebook or antiguidebook to Italy, a country whose charm for many lies in the ease with which the tourist can forget himself there. (Simultaneously within and without, he does not feel a foreigner there. He likes to imagine himself living there, even goes as far as to act as he would at home: strolling is the norm in Rome.) But, Italy or not, the figure of the tourist — a tentative being, transitory, traversing with boredom, regret, or disquiet a world that announces to him at every turn that it is not his — is emblematic of the situation of the bourgeois in a world counting before his very eyes the days left him. Since it is clear that his future is not of this world, better that the disoriented visitor manifest his detachment.

Qu'est-ce que la littérature? does not return to Faulkner, who is replaced by Morand ("the consumer par excellence, the traveler, the passer-by"), Drieu la Rochelle, and so on. An aristocracy of speed given to a mad consumption of space, a "bird's-eye view aristocracy," in Sartre's phrase, against which he would introduce the writer to "constructive freedom." Sartre places on his agenda a literature of praxis which no longer gives "the world to see, but to change." Which takes into account the fact that we see or perceive the world only because we are engaged in it: literary commitment, or engagement, is only a consequence of perceptual engagement. The times demand a literature of production, and to the phenomenology of perception accrues the task of demolishing a literature of consumption. Husserl will once again deliver us from, say, Proust. Will teach us that a landscape is not described but traversed and that it is not the same for a pedestrian and a driver, for a driver and an aviator, for the chauffeur and the passenger of an auto. Perception is already in itself behavior [*conduite*]. All the more reason for the novelist to take control, neither as tourist, nor even fellow traveler, but driver [*conducteur*]. Sartre: "It is the speed of our auto, our plane, which organizes major land masses." "Our": admire the shifter. The writer has left the rear seat and will take the steering wheel. In order to be in his novel as a pilot in his ship.

Elevation

Or his airplane.

Sartre shifts and says "our."

At the end of *Qu'est-ce que la littérature?* note 9 helps interpret that relatively personal pronoun. "When I say 'us,'" writes Sartre, "I might also be speaking of them." "Them" — namely, Malraux and Saint-Exupéry.

The appeal, in the same text, to a literature of praxis ("for us, *doing* is revelatory of being") invoked explicitly, moreover, the writer-pilot: "Saint-Exupery opened the way for us. He showed that for its pilot an airplane is an organ of perception." One does not choose one's epoch. The last words of the *Phénoménologie de la perception* are borrowed from Saint-Ex, all but imposed by the postwar agenda. That reference in Sartre takes on its full significance when we recall that the literature of praxis is expected to break, first of all, with the consumer's aestheticism of the "'aristocrats of the bird's eye-view."

Barely has the decision been made to set the machine aright than it takes off [*décolle*].

The article on Faulkner had already seen another machine *décoller*. But it was in a different sense. Faulkner's narrative apparatus had been accused of decapitating [*décoller*] time, amputating it of its future, "the dimension of actions and freedom." Benjy, the idiot of *The Sound and the Fury*, had moreover, in a sense, lost his head. Ought we not to see an anticipation of Sartre's reticences in the fact that Roquentin, in *La Nausée*, is a full head taller than his contemporaries. A head more. In *Le Cheval de Troie*, Nizan calls him Lange. One more or one less? Roquentin, in effect, lives on the *rue des Mutilés*. But the divergence is not so great between a beheading [*décollation*] and a take-off [*décollage*]. A vanguard, in the last analysis, is merely a detachment of the head. *Décollation*: the head is detached. *Décollage*: the detachment moves ahead. From *Jean sans terre* to *Terre des hommes*. According to the definition in "Matérialisme et révolution" ("That possibility to take off [*décoller*] from a situation and gain a perspective on it is precisely what is called freedom"), *Les Chemins de la liberté* should have been constructed on the model of an airstrip. Freud, in his *Leonardo*, had briefly evoked the impact of aerotechnology on the future of sublimation. We should say the future as sublimation. When consciousness sets the machine aright, "redresses" it, re-rights it, consciousness takes off. It separates from it and [sur]passes it — always by at least a full head. The same process has other names in Sartre: he sometimes speaks of purifying reflection, as well as of acceleration [*reprise*] ("spiritualization, that is, acceleration"). In Sartre's terms it is not the engine but the pilot who is to have jolts of acceleration. The pilot must know how to (sur)pass the machine he is driving. Or, to drive or operate a machine *is* to (sur)pass it. What the Germans, no doubt, would call *Aufhebung*.

One of Sartre's most enduring theses, the objectivity of the future, posits that the future contains more objective reality than the present. The present's reality is what comes back to it from the future. The future, the *binding* principle of the present, gives it consistency and makes it available to perception. The gerundial infinitive is the privileged mode of objectivity: an object is a project, the road is to-be-traveled, the mountain to-be-avoided. "The arrow," as he says, "indicates the road." To assert that the world is "hodological" is to argue that its space is arrowed, its every line a vector, every point a vehicle. The portrait of the artist in an auto, sketched in 1939 concerning Faulkner, will prove similarly rich in future developments, indeed already contains its own future toward which, objectively, it cannot *not* direct itself. For in order that Faulkner, Baudelaire, and Proust be free to indulge in their decadent extasies in the back seat, someone is all the same needed to make the car move forward, a progressive being, up front, who (constrained as he is to submit to the reality principle) has sold his capacity for work in order to operate an instrument of production that plainly does not belong to him. That vehicle, which had been introduced in the context of thoughts on the theory of the novel, is about to veer in the direction of political analysis. The technological model offered to novelistic perception will be transformed into an allegory of the class struggle. We expect Sartre to pursue it and produce at the vehicle's steering wheel the proletariat, the "synthetic class," which looks straight ahead and well knows where it is going: its class consciousness teaches it that the future belongs to it alone. Sartre himself announces as much. The proletariat, he writes, is "the subject par excellence of a literature of praxis." But it does not happen. The automobile's front seat remains empty. Or rather, as soon as it is occupied and someone takes the steering wheel, the auto turns into an airplane and takes off. So long as it remains earthbound, a curse condemns the vehicle to dash along at breakneck speed with no one at the wheel, like a phantom coupé. Sartre calls it elsewhere the determination of the present by the future, of what is by what does not exist. But that is not all. Not only do we never see the proletariat or its vanguard take the controls, but when the airplane takes off, it is the Count (or Viscount) de Saint-Exupéry who is at the wheel — the author as well, as everyone knows, of *Le Petit Prince*. The bourgeoisie is not surpassed by the proletarian future it feared but by a return of the aristocratic past — the ex- in place of the neo-.

A few points in suspension:
— We read in *Les Mots*:

In 1948, in Utrecht, Professor van Lennep showed me some psychological projection tests. One card retained my attention. On it there were drawings of a horse galloping, a man walking, an eagle in full flight, and a motorboat surging forward; the subject was to indicate the drawing that gave him the most intense feeling of speed. I said: "It's the boat." Then I looked with curiosity at the figure that had imposed itself so brutally: the boat seemed to be taking off [*décoller*] from the lake; in an instant, it would be cruising above the undulating stagnant stretch [*marasme onduleux*].

A few lines later Sartre concludes the analysis of his choice. Speed, for him, is characterized not so much by distance traversed as by its power to uproot. Wherein we again encounter the rapidity of the nomads in place. Concerning the *marasme onduleux* from which he takes off, I will recall the etymology of *nausée*: "from the Latin, *nausea*, seasickness, from the Greek *nausia*, from *naus*, boat (see NOISE)." And concerning the takeoff [*décollage*] itself, in order to effect a beheading [*décollation*], this definition given in *L'Etre et le néant*: "The body is what is left behind."
— Saint-Exupéry surfaces again in the *Critique de la raison dialectique* and is dubbed "the first technical agent to have grasped and fixed in his experience the social moment of unveiling through tool-related *praxis*." There is a reference to *Terre des hommes*. A footnote specifies that Saint-Exupéry is mentioned because of his experience as an airline pilot. The airplane here is no longer homologous with the automobile. It is an instrument of mass transport whose proper functioning requires that it retain the hierarchy pilot-passenger ("the inert passenger," says Sartre). Elites and hierarchies are Sartre's preferred targets. All with one exception, which he recalls at the end of *Les Mots*: the "chronological hierarchy," that is, the primacy of the future. But hierarchy itself is but an exception: an exception thus suffices to reinstate it. As required by the structure of the coupé. Every hierarchy produces a kind of take off. It is to be feared that one can never achieve elevation without contributing to the power of Varuna. "Les Communistes et la paix" will show that such a division is operative in the functioning of every apparatus. With all due deference to the novel's passengers,

the mass of readers. The hierarchy of mass transport implies ipso facto the condemnation of the automobile, one of the most demobilizing of all the isolating factors engendered by liberal serialization: "As soon as a man takes the steering wheel of his auto, he is no more than one more driver among all the rest and, for that reason, contributes to reducing the speed of all, including himself." If freedom is a good conductor, in Sartrean electricity, it is because it never insulates.

— Upon breaking with Camus, Sartre would not fail to remind him that freedom is essentially a breaking away. The broken path: from *route* to *rupture* the distance is indeed short. *Les Chemins de la liberté* would be strewn with breaks, from one *rupture* to the next, one rout to the next. A first break, in 1938–40, would attempt to put an end to *La Nausée* by providing *Les Chemins* with their impetus. The war would contribute to the momentum. But already it was not the first. In 1952, the Korean War would trigger an additional one, or rather an additional series: the break with Camus, with Merleau-Ponty; the break with Jean-Paul Sartre the neurotic writer; the break with *Les Chemins de la liberté*. He condemns the novelistic vehicle to a definitive breakdown. Decides that literature is neurosis. Initiates, as a result, a self-portrait of the artist in self-analysis or, rather (to be Bolshevik), in self-criticism: *Les Mots*. The literary tool would never assist in setting the machine aright; only one recourse: the Communist party. "Les Communistes et la paix" constitutes the finest testimony to that development, which seems to be responding in advance to the suggestions made a few years later by Caillois to the Soviet writer Simonov:

> I would not happily board the plane of a pilot who would claim to be irresponsible and would boast of the fact. I should prefer a pilot who knew his trade — mechanics, meteorology, the evaluation of skies and winds — and who would perpetually have in mind the fact that he was transporting human lives. Nevertheless, I must confess that I would be no less suspicious of a pilot who would speak endlessly of the public welfare and of means for assuring the happiness of peoples. Him I would advise instead to go quite openly into politics.

Which is what Sartre decided to do, quite openly, without the slightest affectation, in 1952, when he (almost) abandoned literature, but (definitively) abandoned *Les Chemins de la liberté*, the novel, and literary commitment.

Speed is not conveyed in terms of distance traversed. From 1938 to 1952, the distance traversed between the end of *La Nausée* and that of *Les Chemins* is minimal. Roquentin had been left waiting for the train on the platform of the station in Bouville. In the last sequence of *La Mort dans l'âme*, the train is there:

The prisoners have been herded into the car of a train. A freight car or an animal car, not one for passengers. Brunet, Schneider, and the typesetter, seated in the opening of the corridor door, watch outside as a defeated, sinful, and Pétainist France passes before them. The rest, inside, allow themselves the luxury of confidence. The war is over. The Germans will thus free them. This is their freedom train. Moreover, Moûlu, the former traveling salesman, knows the train line by heart. He used to take it once a week, sometimes twice. He comments on every turn, assesses every switch. "To the right is Germany. To the left, Nancy, Bar-le-Duc, and Châlons." The future is written into the rails veering to the left, toward France and liberation. They think of their wives and homes. The train stops. German soldiers step down to stretch their legs. Schneider asks them where the train is headed. "To Trèves." End of *Les Chemins de la liberté*; they were the paths of captivity.

How is that ending to be read?

It rhymes *La Mort dans l'âme* with *La Nausée*: "Tomorrow it will rain in Bouville," "Tomorrow, the dawn will cover them with the same dew." Sartre had done his military service in the meteorological division. It was there, no doubt, engaged in spite of himself after the expiration of his deferment, that he began to envisage the future in terms of precipitations.

— Few people drive in Sartre's novels. Roquentin, when he is not walking, takes the trolley or, to get to Paris, the train. No car ever appears driven by a character whose name we are given. Sartrean man pays relatively little attention to traffic. Mathieu (who moves about in taxis) is even bumped into by one of those vehicles, which remain intruders in the space of the existentialist novel. Moreover, in *Les Mots*, the speedboat of the projection test is an exception. The standard image is of the clandestine traveler falling asleep on the seat of the Paris-Dijon train.

In the middle of *La Force des choses*, Simone de Beauvoir gives her version of the crisis that the year 1952 had been for Sartre. For her part, things had been going rather well. She was completing her own *Chemins de la liberté* under the title *Les Mandarins*. She had purchased an auto. ("At once driver and passenger, I had all the time I might want to thank myself".) But she does not give the make. And she was in love with the young Claude Lanzmann. "Sartre and I," she writes, "were no longer leading quite the same existence."

One does not stop a writer to ask for his papers. In any event, he has no need of any rights. In a recently published photo album, *Images d'une vie*, Sartre can be seen only once entering an auto. Just after the Nobel Prize, he rushes into the back seat of a taxi in order to escape pursuing journalists. Does he have a driver's license? "One would have to know him."

1. In reality, two drivers of land vehicles appear in Sartre's work, contrary to what I gave to understand in the preceding pages. It is thus not quite exact to affirm, as I did, that in accordance with the stucture of the coupé, it is enough for a Sartrean character to take control of the vehicle in which he finds himself for it to begin rising and take off. Almost exactly contemporary with each other, the two exceptions date from the end of the fifties and the beginning of the sixties. One belongs to fiction, the other

to history. But I had not yet read, last year, *Les Séquestrés d'Altona*, whose ending, all the same, ought to be taken into account in a "portrait of the artist in an auto." Von Gerlach entrusts his Porsche to his son, who has never driven it (since he has not left his room in years), and in a suicidal gesture takes his seat alongside his son.

As for Flaubert, the second exception, he does not drive an automobile (1844 was a bit early for that) but a team of horses, when he experiences the crisis whose analysis constitutes the conclusion of the first part of *L'Idiot de la famille*. The crisis is described in terms that may recall the end of *Les Séquestrés*. During that late January night as he was coming back from Deauville to Pont-l'Evêque, "a man died," writes Sartre. "Gustave himself was driving the cabriolet. Suddenly, in the vicinity of Pont-l'Evêque, as a carter passed to the right of the vehicle, Gustave dropped the reins and fell at his brother's feet, dumbstruck." Further on, Sartre wonders: "Was Achille [Gustave's brother] tired? Had they decided to alternate driving? Or did the demon of masochism impel Gustave to take up the reins?".

(To be linked to the hypertension that would overcome Sartre himself when he approached the administrative spheres of the Communist party. Summer 1962: he is in Rome on vacation. In France an anti-American demonstration organized by the Party has just failed. Sartre, furious, does not want the bourgeoisie to realize that it has happened. "When I got back to Paris, precipitously, I had to either write or suffocate." That sentence could have been signed by Flaubert in 1844. "In fact, I had been writing at a galloping pace," he specifies further on in pages of the text on Merleau-Ponty recalling the circumstances under which "Les Communistes et la paix" had been written. He had already let himself be carried away. Two years later, in Moscow, overworked and bruised by Simonov's unrelenting demands, he breaks down: hypertension. He has to be hospitalized. Was it the demon of masochism that had impelled him to be so close to the reins of the party apparatus?)

From the article on Faulkner to *Qu'est-ce que la littérature?* the driving of an automobile had been proposed as the model of perceptual behavior. To take the wheel was to gain consciousness. But here it is to lose it. Sartre's analysis of Flaubert's crisis insists on how impossible it is for the future novelist to really do what he is doing: he takes up the reins in order to be serious, but he succeeds only in pretending to be serious. Which he does neither seriously nor deeply. He is serious only in order to distract himself, to be more available, more attentive to a deeper distraction haunting him. Even with the reins in his hands, he is not really driving but imagining he is driving. The team is the instrument of his depersonalization. The swoon merely allows him to go a step further: it is he himself who becomes "entirely imaginary." But by seating himself in the direction of travel, in the driver's seat, Flaubert, too, "undoes himself," exactly as Baudelaire did by staring at the road behind him. He is prey to an identical "dissociation of his person" accompanied by an identical "dispersion of images."

2. Orpheus also turns back, like Baudelaire, Faulkner, and Genet. He takes everything backward, in the wrong direction, from behind. The first of those dominated by the past. The consequences of that retrospection furnish the substance of myth: the object (Eurydice) disappears, and the subject (Orpheus) is dismembered. Again, a dissociation of the individual (another depersonalization) linked to a collapse of the perceptual schema. Orpheus does not belong to the world of the front.

It is in *L'Espace littéraire*, a collection concerning which it would not be difficult to show that each of its theses is a detailed response to *Qu'est-ce que la littérature?* that Blanchot develops his analyses concerning Orpheus's gaze. Sartre always wanted the image to follow perception, literature to second reality. (If it was to transcend the present, let it be toward a future more real than the present, and so on.) There are words because there are things and so that human praxis can submit them to itself; the verbal phase is but "a secondary structure of the enterprise" (= the literary enterprise).

It is all the more significant, in the light of those Sartrean postulates, to see Blanchot endeavor to show, concerning the myth of Orpheus (white Orpheus?), that literature would be the specific locus in which is effected the experience of an imaginary more original than any origin, an imaginary which is no longer a simple consequence of the real, a complex and inconsistent imaginary of which the real in turn would be a mere repetition: the experience of the imperceptible. *L'Espace littéraire* might be read as an anti–*Phénoménologie de la perception* or, rather (to imagine a more Sartrean title), an anti–*Technologie de la perception*. Such is the lesson of the Orphic turn. One does not write while looking in front of oneself.

3. It was in 1948, in Utrecht, that Sartre came to know Professor van Lennep's projection tests and chose the motorboat [*canot automobile*] which seemed to "take off from the lake." He was undoubtedly not entirely ignorant on the subject (of nautical crafts) since his stepfather, Monsieur Mancy, had been a naval engineer. And since it was for that reason that he had brought his new family to the port city of La Rochelle. Don't miss me, honey.

But it was also in 1948 that *Les Temps modernes* ("a ship without a captain," Sartre would say of their situation at the time) was filled with references to a motorboat that were nonetheless not at all due to Sartre's pen. The motorboat belonged to Lawrence — Lawrence (like Aden, or almost) of Arabia. Two articles by Etiemble ("338171 T. E.," in March 1948, and "Un Saint en salopette," in October) and three installments (in the May, June, and July issues) of the correspondence of the celebrated British adventurer, translated by the same Etiemble and Yassu Gauclère, launch a crusade on behalf of the order of machines (= the religious and even monastic order of machines), a world to which women have no access.

"The mechanic is cut off from any real communication with women," wrote T. E. Lawrence to his friend and biographer Robert Graves in February 1935, shortly before his death. "There are no women in machines, whatever the machine may be." "All this, he continues, "reads like a paragraph of D. H. L., my step-namesake." At the beginning of the letter, he had insisted that he was far more proud of the part he had played in the conquest of "the last element, the air," than of his role in Middle Eastern politics. He refers explicitly to the "flying boats" on which he had been working for the RAF since 1929. "As their speed increases, they rise out of the water and run over its face."

Lawrence, according to Etiemble, used to race airplanes on his motorcycle, and outrun them. It was on that machine that he died, like a man. Like a von Gerlach.

Chapter 2
Sartre's Ends

. . . et que cache un discours
Commencé tant de fois, interrompu toujours?
Racine, Phèdre

The most beautiful thing in *L'Education sentimentale*, according to Proust, is the "extraordinary shift in velocity," the twenty years that Flaubert, like an onset of old age, bestows on Frédéric in the course of a blank space between paragraphs.

After the publication of the first two volumes of *Les Chemins de la liberté*, *L'Age de raison* and *Le Sursis*, Blanchot — who deemed Sartre's novel "as yet entirely to come" — implied that its incompletion constituted the principal strength of a work which, he added, "at present enjoys the advantage of appearing to elude us forever."

That was in 1945, right after the Liberation. Sartre at the time announced a sequel and conclusion, to be entitled *La Dernière Chance*. Four years later, a third volume did indeed appear. But it was *La Mort dans l'âme*, a sequel without conclusion, which persisted in announcing the future it had replaced: *La Dernière Chance* would now come fourth; it had to be temporarily delayed but was in no way diminished for the wait. Or so he said. *La Mort dans l'âme*, after fulfilling its role for a few years as temporary conclusion, would end up confirming the definitive incompleteness of the work. It is, in fact, the case that *Les Chemins de la liberté*, now and forever, end on a page which no one, neither their author, their publisher, nor their characters, had predicted would be terminal. They would thus end without losing anything of the advantage with which Blanchot

27

had credited them at their inception. No less "to come," now that they were over, than they had been in their beginning. They botched their *dernière chance* [last chance]. You missed me, honey.

"Every existent thing," according to Roquentin, "is born without reason, prolongs itself out of weakness, and perishes by chance encounter." Although they were sufficiently strong not to prolong themselves, the *Chemins* were cut short in the manner in which existent things perish, suddenly running up against an ending they failed to recognize — not at all the one they were awaiting. They did not contain it as an internal necessity. A swoon cuts short the future of a narrative which has not even broached its finale. And which it leaves in suspension, truncated, as though mutilated, on an unresolved chord.

The following pages deal, in a way, with a book that has not been written: *La Dernière Chance*. It will not be a matter of guessing what it might have contained and how *Les Chemins de la liberté* might have ended. Sufficient answer has already been given to those questions (which are not without interest) in remarks published by Sartre in various journals. In *La Force des choses*, Simone de Beauvoir also takes it upon herself to summarize Sartre's intentions. It is not necessary for a book to be written for its contents to be known — at least to a certain point. It will be a matter, rather, of weighing: What is the specific gravity of such a failure? Within Sartre's work, what is the weight of the futures it will have allowed to pass without seeing the light of day?

To which we shall return.

Among the lessons of this failure of 1952 should be counted Sartre's definitive renunciation of the novelistic genre, which revealed its ineptness in realizing the ends toward which it had been chosen. In a more fundamental way, it was in the wake of this failure that Sartre decided that the ideal of committed literature was utopian: the bourgeoisie is literature's only audience. One can write for it, or one can write against it; but in any event, the workers don't read. Worse still: those who do read are already on their way into the bourgeoisie. In other words, a writer should be committed, but he can no longer be so through the means provided by literature. As a writer, he must renounce literature. And militate. Not only his intentions but also his interventions must be political. They must be so directly, to the first degree. Sartre puts it as follows: "The P.C. rid me of my writer's neurosis."

It was also on the occasion of this crisis in 1952, the revisions and frequently radical breaks that accompanied it, that Sartre came to elaborate the concept *series*, a polemical concept based on which one can envision a first approach to the singularly abrupt breakdown cutting short *Les Chemins de la liberté*. It is at the center of the *Critique de la raison dialectique*.

The *Critique* distinguishes between two types of sociality, the serial group and the group in fusion.

Seriality is understood as the social organization of solitude in the world of capitalism, the atomization of the collective into a scattering of countless individuals who, in order to relate to one another, know only the abstract and narcissistic bonds of identity. Social classes in action, another term for groups in fusion, accomplish this, on the contrary, through concrete bonds, those of unity. Men in such a mode no longer stand alongside one another; they are together. Based on the model of what industrial technology calls "assembly-line production" [*production en série*], seriality here connotes an interminable, vain, and monotonous reproduction, the proliferation of the same. Rigorously coextensive with the bourgeoisie's abstract universalism, liberalism, and mechanistic rationalism, serial ideology functions through the recurrence of the practico-inert within the body of society which it detotalizes. Remember, Man, that thou art but dust.

Sartre's concept of series dates from the fifties, but it responds to a long-standing preoccupation. We could go quite far back but will content ourselves, in the present context, with stopping at the period in which the motif, without yet bearing the name *series*, appears for the first time in relation with a political problematic.

We could go quite far back. Specifically, we could go back to the scene in the public garden in *La Nausée* in the course of which Roquentin discovers existence to be a process of indifferent reproduction of anonymous and defective entities. "Why so many existences, if they all resemble one another?" This experience of the depersonalization of space — which is also the depersonalizing experience of space — is surmounted in *La Nausée* by the work of art (the melody "Some of These Days"), which escapes from reproduction: from both multiplication and division. That is: from partition. From that pulverization described by the article on Faulkner (flickering, filtered tremors, confetti of light). The work of art, in Sartre's conception, thus escapes impressionist and pointillist sensualism; it consists of a unity which is unbroachable because without support.

After the war, it is the group in fusion which will take its place and will constitute the totality destined to resist analytic serialization. The break of the forties, culminating in the insurrectional festivities of the Liberation, thus marks a decisive break in the Sartrean thematic, which passes from esthetics to politics. Each of them, however, has in common the fact of heeding the call to resist serial reproduction.

At the time of the Liberation, Sartre accepted two journalistic assignments. The first set of articles, ordered by Camus, appeared in *Combat*. It followed day by day the popular insurrection in the streets of Paris accompanying the arrival of the Allies at the gates of the capital. Seven articles appeared, composed in the heat of action, between 22 August and 2 September. The first began with a declaration of realism: "I tell only what I have seen." The second set of articles, a little less than a year later, appeared alternately in *Le Figaro* (eleven articles) and *Combat* (twenty), between January and June 1946. This was Sartre's account of his first stay in the United States (a trip which was the occasion of his first nonmetaphorical use of the airplane). The two scenes which history and geography placed at his disposition (Paris and America) prefigure quite precisely the two types of sociality to be distinguished in the *Critique*.

1. It was the Liberation that accorded him for the first time an experience of the group in fusion, which can be described as the irruption in a public space of a collective self-consciousness or even as the collectivization of self-consciousness. Society therein becomes an act of freedoms realizing themselves by the simple fact of being together. Sartre speaks unhesitatingly of celebration [*fête*] in describing such moments: being together is an end in itself. After years of clandestine resistance, liberated Paris demonstrates — demonstrates together, demonstrates that it is together, demonstrates in order to be together. The group in fusion is autotelic: it contains its own end within itself. One demonstrates for no other reason than to demonstrate. At that time, Sartre comments in the *Critique*, "*addition* becomes a synthetic act for all concerned: the growth of the group becomes the activity of each person." The operations of revolutionary arithmetic bear the imprint of the class struggle. To this synthetic addition, which is not a simple juxtaposition of supplementary units but the medium within which is elaborated an organic whole (that is more than the simple sum of its parts), "Réponse à Claude Lefort" would oppose a neo-capitalist practice defined as the multiplication of division ("Why would the division not be multiplied until infinity?" he asks), precisely the practice which progressivist addition takes it upon itself to resist.

But it is not the Liberation of Paris which the *Critique de la raison dialectique* takes as its example of the group in fusion, but the storming of the Bastille. There would be several ways of explaining this displacement of the model. First, the Liberation is too far from our present existence (it was during the fifties that Sartre was working on the *Critique* — ten years later). On the one hand, the promises of the Liberation had not been kept. The Fourth Republic was liberation betrayed. But on the other hand, the ideology of liberation had promoted an exaggerated cult of heroism. At the time, it was no longer a matter of dying on the right side that counted, but surviving there. "Things were too simple," he said to Kenneth Tynan. He had already told Camus that he was dated. There is a second way of explaining the displacement — from the Liberation to the Bastille — of the model of the group in fusion, and it is the inverse of the previous one. The Liberation remained too close and had not yet found its Mathieus, Lefebvres, and Guérins. A third explanation? Perhaps Sartre continued to reserve the Liberation for a different book. But in the last analysis, the displacement itself is of little import. The Liberation, with the shock of lived experience, remains for Sartre the prototype of the group in fusion. Which is why it would not be vain to introduce at this point a few reminders relating to chronology.

The first concerns the date of publication of *Les Chemins de la liberté*. It was 1945, that is, precisely one year after Paris was liberated or — to formulate it otherwise — a year after Sartre, in the articles assigned him by *Combat*, composed his first-person, live account of that historic event.

The second chronological factor that I would like to introduce does not belong to the same order of duration. It finds its place not in the shared time of common memories and collective experience but, rather, within the fictive temporality prevailing within novels. The publisher's blurb for the two first volumes of *Les Chemins de la liberté*, in fact, informs us that the series would eventually bring its characters to an end defined as the liberation of Paris. A date — 1944, for example — does not have the same status on either side of the novelistic frame. It may even be that, as in the case of the constellation named after a dog and the barking animal of that name, we are dealing with a mere homonymical coincidence. Or as in the case of someone named Gerlach in real life and someone who would be named Gerlach in *Les Séquestrés d'Altona*. Whatever the case may be, the conclusion that the narrative of the *Chemins* adopts as its own, its end point, is the fictive internalization of the historical context which was the actual backdrop of their first publication. By which I mean that it is improbable that Sartre had thought of the liberation of Paris as the end point of his novel before the course of history allowed him to participate in it and to live it in person in the reality of a Parisian summer. The Germans departed, censorship was lifted, printers returned to their presses. It was only at the time he was able to publish his novel that he realized what its ending would be: the moment at which he published the novel. As though it were possible for the two 1944s, the 1944 outside the text and the 1944 within it, that of Paris and that of the *Chemins*, to end up one day by converging. It should be recalled in this context that Sartre never reincorporated his articles of August 1944 in a published volume, probably because he intended to integrate them into *La Dernière Chance*. But it happened that what it had been possible to narrate in the heat of the event as a journalistic event was consumed in the process, leaving behind nothing but its ashes to the memory of the novel. *Les Chemins* were never to reach the liberation of Paris.

Which might constitute a clue that the novel, as such, does not — and could not — have any relation with the group in fusion. It does not tolerate victory.

That's not its style.

2. "The group in fusion," says Sartre, "is the city." By which is meant Paris. 1789, 1848, 1870, 1944: always the same. Above all it is not an American city.

The Parisian insurrection had brought the archetype of the group in fusion down to earth. The second journalistic report revealed to Sartre, as he discovered the space of America, the archetype of seriality. Page after page, to the point of dizziness, we are confronted with the puzzle of homogeneity, the platitude of what lies side by side. Touching was not the sensory register that Sartre was most inclined to trust. And in America, everything was in contact. But no more than that. Contiguity was the sole legal form of association. Individualism and conformity competed in the somnolent celebration of private property and neighborhood. Politics was not to be conducted in the street: everyone might see you.

The best articles inspired by that trip are reproduced in *Situations* III: one finds in them the matrix of what the *Critique* would subsequently elaborate on the subject of series. Since all citizens resemble one another, as fashion dictates, they are given a number that will prevent any confusion. All the same, but each in turn. Precisely like the N + 1 streets of New York. Or like soldiers with their dogtag numbers. It is Sartre himself, to be sure, who makes the connection. The sequence of numerals being infinite, the realm of series is the genesis of that which knows no end. Are there any proper numbers? A numeral, all the same, cannot be addressed by its first name.

But the *Critique* does not return to survey the topography of New York. In that work, Sartre finds by looking out his own window the example allowing him to analyze the serial group: the line forming at a Parisian taxi station. Each individual has taken his number and waits for his turn to come. Paris has become Americanized. The group in fusion was the mobilization of an impatient city beginning its march forward. The series is a group of stationary pedestrians waiting at the corner of the place Saint-Germain-des-Prés.

There can be no question, in this context, of simply confronting — without further precaution — these two quite different forms of incompletion, that of the series and that of *Les Chemins de la liberté*. The first is part of its definition; the second is a developmental contingency. A series can, in fact, come to a halt, although it could, in principle, continue indefinitely. There is always room in it for one more, for as far as one can see. It never declares itself complete but nonetheless is in no way lacking. It can very well make do with what it does not have. It is too early, however, to suggest that there is not necessarily anything missing from *Les Chemins de la liberté* just because they came to a halt before reaching the ending they had anticipated.

INSERT. It is well to return to the date on which — the event through which — Sartre understood what the ending of *Les Chemins de la liberté* was to be. He learned where he was headed precisely at the moment of their publication. The starting point had long been known. From the very beginning, it was clear that the machine of *La Nausée* had to be set aright, that first Munich, then the declaration of war of 1939 and the captivity of 1940 constituted excellent occasions for a break, opportunely furnished by history to the novelist intent on exploiting them. But he started off without knowing where *Les Chemins de la liberté* would take him. The first two volumes were no doubt already completed when Sartre received the revelation of what their ending would be. They were thus completed — without knowing their completion. Ended without an ending. Were they waiting to appear (to be able to appear) in order to know where they would lead? At the very least, it is a fact that they waited to appear until their ending had already transpired. The departure of the Germans and the collapse of the Vichy regime, as we have seen, were simultaneously the occasion on which the work's first two volumes (*L'Age de raison* and *Le Sursis*) were to appear and the event to which Sartre promises (on the work's cover), and promises himself, to devote the following and concluding volume of *Les Chemins*.

This can be formulated slightly differently by saying that Sartre wanted the writing of *Les Chemins* to make contact with the precise moment in which their reading began. *A la recherche du temps perdu* retraces everything which precedes its own writing; it brings the narrative to the inception of its own narration. *Les Chemins*, for their part, would like to bring it to the point of its own reading. To the point of an encounter not with the imaginary, but with the real. Not to the moment when the writer takes control of the narrative, but to the moment the narrative leaves the author's hands, the moment it escapes him. Which means, since they appeared before their composition was completed ("I request that my characters not be judged on the basis of these two first volumes," wrote the author in his blurb), that while one part of *Les Chemins* was being written by the novelist, another would already be in the process of being read by its readers. Which means, consequently, that a single work (*Les Chemins de la liberté*) might be written and read simultaneously. In the years following the liberation of Paris, readers could indeed read the first volumes of the whole while the author was still writing the last.

This situation, as such, bears a direct relation to what has been called the work's incompletion. In a certain sense, the project of bringing the narrative to a halt at the precise moment of its publication is in perfect harmony with the definition of literary practice given in the second chapter of *Qu'est-ce que la littérature?* "Why Write?" Sartre precisely demonstrates there that reading is the specific end of writing. A work does not exist, is not finished, is not even yet written so long as it has not yet been objectivized in a reading. The global project of *Les Chemins*, insofar as they propose to end at their date of publication, adheres faithfully to the economy mobilized by that definition.

"A writer cannot read what he writes," according to Sartre. But he does not write until he has been read. He thus needs a second person, the reader, who constitutes, in every sense of the word, the end of his work — the goal he pursues along with its final interruption. From which it follows, just as rigorously, that reading cannot be contemporary with writing or that a text (*Les Chemins de la liberté*, for example) could in no case be simultaneously in the hands of its author and those of its readers, could not be read and written simultaneously. "As far as the reader may go,"

Sartre declares, "the author has gone further than him." At the end of *Les Mots*, he tells of how he feeds critics the books he is no longer writing to graze on, a bit like Cartouche distributing gold coins to delay his pursuers. Clearly this difference disjoining the two constitutive edges of the literary object will not be without consequence for the Sartrean program of writing for his age. Will literature, like bananas, be able to be consumed on the spot if the reader cannot be the author's contemporary? If it is forbidden them to meet and be co-present to each other? If writing is above all an energy which defends against being read?

Moreover: What is an unfinished book? What is missing from *Lamiel*, *Bouvard et Pécuchet*, *The Man without Qualities*, *The Castle*? What more does *La Nausée* have than *Les Chemins de la liberté*? Perhaps we would never have been able to know that the last mentioned were not finished if the author had not proclaimed so from the rooftops. Moreover, concerning *La Nausée* itself, we have seen that Sartre, after completing and publishing it, was to state, after the fact, that it was unfinished. An unfinished book, arbitrarily and tautologically, is but a book whose author has decided — or at least concerning which he has said — that it is unfinished (concerning which he did not say, in the event of death, that it was finished). We shall see that however completed it is, *La Nausée* is not very well ended. Even if (in theory) it bears its end within itself, its conclusion leaves something to be desired. But it does not belong to the literary genre or subvariety of books pretending to incompletion. Which are published with the label "incomplete." Which want to appear incomplete. Abortion as a literary genre: Sartre did all he could to let it be known that his books were not carried to term.

But for whom does one write unfinished books, and why choose such a genre? There is a partial response in the interview with Contat: "As long as he is alive," Sartre tells him, "the work he has written belongs to the author. In particular it belongs to him if it is not finished." In this sense, Sartre's life work, which as long as he was alive would have been a kind of prepublication, a generous mass of preview-extracts, can be considered as governed by a strategy whose aim has been, in every sense of the word, to retain the reader. Wait: don't go, don't speak. Make sure he is on the line, but reduced to silence. I'm not done; it's not yet your turn.

Two consequences issue from the definition according to which a book cannot be read before being finished, that the end of a book coincides with its reading. The first corresponds to a strict interpretation of the formula. It posits that from the very instant a text has been read, it takes on the property of completion. In this sense, Sartre insisted in vain. *Les Chemins de la liberté* come to a halt at the moment when they appear, even if they have not had the time to give, as planned, an account of that moment. The second interpretation is far looser. It is the one through which Sartre defends himself against being read. An author can always say, "Truce!" He can always say he hasn't finished, in order to delay his readers.

To come back to *Les Chemins*, their incompleteness is undoubtedly a retroactive effect of their precipitous manifestation. If they wanted to conclude with an account of the Liberation, they should have ended with the anthology of articles of August 1944, written in the heat of the insurrection. A premature contact with their reader cut them off from their end. No one asked him for his papers. It was Sartre who insisted on showing them. And who stopped short by himself.

I would rather indicate, in far more general terms, several features linking the novel as a genre and the Sartrean problematic of the series.

Les Chemins thus missed the objective they had taken on, the group in fusion. Might the novel per se be condemned to seriality? But in that case, ought one not to consider the topography of America — whose discovery by Sartre followed by only a few months that of the group in fusion and which would subsequently serve as matrix for the other central concept of the *Critique*, seriality — ought one not to consider it (as a serialized space) a particularly propitious terrain for the development of the novel, literally speaking, its terrain par excellence?

It would thus be impossible to attack the one without sooner or later entering into contact with the other. It is well known that Sartre's discovery of Dos Passos, Faulkner, and Hemingway, the shock elicited by their novelistic technique, were decisive in the conception of *Les Chemins de la liberté*. We should ask, at this point, in what way those writers are American. More specifically, it was concerning Faulkner that Sartre first mentioned idiocy. The term would be crucial in his reading of Flaubert. Does the temptation of idiocy have an essential relation with seriality, the novel, and social fragmentation? Idiocy is separation, schizophrenic or not. There is no social link. But Sartre seeks growing awareness, which is on the side of the *koinos*, not the *idios*. His relation with American novelists is not simple: "I love his art," he says of Faulkner, "but I do not believe in his metaphysics." A tragedy of fate, the American novel shows the impasses of capitalism, but goes no further. The committed novel will disclose the future, which is socialist. The epic of freedom is not to be a tale told by an idiot, filled solely with sound and fury and signifying nothing. It is to be a hesitation — not to be overly prolonged — between meaning and fury.

INSERT (*MADE IN U.S.A.*). In the author's insert accompanying the two first volumes of *Les Chemins*, instead of summarizing events or introducing characters, Sartre explains his reasons for using different novelistic techniques in *L'Age de raison* than in *Le Sursis*. In the first volume, he says, he remained faithful to traditional narrative forms (which include interior monologue), in which individuals are seen to evolve in relation to one another, but without their identity itself, their individuality, being called into question. "During the deceptive lull of 1937–38," he writes in justifying his choice, "there were those who managed to retain the illusion in certain circles of having an impervious and discrete individual history." Now it is precisely the collapse of that illusion which is the subject of the second novel. *Le Sursis* effectively retraces the Munich crisis, a situation, that is, in which historical urgency inculcates in the individuals it sweeps away an experience of collectivity. The individual is surprised to find himself "in a process of generalization and dissolution." In depicting that violent osmosis, in which characters lose themselves in their discovery of a social dimension, traditional narrative technique proves inadequate. I have thus borrowed, says Sartre, from the novelists of simultaneity their technological innovations. Whereupon he mentions two names: Virginia Woolf and Dos Passos. The first is English; the second, American. Both are Anglo-Saxon.

In *L'Age de raison*, history is not absent, simply distant. The Spanish Civil War remains contained within its borders, and Mathieu is able to live in Paris without living it as such, indeed even regretting not living it. The centers of crisis are circumscribed, thus affording the narrative a stability respectful of the unity of place. In *Le Sursis*, by contrast, the so-called Munich crisis explodes, in a certain sense, everywhere at once, not only in Munich but also in Paris, in Czechoslovakia, in Spain, everywhere without exception. In opposition to the immobilism of the preceding novel, it is this general mobilization of characters and this overlapping of places which requires recourse to the procedure of simultaneous narration borrowed by Sartre from what he elsewhere calls the "American technique." The traditional narrator is in solidarity with what is called in *Qu'est-ce que la littérature?* a stabilized society. The narrative innovations of the second volume — Sartre asks us not to see them as mere formal experiments — are quite precisely intended to account for the collapse of that society as it observes itself rocked by crisis and swept away in a historical debacle.

But it should be recalled that Sartre is not an unconditional admirer of the American novelists. If he likes them, it is above all because he likes to criticize them. He is quite severe, for instance, with Faulkner, whose "technique of disorder" will not resist, in his opinion, a rudimentary reading of Heidegger. In the article on *L'Etranger*, he will similarly reproach Camus with all too facile effects of absurdity and non-sense which such procedures allow him to produce. Moreover, even the more-than-admiring article he wrote on Dos Passos' *1919* restricts the validity of the formal inventions of the American novelist to the limits of mimetic referentiality. It was because that was the only manner in which to tell the truth about American capitalism that he was right to resort to them. A chaotic novel for a chaotic world. An inhuman novel for an inhuman world.

But (with the exception of the first scenes of *La Mort dans l'âme*, showing Gomez in refuge at New York), it is not in the United States that *Les Chemins de la liberté* take place. It is even precisely in Paris that Sartre wants to bring them to an end, and in a historical and social situation that makes of it the exact antithesis of American space. No doubt the technique of simultaneity (*Made in U.S.A.*) is marvelously well suited to depict moments of personal disintegration, the negative effects exercised by a chaotic social order on the subjective synthesis. But the group in fusion, the one, for example, to be embodied by the Parisian insurrection of 1944, constitutes precisely the transcendence of such moments. It is a matter not of a return to the prior subjective immobility, but of a metamorphosis of disorder into movement, an epic exploitation of the energy emergent from the fission of individualities. It goes without saying that the narration of this third moment cannot be entrusted to the technology perfected in the interests of the second. One might consequently wonder at this point to what extent the incompletion of *Les Chemins de la liberté* is not a function of the fact that Sartre was unable to transcend, as he had proposed, American narrative innovations, that he failed to invent the style allowing the group in fusion to tell (of) itself, the style without which it was condemned to mark time in the limbo of the unspeakable. *L'Age de raison* is the stability of the ego (thesis). In *Le Sursis*, it collapses (antithesis). But as in Bataille, whom Sartre reproaches for it, the synthesis does not come. The third section, *La Mort dans l'âme*, barely prolongs the situation in *Le Sursis*: opening night after the dress rehearsal. The mobilization had been for nothing. Now it was for something. But to be a soldier is first of all to receive a registration number — to serve an apprenticeship in seriality, the exact opposite of the group in fusion. The novel never manages to stop being American. It is not by following the paths of the novel that one steps out of series.

On the occasion of republishing *Puissances du roman* (in *Approches de l'imaginaire*), Caillois recalled the atmosphere in which he had composed his brief work: "In the 'full' society dreamed of by the Collège de Sociologie, the novel would not have its place."

Elaborated on the morrow of the defeat, *Puissances du roman* does not limit itself to being merely contemporary with the project of *Les Chemins*. It also undertakes to put an end to the serialized space of dispersive sociality. For one as for the other, society is a duty to be *fulfilled*. It is incumbent to put an end to a society that is no more than an institutionalization of solitude and rests on the absence of the other. But unlike Caillois's book, Sartre's is a novel: can one step out of seriality through novelistic channels? Caillois's full society corresponds approximately to Sartre's group in fusion. In that full society, "There exists no place for a novel: no void, no interstice, no solitude in which the desire for a different life might grow. The individual thinks only of history."

No doubt the novel, too — Sartre's, for example (Caillois mentions those of Hemingway, Montherlant, Saint-Exupéry, W. Faulkner, A. Malraux, E. von Salomon) — can eventually be brought to subscribe to such a program. It can propose its own variations on the theme of "man's misery outside of society" and dream in turn of a society with no room for itself. It will nevertheless be appreciated only in reading rooms. In a certain sense, the novel has never done anything other than denounce a society without principle of cohesion, which separates instead of joining, and so forth. It is nonetheless one of the most virulent agents of individualist entropy. It begins by detaching its reader from what surrounds him. There is no social relation.

In 1972, a French Maoist wished that Sartre, instead of wasting his time on *L'Idiot de la famille*, would write a popular novel. The political yield would be more apparent. Sartre's answer: "How might one go about striking the attention of the masses? A popular revolutionary novel ought not to be read by everyone alone in his corner: it would be necessary to be able to read it together." But who would be reading? The mass of readers — or the masses' (delegated) readers — added up synthetically? It would seem that the author, a striking intelligence, would remove himself from the collectivity: necessarily? The question has its importance, since for Sartre the writer is incapable of joining both ends; he will never succeed in reading himself. He may politely announce to his readers that he will rejoin them in an instant, but that is a pure formality. He will do nothing of the sort. He is not on the same side. "However far the reader may go, the author has gone further than him." *Qu'est-ce que la littérature?* puts things in their place. Moreover, one wonders why collectivization should affect reading alone. Why not also collectivize writing while one is at it? Such a move would surely be no less popular or revolutionary. But the problem in such an event would lie in finding a reader, that is, someone who would not have written. In addition, Sartre gives no specification concerning the scenographic modalities of the collective reading he dreams of in *On a raison de se révolter*. Would everyone meet in the same auditorium, each reading in a low voice? or a loud one? reading his personal copy? or the text projected on a screen? listening to the voice of a (present or recorded) reader who would speak the text before the assembled public?

Before *Les Chemins de la liberté*, Sartre had his theory, one of man alone. With *Les Chemins*, he moved to one of men together. It is not a matter of a simple multiplication of the first. But one is hard put to see what men, once together, would do with a book. This utopia of a collective reader, this desire to group around a text, to ignite a readers' hearth whose heat, by contagion, would generate a group in fusion, is not unrelated to the suspension of *Les Chemins de la liberté*, which will not succeed in saying from where they came. Caillois, in *Puissances du roman*, dreamed of a full society. With negligible disparities, such is the exact program of Sartre's novelistic project. With the difference, nevertheless, that we are confronted with a novel dreaming of a society where there would be no more room for the solitary pleasures of novel reading.

What would be the difference, moreover, between such a collective reading and a theatrical event on the order of a "happening" (which Sartre defined in

1966 as "the concrete organization of the assembled members of the audience into a group ")? Although matters are more complicated — in particular because Sartre's conception of the theater remains (in spite of everything) essentially literary, that is, intent on maintaining the primacy of a text which must have been written before being dramatized, but also because Sartre will, on occasion, denounce what he finds irremediably bourgeois in the institution of the theater, which he contrasts with more popular and less elevated art forms such as film — it is nonetheless the case that the theater auditorium constitutes for Sartre the matrix and prototype of being-together, if not of the group in fusion. The important section of *L'Etre et le néant* devoted to the existence of others is dominated by the description of the crucial but painful experience of what Sartre calls the other's gaze — that which reveals to me my own objectivity and contingency. The experience is illustrated by a reduced scene during which a third party surprises a voyeur with his eye glued to the keyhole, through which he spies on gestures not addressed to him. But even as the voyeur's gaze requires solitude, just as surely does the spectator's imply community. The arrival of the third party is a source of discomfort for the gaze whose solitary vocation it disturbs. In the theater, the exact inverse holds: there, one would be uncomfortable to find oneself alone. "Everyone knows," says Sartre, "that unacknowledged sense of embarrassment that seizes us in a half-empty auditorium." A spectator is always already a "co-spectator." The theater, in fact, allows one to escape simultaneously from solitude and the other's gaze. It allows one to be with others without facing them. Being together is, first of all, being seated in the same direction (as in the back seat of an automobile, everyone facing forward). People don't look at one another, but they look together at the same thing. The respite of the theater offers a pause from jealous spying, but that implies, plainly, that the spectacle is not in the auditorium (in which, to ensure the operation's success, one begins by turning out the lights). One is together only in the dark. And it is precisely there that novelistic literature fails to produce an authentic collectivity: lights have to be turned on before one can begin to read.

The bourgeois novel and the people's theater are like day and night. Between them there passes for Sartre one of the first lines of demarcation of the class struggle. It was in 1940, in Stalag XII D, while performing before his companions in captivity a play he had written for them, that he rediscovered that object he had believed to be lost, the crowd. On the same occasion, he discovered the religious nature of the theater. That was the word he employed. The etymology of religion is common knowledge: that nature is political.

. . . Since the advent of Schönberg and his school, there exists another — musical — sense of the term *series*.

As is known, the introduction of twelve-tone music in France was to a considerable extent the accomplishment, after the war, of René Leibowitz, who on occasion wrote for *Les Temps modernes*. The book he published in 1950, *L'Artiste et sa conscience*, would even be preceded by a study by Sartre. Alas, like the book itself, the study speaks of Jdanov but very little of Schönberg or Webern. The sole allusion it contains is in the form of an act of disavowal: "It is not my intent, as may be imagined, to explain tonal music by the regime of private property." In addition — that is, in sum — Sartre describes and strains to "dialecticize" the conflict between "the laboring masses who want music" and "modern music which demands an elite." Might music, which is not committed [*engagée*] by virtue of its content, achieve that status, even in spite of itself, by virtue of its addressee and the social conditions of its consumption? The question here is: For whom does one write modern music?

The social series was defined in *Critique* by the juxtaposition of individuals along a chain in which they are distinguished from one another solely by their number in order. An abstract relation, says Sartre, since it fails to take into account what those individuals are, who they are. Serial music has also frequently been accused of being an abstract music. In his introduction to Leibowitz, Sartre formulates the alternative at which he arrives in these terms: a "free but abstract art" (Schönberg) versus a "concrete but encumbered art" (Jdanov). The juxtaposition of the twelve tones of the series in a kind of formal equality destroys the organic unity and internal hierarchy of the tonal scale. Tonality was onerous. The series suspends the sonorous ponderousness whose laws, during the classical era, had regulated the development of melodic lines right to their cadence. It reveals to musical cosmology a decisive decentering: the music of the spheres will not survive it. Insofar as it gravitates around effects of resolution and unison, tonal music remained Newtonian, not to say Aristotelian. But Boulez was to evoke "the total absence of weightiness" within which Webern's music develops. Man has sung on the moon. The baritone's humility impossible: even the deepest voices no longer able to descend. Delivered of the weight of existence, they negotiate the silence of infinite space. Concord or discord: the difference can no longer be heard. The theme takes flight in a fugue without coda. Serial proliferation sounds still again the end of the end . . .

. . . To return to *Les Chemins de la liberté*, relieved in extremis of their final movement: their very project, as we have seen and will see, answered the desire for an end, a descent, a chance that might be authentically the last, a falling due from which there would be no possibility of recovery. But *La Mort dans l'âme*, in holding *La Dernière Chance* at bay, committed the narrative to a movement such that it would perpetually remain equidistant from its end. The failure bringing it to a halt before term would thus respond to a secret calculation by means of which the novel would at least spare itself infinity. An internal resistance would cause the novelistic discourse to bridle at the approach of the narrative seriality of sequences without end. What might a chromatic, atonal, or serial novel be? With its final chord unresolved, suspended, it would seem that Sartre's novel holds back, discordant, at the very brink of its series . . .

In speaking of the "advantage" accruing to *Les Chemins de la liberté* by dint of their incompletion, Blanchot was referring to the discomfort of the situation in which Sartre unabashedly abandons his reader and leaves him on his own.

For every critical judgment of the novelistic fragment he has published, the author of an unfinished work can always invoke in his defense what has not yet appeared. Wait before making any pronouncement. This is only the beginning. The future holds many surprises. In his author's insert, Sartre did indeed take advantage of such a case of incompletion in order to ask critics to hold back, to accord him a reprieve: "I request that my characters not be judged on the basis of these first two volumes."

But on what else might they be judged, since these are the sole documents in the case? And how is one to read a book that is intent on being unfinished? How is one to describe the act of reading when its object is a book that claims to be "entirely still to come" or, in Blanchot's words, "does not yet exist"?

Sartre remains silent.

We might parody Proust and say that the most beautiful thing in Sartre is the books that he did not write, those endings concerning which he did everything so that we see them as missing, the obstinacy with which not only *Les Chemins* but also each of his other books ends up imperturbably cutting itself off from its end, separating itself from it, achieving its own detachment. Like the cathedrals that the Middle Ages abandoned in midconstruction all over Europe, each of his projects ends up colliding with a "to be continued" bereft of future, prolonging the series of solitary Volumes I which no longer even wait for their ends to reunite with them.

BERKELEY. 15 April 1980. 7 P.M. Pacific Time. Tuesday, I believe. The evening news announces that "French philosopher Jean-Paul Sartre is dead." Immediately, I think of a verse by the late Queneau: "If I speak of a man, he will soon be dead." In what way does the news affect me? Do these pages owe it to him to say? Should a text allow itself to be overtaken by the death of its object? And if it should, is it capable of doing so? I was going to say his disappearance, but it is not easy to take inventory of just what is disappearing with this death. Perhaps nothing. He is survived by — his name. The event undoubtedly was factored into the text's calculations, and yet there is no way in which its title could be some version of *Sartre Is Dead* (but even less *The Living Sartre*).

Conan Doyle, at the behest of his readers, had been obliged to resuscitate Sherlock Holmes. I am not about to attempt a "Sartre, *veni foras!*" There is also the beautiful anecdote Leiris tells about Puccini. He was in the process of writing *Turandot* when he realized, rather quickly, that his sickness would not allow him the time to finish. Whereupon he ordered the executor of his will to see to it that his opera be completed in accordance with his instructions and that on opening night, at the last note he would have written in his hand, the performance be interrupted just long enough for the conductor to announce: "At this moment, the *Maestro* died" — and then be continued until the final curtain. Sartre used to wonder what would happen to the Seventh Symphony if Furtwängler were felled by a heart attack in the middle of its performance. But unlike Sherlock Holmes, Sartre is not — or not merely — a character in this book; unlike Puccini, he is not simply its author or composer. As for myself, at this point I already hesitate to say that I am conducting him.

"If I speak of time, it already no longer exists." *Esse est percipi.* Certain messages limit themselves to letting you know where they reach you. For example, in the serialized suburbs of paradise, from which I imagine that his death is instilling, will instill, has instilled, will have instilled — given the change in time, what is the proper tense? — a bit of fusion in the streets of Paris.

Chapter 3
The Taste of the Future

"Twenty times I reread the last pages of *Madame Bovary*; when it was over, I knew whole paragraphs by heart." A relationship without a future (it is said) is a relationship that is already over. Along with the future, the present evaporates. But the past does not survive them: the energy to endure and to have taken place disappear simultaneously. The happiness of making a break would be free of all shadow if such retroactive annulments did not condemn what they cut short to not having occurred. Blanchot proposes the following definition of the novel: "Something has happened, which one has lived through and subsequently recounts." The ending can be a stroke of good fortune when it allows the event to be accomplished, and through its accomplishment, for memory to embrace it. But malign fate, by causing the letters that Léon had addressed to his wife to fall into Charles's hands, simultaneously deprives the latter of the healing grief in which he might lament what had just come to an end. It consigns him to the imponderable realm of the unfulfilled. Auguste Comte considered widowhood the completed form of marriage: love in its perfect tense. Charles had just settled into the perfection of such morose delectation when it befell him to open the secret drawer of the rosewood dresser. Until then, he was grieving over the loss of Emma. He was now obliged to lose that very loss and to lose himself in that loss thereafter bereft of any object. Sartre was to condemn the security of the perfect tense from which classical narrative issued: "It is disengaged from the story it recounts; it looks backward to consider it in its truth." But when Charles turned to look back on it, his story crumbled into dust. Emma, twice lost like Eurydice, deprived him even of the posthumous consolation of a mourning he no longer was entitled to conduct. What you lost you never had. Flaubert wanted to write a book about nothing — and nothing happened. Who mentioned the perfect? The end of *Madame Bovary* participates, rather, in what Proust called, in a different context, the "eternal imperfect."

It is in *Les Mots* that Sartre recounts his precocious fascination before the opaqueness of the last pages of *Madame Bovary*. Did the rest of the novel interest him less? Should the end of a book always interest more than the rest? And outside of books? But are there any ends outside of books? To all these questions Sartre offers several answers. At times, he speaks of the "end illuminating the world"; at others, he denounces it under the heading "retrospective illusion."

1936: the year in which Sartre published his first book, *L'Imagination*, a passing interest in the Popular Front inspired Thorez, secretary general of the Communist party, to issue his famous aphorism: "It is necessary to know how to end a strike." But Sartre at the time was no more than a spectator (he did not frequent any groups in fusion). He ends his first book with an announcement: "At this point it would be necessary to broach the phenomenological description of the image 'structure.' We shall attempt this in another work." The book, in ending, effaces itself before the one that it announces. The king is dead! Long live the king! It is a paschal, Easter-like ending: death and resurrection. It falls under the category recently invoked to assemble — under the oxymoron *opening closing* — those concluding words triggering in the reader "a prospective activity of *expectation*." Instead of a retrospective balance sheet recapitulating the terrain covered, they sketch the future. In a single and common gesture, they close and open, conclude and introduce. A peaceful solution to the conflict between end and future, the fear of ending and that of not ending, the wish to have been and that to continue being — preservation and creation.

Let there be no error: there is absolutely nothing abnormal in such a closing. On the contrary, composition manuals recommend that the subject be expanded in conclusion. It is considered good taste for an author to finish with a sentence (like an *Au revoir*) announcing his future works. Such a foretaste plainly does not imply that the book he is concluding is in any way lacking. *L'Imagination* covered the complete itinerary that it had assigned itself. It concluded its program: to demonstrate that the starting point of classical theories of the image entailed a confusion between imagination and perception. The future of his opening conclusion thus did not introduce any mark of incompleteness in the book it closed.

Concerning this first conclusion, presented in the future, it will perhaps not be unhelpful to recall the analyses found in Sartre's philosophy of this fundamental temporal dimension. Analyses as numerous as they are unstable, at once insistent and indecisive, repetitive and contradictory: the circle they run traces the whirligig generating the Sartrean text at what is undoubtedly its most idiosyncratic. Its terrain is constituted by what can be called the rivalry of the present and the future.

We will come back to the point, but the theory of commitment can be defined briefly as a conquest of the present. One writes for one'e age. Art cannot be reduced to a dialogue "with men who are not yet born." Aphorisms abound: "We have no desire to win our case on appeal." Or: "We do not want to look on our world with future eyes." The title he gave to his journal, *Les Temps modernes*, has programmatic value. Blanchot was to link the experience of writing with what he calls the absence of time, a time lost in each of its dimensions: the past, to be sure, but also the future and, above all, the present. Writing, for Sartre, is, on the contrary, the only means for a man, for every man, to belong to his own time. The verb *écrire* must be conjugated in the present.

Must be: the Sartrean present, in point of fact, has nothing of an impassive indicative. It is not something to be described but, rather, to be prescribed: committed literature will denounce the objectivist postulates of the realist aesthetic. It is a voluntaristic present, a program, almost an obligation. Its maxim of impatience rejects the structures of expectation. The present, in its minimal definition, is that which cannot wait. It rejects preoccupation: the future is none of its business. In 1946, Sartre published a short text eloquently entitled "Writing for One's Age" [Ecrire pour son époque]. Its ending is no less eloquent: "Afterward — the deluge!" it concludes. But this was already not new. The first page of *La Nausée* did nothing but affirm, to the point of saturation, the imperative of the present: "It would be best to write down events day by day. . . . I have to say how I see this table, the street, the people." As for the deluge, Roquentin concludes his diary by noting: "Tomorrow rain will fall over Bouville." To be continued.

It is at this juncture that the whirligig emerges. For what ought to be, is not. And if it is necessary for it to exist, that is because it is lacking. Now, as soon as one has made a goal of it, how is one to distinguish the present from the future against which it was set up? The next step will be that of rivalry. It is formulated at the end of *Saint Genet* (as well as elsewhere): "The future is there, more present than the present." This is a matter of course as soon as one has decided that the present has a greater future than the future, defined the present by its ability to anticipate itself (that it exists only on the condition of being in advance of itself), and posited that the specificity of the present is to move beyond itself. In the same vein, "Les Communistes et la paix" will propose, "The immediate reality is the future." The present here has precipitated itself into the future, which has taken priority over it. The present is a process, but a process given consistency by the future. There is no present if it is not introduced by the future. More even than introduced, we should say — in the sense in which Sartre, precisely, wrote a "Présentation des *Temps modernes*" — that there is no present unless it is presented by the future. There occurs at this point what Sartre calls "something of an inversion of time": life is introduced to its present by its future, to what it is by what it is not. Or, differently stated, there is but one reserve of capital, the future, for which the present is a kind of revenue. The present is granted as a bonus to whoever has the grace of being in his entirety yet to come.

But the spiral continues. A second turn, which is not a return, ensues. We began by wanting the present against the future. Whereupon we ended up realizing that the present is in its entirety yet to come. Now it is the future's turn to break free of the present, to affirm itself against it. Sartre's formula for this moment: "The future is blocked." *Fort/Da*: as close and as far as can be. Man in the future will be what Heidegger called a being of distances. "The future is not *realized*," does not allow itself to be "caught," according to *L'Etre et le néant*. And *Les Mots*: "Such is the mirage, the future more real than the present." It is not certain that grammar allows for the present to be used in the imperative. It is doubtful, on the other hand, that the future, whatever the grammar books say, can ever participate in the indicative. It is a promise, a mortgage, a commitment — which is not used without risk.

1. Sartre's first book ended with these words: "We shall attempt as much in a different work." The future proved to be quite indulgent. It was willing to confirm the future of 1936, and in 1940, Sartre brought out *L'Imaginaire*, the volume announced at the end of *L'Imagination*. But a single occurrence does not prove any rule. This was a first and only chance. Simone de Beauvoir explains why. Sartre, who had been asked to write a work on the imagination, submitted to his publisher a manuscript too voluminous for the collection in which it was to appear. His editor asked him to split it in two and published only the first half. The future of the closing is future only out of diplomacy: the work it announces was already written, and merely needed a publisher.

2. The case is not the same for *L'Etre et le néant*, which nevertheless reemploys in its conclusion the precise formula that had been used in *L'Imagination*, and announces a treatise on ethics: "We shall devote our next work to that task." But we are no longer in 1936. Sartre is far more occupied. Contrary to the case of his first book, the announcement concluding the 1943 volume refers to a work that is not yet written: it would not be subsequently. Not written, not finished — not published, in any event: it would not be read. The diplomatic future has yielded to an imprudent future. What weight should be attributed to the failure constituted by this unhonored commitment, this violated pledge? It might well be the case, moreover, that ethics never asked for any more than this. That it found safety in the future. That the intention was enough for it. It is of little consequence, moreover. The loss of its future is of little importance for *L'Etre et le néant*,

which remains, as such, a completed work whose coherence is not jeopardized by the defection of its successor.

3. It is with *Critique de la raison dialectique* that the "critical" threshhold is crossed. Like the previous works, it ends with the by now traditional opening closing: "The reflexive experience of this as yet formal adventure will be the object of our second volume." As in *L'Etre et le néant*, this closing will not be followed by any effects. The announced volume will never see the light of day. But that is not new. What is new is the status of this missing volume. Until now, Sartre had announced "another work" or "a next work." What he announces at the end of the *Critique* is "our second volume." One has to choose: one is either the only son or the firstborn. It is difficult to be simultaneously alone and first. What had to have happened in order for a first volume to remain by itself? Was it its brother's keeper? One would have to have Ponge's irony to entitle abruptly, after the fact, *Tome premier* the anthology (followed by no other) of his early writings. The solitude of the *Critique* is no longer the splendid isolation of *L'Etre et le néant*, the proud solipsism of man by himself; it is guilty of the absence of the other which undermines it. The fact that its closing opens onto a future that will not allow itself to be broached now cleaves the present and introduces a retroactive lack. The unwritten book filters back into the written one. The future, as it aborts, forms an enclave within its walls.

4. The Flaubert study only confirms the curve of these closings, the growing virulence of their morrow-less futures. The first part of *L'Idiot de la famille* appeared in 1971, ending on the expected words: "We shall be able to understand what that means only at the end of this work, after rereading *Madame Bovary*." This much should have been expected. And yet a new step has been taken. A supplementary step into incompletion, one more step less. The fact that Sartre, in the course of writing *L'Etre et le néant*, encountered the imperative of an ethics is one thing, but it did not entail that *L'Etre et le néant* itself had to respond to that imperative. The situation of *Idiot* is radically different. There Sartre specifically proposed to study him whom (in an interview) he had called "the individual Flaubert who wrote *Madame Bovary*." And it is precisely when he is about to broach *Madame Bovary* that the work comes to a stop. It is cut short at the precise moment when it is about to approach its subject, at the moment when — with all the preliminaries properly disposed of — it would at last examine that in view of which the book had been undertaken. Until this juncture, the opening closings had announced a work other than the one they were concluding. Those of *L'Idiot* bizarrely announce a book that differs from the one being read only because it is not written. That is the sole — imponderable — difference. The last lines of *L'Idiot de la famille* announce *L'Idiot de la famille*. Sartre's last book stops at the threshold of itself, concluding by introducing itself. It is fully entitled to the judgment formulated by Blanchot with reference

to *Les Chemins de la liberté*: the book is "in its entirety" yet to come. That is not the only thing the two projects have in common. *L'Idiot* and *Les Chemins* stop at "a quarter to," with a third volume expecting a fourth that fails to come: $3 + (-1)$.

If one observes that these books, even as they succeed one another in an order of expanding incompletion, end up as publications that are increasingly voluminous (*L'Imagination* has 162 pages, *L'Etre et le néant* 722, *L'Idiot de la famille*, 2,800), one feels inclined to propose as a formula for Sartre's writing that he needs more and more time in order not to finish his books, to put off their ends. In other words, his books, even as they come to a halt earlier and earlier (in relation to the end initially projected), do so later and later (in relation to their starting point). They are cut shorter and shorter the longer they get, condemned in perpetuity to stop too early and, simultaneously, too late.

5. Plainly, there is no reason to restrict these remarks to the philosphical works. The last words of *La Nausée* are no exception to the rule. The characteristic suffix of the Sartrean coda is there, as expected: "Tomorrow rain will fall over Bouville." That all too literal future does not announce any book, to be sure. But does it completely escape contamination by the lines preceding it, in the course of which Roquentin decides precisely to write one, decides, rather, to have finished one — that is, to write one which, like a melody (and unlike a series), would contain its own end within itself. An opening closing, then, in both its letter and its message. Roquentin dreams therein less of a future of writing than of its *futur antérieur*: "There would come a moment when the book would be written — would be behind me." It remains to be determined whether Roquentin's announcements are more trustworthy than his author's. And whether it did indeed rain in Bouville. You missed me, honey. To be continued.

6. The same note is sounded at the end of *Les Chemins de la liberté*: "Tomorrow the dawn will cover them with the same dew, the dead flesh and the rusting steel will drip with the same sweat. Tomorrow the black birds will come." The rhyme is impeccable. As for the short stories of *Le Mur*, the last line in "La Chambre" is reserved for Eve: "I will kill you first"; that of "L'Enfance d'un chef," for Lucien: "I'll grow a moustache." And if neither "Le Mur" nor "Erostrate" ends on a sentence in the future, their closings are no less opening. They spring from the panic-stricken and claustrophobic depth that is reactivated in Sartre's texts whenever something on the order of an authentic ending approaches, whenever the future is blocked, whenever — precisely — there is no future. No exit. "Erostrate"'s ending could not be more literally an opening: "Then I opened the door to them." Which it is also in thematic terms. By renouncing the suicide for which the narrative in its entirety had been preparing, by opening the door to his pursuers, Paul Hilbert decides in a single dramatic stroke to have a future. He will indeed be arrested, brought to trial, and so on. All is not over. The same

reversal in "Le Mur" stops the countdown that could not but have led to Pablo's execution. It was to be the end, in place of which he is granted a reprieve. One of reason's ruses — or history's slip-ups — allows these tales to avoid categorization as ghostlike "Memoires from beyond the Grave" and their heroes — recently returned from Acheron — to take up in the first person the narration of their resurrection. "Le Mur" — or it was only a joke.

However spectacular or unexpected, the sensational turns that end these two tales are, in a certain way, prepared for and even demanded by the formal structure of the narrative, its very narration. To the extent that it accepts the clauses of the realist contract, a narrative conducted in the first person, past tense implies that its "hero" has survived his misfortunes. Since they are recounting them, Pablo and Paul Hilbert must have managed to emerge from them. The stories of Le Mur are far more coherent in their realism than L'Etranger. Meursault's account, similarly conducted in the first person, past tense, in no way implies that its utterance benefited from any act of pardon. But Sartre does not comment on this point in his article on Camus.

The parallel narrative resurrections on which "Le Mur" and "Erostrate" end are emblematic with regard to the place in their text in which they occur, combining the twofold impossibility for the Sartrean text to conclude and for its hero to die. But they are not exceptional. In a general way, Sartrean characters do not die easily. L'Etre et le néant explains that death does not count among the number of my possibilities: "There is no place for death in being-for-itself." Nor is there any more in the Sartrean text. I will mention only the false death of M. Fasquelle in La Nausée. But it would seem that Sartre, with respect to his characters, behaves in the same manner as Daniel, in L'Age de raison, does with his cats: he goes to great lengths to put an end to them but then, at the last moment, cannot manage to get rid of them. Moreover, the end of L'Age de raison offers a good example of this paschal turn when we see Lola resurface beneath the sun of the living after she had already been buried and mourned by all concerned. Mathieu had even seen her corpse. A happy ending again (if such be one's notion of happiness) in Le Sursis: with the September mobilization, all the males take off for the slaughter, but the gentlemen in the Chanceries content themselves with that gesture and ask no more of them. There is no need to risk one's life for real. One thinks of the sacrifice of Isaac. Thanks to Munich, one emerges from the postwar period, thank God, but without entering into war, thank God. Not this time. The most resistant of all is Mathieu. He is abandoned in the middle of La Mort dans l'âme in a situation even more desperate than Pablo's and Paul's. And all the more desperate in that it is recounted in the third person. From atop his steeple, he fires, alone against the German army. The impasse is absolute. Under such conditions, any evocation of the possibility of his escape is both the most gratuitous, the most rhetorical of considerations and an insult to verisimilitude: which did not at all daunt Sartre. Simone de Beauvoir notes in *La Force des choses*: "In his author's preface, Sartre indicated that he survived, but that did not at all emerge from the narrative."

7. We could continue with the plays. With *Huis clos*, for example, which ends: "Very well, let's continue." With *Le Diable et le bon dieu*: "There is a war to be waged and I will wage it. Or *Les Séquestrés d'Altona*: "I will answer for it. Today and forever after." And so on.

CURTAIN

Chapter 4
The Reality Principle

Making use — as the fine novelist he is — of what he has beneath his
eyes, Jean-Paul Sartre . . .
Claudine Chonez, "A qui les lauriers des
Goncourt?", *Marianne*, December 1938.

The first book published by Sartre, as we have seen, is entitled *L'Imagination*. A second would follow shortly thereafter on the same subject. That primal condition, however, does not entail any primacy. First of all, perhaps, because we are dealing not with works of imagination but works *on* it. The mood of the day, moreover, so blatantly postsurrealist, was inclined toward severity regarding the freedoms that this faculty had arrogated to itself throughout the period called in French *les années folles*.

If (as its title indicates) the imagination does indeed constitute the subject of Sartre's first book, the first page, the first line, the first word of that first book is nevertheless given over to perception: "I look at this blank sheet, placed on my table; I perceive its shape, its color, its position." Imagination is not capable of introducing itself on its own. *L'Imagination* must thus begin with perception, which starts things off, which, of itself, is the starting point. For the inverse is not true: imagination is unable to establish the difference. "To affirm: I perceive, which is to deny that I am dreaming." That is an irreversible, nonspeculative proposition. If it begins by examining the question of the mental image, Sartre's life's work does so only in order to put it in its proper place, which is second. In conformity with the dictates of phenomenology, one must begin with what

51

one has before one's eyes. Brief interlude in a café. It takes place at the Bec de Gaz on rue Montparnasse, Paris. Aron, back from Berlin, pronounces Husserl's name in Sartre's presence: "You see, my little friend, if you are a phenomenologist, you can talk about this cocktail and it'll be philosophy!" Simone de Beauvoir: "Sartre grew pale with emotion." The key to this dramatic episode lies entirely in what I shall call its phenomenological demonstration, that is, the use of the demonstrative in order to transcend reference and ground exemplarity: "this" cocktail, "this" blank sheet. The first lines of *L'Imagination*, if we exclude the imperative, will be found again at the beginning of *La Nausée*: "I have to tell how I see this table, the street, the people, my tobacco pouch."
The imagination will follow.

It appears, in fact, in the book in which it plays the title role, about twenty lines from the beginning: "But now, here I am turning my head away. I no longer see the blank sheet. I now see the white paper on the wall. The sheet is no longer present. It is no longer *there*."

The sequence is thus as follows: "I" myself, who a moment ago was looking at "this" blank sheet, now, without ceasing to be "I" myself, stop looking at it, which allows "me" myself to imagine it. In other words, "I" begin by positing this sheet as present, then "I" posit it as absent. Imagination presupposes the reality which it denies. The absence is secondary in relation to the presence whose lack it thematizes. *L'Imagination*, which begins Sartre's complete works, begins by putting imagination in the position of a successor.

At first sight, at least. And if, like Sartre himself, we attend only to its message — if we decide that the "verbal moment," as such, can and should be passed over in silence, that there is no basis for taking into account the utterance of this inaugural scene in which we see someone called "I" begin, in an initial phase, to perceive in the first person, in order to proceed in a second phase to imagine the object of his prior perception.

Paulhan linked the interest in collage techniques that flourished during the cubist period to the fact that in a world whose reality, axes of reference, and frames of representation had been systematically unsettled by the latest theories of physics, painters had no recourse but to latch onto whatever they could find within reach: their cigarette packs, newspapers, a Métro ticket. Sartre's motifs are perhaps not of the same order. And yet we find in his first works (up to and including *L'Etre et le néant*), with an insistence all the more remarkable in that it does not take into account the specificity of contexts, the repetition of an analogous gesture in which something like a fragment of reality manages to insert its way into the text under cover of what might be called the "example of writing."

From dozens of cases, an example of this example, drawn from the *Esquisse d'une théorie des émotions*, reads: "For example, at this instant, I am writing." The beginning of *L'Imagination* would be another: "This blank sheet on my table." Sartre likes to draw support from his writing. To write, for example, on what he is writing on. The enunciation of Sartre's phenomenology is thus the exact opposite of a tabula rasa. It is effected by producing the instruments of its production, those accompanying the writer's task, what he has in sight and at hand: his table ("this" table), his paper, his pen, his pack of cigarettes, and even, should the case come up, his hand, his own hand.

In its complete formulation, the example of the example of writing just borrowed from the *Esquisse d'une théorie des émotions* leads to a proposition that is not without a measure of strangeness. "For example, at this instant I am writing," said Sartre, "but do not realize I am writing." It is perhaps possible to write without realizing it (and such, at least, is what happens to Roquentin throughout *La Nausée*); it is far more doubtful that one does not realize one is writing while writing "I am writing."

INSERT. (*I write. I reread myself. I will never have read myself.*) In a certain sense, it is quite true that, as the example states — and precisely because it does not hold up — Sartre does not realize he is writing what he is writing, consequently does not realize (if not that he is writing) what it is he is writing when he writes "at this instant I am writing, but do not realize I am writing."

(I say Sartre, but Sartre says "I" without specifying whom he is speaking of. Should we understand himself? It is indeed he who writes "I am writing," but the prohibition he directs against self-affection — I must not understand myself — condemns "I" to be no more for him than an example.)

It is probable that had he managed to read himself, to hear and understand what he was saying, to hear himself and lend himself an ear, he would have corrected what he had written. He would have changed the modes: "I am able to write without realizing I am writing." Or still better: "For example, a while ago I was writing, but I did not realize I was writing." But he who writes does not succeed in understanding what he says. He is unable to read himself. That is what makes him exemplary — and exceptional. The Sartrean conception of literature and writing issues from an unyielding prohibition aimed at every form of self-affection, folding back on self, autoerotic sinuousness. "What is literature?" "Whereas the shoemaker can wear the shoes he has just made if they are his size and the architect inhabit the house he has just constructed, the writer cannot read what he has just written." Literature has always already transcended the subsistance level.

No doubt intentional transcendence (the fact that consciousness is always conscious of something other than itself) has as a prior condition that consciousness is initially conscious of itself, but the very definition of that self-consciousness requires that it cannot be thematized, that it never attain the status of reflection, that it be, by definition, unreflected. Since it is empty and transparent, consciousness traverses itself without ever finding anything in its path to stop it.

The bizarreness of the example borrowed from the *Esquisse d'une théorie des émotions* (that writing might claim to succeed in not being aware of itself at the very instant it singles itself out as an example) is systematically related in Sartre's text to the state of distraction (to which we shall return) preventing Roquentin, at work writing *La Nausée*, from realizing that he is writing even though that very circumstance — which is, nevertheless, within his grasp — constitutes the crucial medium of the difficulties amidst which he claims to be coping. It is also systematically related to Sartre's reproach of the same period (1939) to Nabokov that he "never writes without *seeing himself write*, the way others listen to themselves speak."

Sartre, as we shall see, does not like writing when it is self-conscious. More generally, he dislikes self-consciousness. All consciousness is, first of all, consciousness of something other then itself. It embraces itself as well, to be sure, but in a nonreflexive, nonthetic manner. (Poor Baudelaire: "For the rest of us, it is enough to see the house or the tree; completely absorbed in contemplating them, we forget our own selves." But Baudelaire "watches himself seeing; he observes in order to see himself observing.") A novel should be the novel of something other than itself. When one uses a rifle, one thinks of the target. When one uses a car, one thinks of the road. An artisan does not think of his tools; he makes use of them in order to produce the object he has in mind. And that is precisely why the seriality of assembly-line production will constitute the principal argument for the condemnation lodged against capitalism. The fragmentation of the process of production effectively rules out any possibility of the operations carried out by each worker at his station being accompanied by an awareness of the final object that his labor nevertheless contributed to produce. In the artisan's studio, means yielded to ends. In the serialized factory, the worker is obsessed by his tools. Sartre has an undeniably artisanal conception of writing. Language is in the order not of a machine, but of a tool. When declaring himself in favor of a literature of praxis, he evokes a mode of production in which the finished product issues from the very hands which began the job. Writing ought to be a craft like any other, a minor but authentic craft — that is, a prosaic activity, fully participant in artisanal democracy. And yet . . .

And yet, at the heart of this egalitarian utopia, not just anyone can serve as an example. The writers' guild, as soon as it appears, moves to the front and breaks off from the squadron. Unlike the shoemaker who can don his shoes, the architect who can inhabit his constructions, the cook who can eat the dishes he prepares, the writer cannot consume what he produces: he cannot read himself. He is alone in being refused such feedback. This first exception immediately entails a second one: he is also absolutely alone in being able to couch in writing what he does, alone in being able to do what he does and in doing it write it down. A shoemaker, to return to that intriguing profession, can say: "I am in the process of making a shoe" at the same time that he does it. But if that utterance is proffered in written form, it is necessarily in the order of fiction, because it is impossible simultaneously to make a shoe and to write that one is making a shoe. The sheer fact that someone has written that sentence with his hand excludes the possibility of his having been able at the same time to perform the action described in his statement. In the literality of its first-person present indicative, such a sentence is a lie or a novel.

It is not a matter here, as with "I am lying," of undecidable statements. (If it is true that I am lying, I am no longer lying in saying that I am doing so; thus, I was not lying in saying that I was lying; and so on.) Rather, it is a matter of statements that are unpronounceable or unutterable for reasons relating to what Mauss called techniques of the body. We are confronted less with a logical trap than a physical, almost gymnastic, impossibility. A certain mobilization of the body in writing is thus at the origin of the fictionalization of statements that other techniques of utterance — oral statement, for example — might potentially endow with truth-value. For instance, it is possible to write, "I am eating"; it is more difficult to emit that sentence at the precise moment of the ingestion of the food it designates. On the other hand, one can say, "I am running" (as long as one is not out of breath), but one cannot write it without fictionalizing the statement. "I am sleeping," insofar as it is concerned, must renounce any realist pretention, in whatever (phonic or graphic) form it appears. Propriety is not the only obstacle to speaking with one's mouth full. Freedom of expression must cope with implicit impediments. In like manner, it is difficult to write when one's hands are busy with something else. Guyotat, I believe, has convincing pages on this subject.

One last point of critical utterance: it happens that one must interrupt one's reading in order to protect it by proclaiming it. I stop reading long enough to say, "I'm reading." But does the fact of writing, "I'm reading" imply as clearly that one was obliged to abandon the activity referred to? that one stopped doing what one is saying? This is an extremely critical point for Sartre (there is no other word to describe it), since for him the prohibition of self-affection governing the literary economy and, more generally, language as a whole ("I can't hear myself speak," we read in L'Etre et le néant; and in the article on Parain ["Aller et retour," Situations I] he subscribes to a philosophy of language which stipulates that "when people understand one another well, they keep silent"), the ban on self-affection rules out the possibility of writing and reading being simultaneous, excluding even more fundamentally any individual from combining both functions. Critics — who write that they are reading — are bastards of a type for which Sartre experiences an unyielding allergy.

Independently of its potential pretensions to democracy, writing is thus the sole practice capable of positing itself as an example. On this count, it holds an absolute privilege it is unable to share with any other guild. And it is a law of Sartre's text that it unabatingly leans on it for support, promotes it as an example, which should be understood, of course, in the most literal sense of the expression, even if it is only to begin with. It takes a strange pleasure in putting itself forward, producing that on which it rests, in order to strike the reader, in something of an ad hominem argument, with an effect of concreteness.

One might thus — and Sartre does it abundantly — in order to illustrate the presence of the future in perceptual behavior, describe the manner in which a tennis player reacts before the ball. Or the skier, who adapts in advance to twists in his path not yet in his purview. Or further still, the revolutionary leader who builds his entire strategy on events that have not yet taken place. But when my description of these "future real beings" invokes the very words that my hand traced while accomplishing it, when it illustrates itself with its own production and — instead of borrowing an example extrinsic to it — offers itself as an example of what it is saying, the stakes are no longer the same: the example suddenly escapes from the series. It is no longer an example among an infinite number of possibilities but becomes an incomparably singular example, an exemplary example: writing, in this, has no equal.

I return to the first words of Sartre's first book, *L'Imagination*: "I look at this blank sheet, placed on my table." They will reappear frequently: "Let us consider this sheet of paper placed on the table" will be *L'Imaginaire*'s version of the refrain. Every tool in his box will be invoked in turn. The author returns tirelessly to their exemplary discretion. As well-behaved as images: just look at how little they are noticed. If the affirmation that writing rests on something itself rests on something, it can be said of Sartre's writing that its first words focus on what they are written on: a blank sheet of paper. It is produced while producing its very basis. I advance unmasked. But perhaps it rested on it only to the extent that it failed to exhibit the fact. Perhaps in revealing its underpinnings, to lean a bit on its proposition, it loses footing in a less than exemplary manner.

There follows, in fact, some twenty lines later *L'Imagination*'s second act: imagination itself. "But it now happens that I turn my head away. I no longer see the sheet of paper." We move from perception to imagination by means of a rotation of the head, which causes the object, the blank sheet, to disappear from the field of vision where it was present a moment before. But plainly Sartre, as a good phenomenologist (if it is he who is the "I" that he says), manages to be attentive to that distraction and continues to record what happens. In particular, he notes the modifications affecting both subject and object of this capital turn. Thus it is that he acknowledges that he no longer sees the sheet every bit as scrupulously as he had previously acknowledged that he saw it. And yet, from one scene to the other, a crucial change has occurred which he curiously does not succeed in taking into account. Something decisive has been set free at the level of utterance. Who is speaking now? Is it possible that it is the same "I" who a while ago was saying "I look at . . . " and now says, "I no longer see . . . "? Is it concerning the same sheet — the one of which he first said that he saw it and now says that he no longer sees it? Is it concerning the sheet on which he is writing that he writes that he is no longer looking at it? For one cannot, in truth, write on an imaginary sheet. It is not even certain that one could write on a sheet one was not looking at. A boundary has been crossed without a word spoken. The move from perception to imagination is not brought about within the enunciatory framework elaborated concerning the former. It entails its complete revision. As long as I am looking at this blank sheet, I can write on it that I am looking at it. The coincidence or coexistence of the two acts is not a problem. But as soon as I write that I do not see it, a dissociation is created between (1) the "I" who does not see the sheet and (2) the "I" writing the sentence in which it is said that the first "I" does not see the said sheet. The same dissociation, moreover, occurs on the side of the object. Now two sheets are needed: one which I do not see and the other on which I write that I do not see it. The deceptive continuity which introduces imagination into the narrative pace of perception thus produces a fallacious appearance of presence. No sooner do "I turn my head away" than the present evaporates. The performative "I" doing what it says in the first sequence gives way to a phantom "I" who never truly imagines but who is imagined imagining: an imaginary "I," no less imagined than imagining.

The two voices — of message and utterance — thus cease singing in unison as soon as they encounter the imaginary. Their agreement in the previous scene (introducing the exemplarity of the perceptual performative) is nevertheless insufficient to authorize us to conclude that there was only one voice. No doubt the second statement alone was clearly fictive. But that characteristic takes no less of a toll on the scene that introduced it and whose perceptuo-performative solidity it retroactively disqualifies. A fictive (re)turn brings a suspicion of duplicity to bear, after the fact, on an all too simple origin. And as a result, despite *L'Imagination*'s insistence, it does not begin with perception but with a fable, a brief narrative forged as an example in order to show just how essential it is to distinguish imagination from perception and to respect the hierarchical order governing their relations: perception first, followed by imagination. Except that as a narrative, the work succeeds in doing so only in the context of a fiction that embraces them both: perception and imagination. Sartre's first order of business was to restore the second to its proper place. He gives the right example and begins his first book, *L'Imagination*, not with imagination itself (which is to follow), but perception. And he elaborates to that end an inaugural fiction: let us begin by imagining that I am perceiving this sheet of paper . . .

This play of cross-purposes has an allegorical value. In each of his future books, Sartre will continue to affirm that everything begins with perception. The definition of reality may change and be formulated in terms that are at times phenomenological, at times Marxist. Reality will occasionally be identified with the present, occasionally with the future. That is of little concern. Beyond such successive versions, Sartrean theory will not relinquish its primordial choice: the affirmation of the primacy of the reality principle. That constancy is all the more remarkable in that in his life (or, at least, in his autobiographical discourse), he always accused himself of having begun with the imaginary.

In the beginning was the word, but subsequent hostilities put things back in their proper place. "I had dreamed my life for nearly forty years," he confided to Jacqueline Piatier. "What I was missing was a sense of realities." And in *On a raison de se révolter*: "The war opened my eyes." The war was needed (such was the nature of things) for me to no longer confuse things with their names. It would be worthwhile pondering the presuppositions of a system of thought for which war alone would be entitled to be qualified as real. The riddle-image through which (a year before the war) the *Esquisse d'une théorie des émotions* clarified what was to be understood by acting perceptively in the world receives from its date emblematic and premonitory status: "Where is the gun?" Perception for Sartre is polemical by vocation: a polemology of perception. We were able to think we were at peace for as long as we were dreaming, but the war opened our eyes. To perceive is always to look for a gun, a secret arm.

We would rather underscore at this point the contours of the surprising chiasmus according to which, concerning these questions of procedure and propriety, the work and life of Jean-Paul Sartre cross over, erase, and overlap with each other. The hierarchy which, he complained, governed his biography (in which, in his version, the imaginary would have benefited from an uncontested head start against a reality he became acquainted with only later) constitutes, in effect, the monotonous target toward which he would obstinately aim a work that never hesitates to insist on the necessity of the inverse imperative: reality must never give up the dictatorship it exercises over the imaginary. That twisted economy results, however, in a single restriction: it is, in fact, to reality alone that the usurpation of its preorogatives by the secondary instance is limited. In other words, it would be in life alone that the parasites of representation would rage. It is in the reality of what he calls his life (in the referent of his autobiographical discourse) that the imaginary found itself endowed with a scandalous primacy, that words got the drop on things, that the secondary passed ahead of the principal.

But Sartre's words, for their part, never manage to be severe enough toward a life that yielded them first place. It is thus the secondary that restores its privileges to a primary instance which had abdicated them to it: it makes the primary withdraw its resignation. Whether it is a matter of signs (words) or of images, there is not a line of Sartre in which the inflationary precipitousness discrediting in advance any initiative that might be accorded to language is not (in one way or another) discredited. The definition from *Qu'est-ce que la littér-ature?* will be recalled: the verbal phase is no more than a "secondary structure" in our enterprise. The work that Sartre in his life put ahead of his life nonetheless does not restrict itself to denouncing its origins. A throbbing nostalgia for gravity constrains it to recognize that words simply do not carry the requisite weight.

Against Inflation: A Few Words

A measure of astonishment may greet Sartre's stubborn indifference to what will have been undoubtedly the major ideological theme of his times: what he (soberly) calls in "Aller et retour," his 1944 article on Brice Parain, "the tiresome problem of language." As false as it is famous, alas . . . Sartre did all he could to avoid stopping at it. It was concerning the same Parain that Simone de Beauvoir, in *La Force de l'âge*, quotes a letter Sartre sent her while negotiating the publication of *La Nausée* with Gallimard: "Brice Parain is rather intelligent, but no more. He is a guy who thinks about language, like Paulhan: that's their business." The author, it will be seen, is not lacking in broad-mindedness.

If we admit, however, that, launched by Husserl, Freud, and Saussure, the thought of our age will no doubt have defined itself as an epoch — from economics to literature, from religion to technology — by evolving under the sign of the sign, it is not without a measure of surprise that we see it dominated by that immense exercise in untimeliness, the work of Jean-Paul Sartre, whose will to modernity ("We don't want to miss anything of our times," in his words) issues on this specific point in an unprecedented anachronism. You missed me, honey. From one end of his work to the other, Sartre never stopped refusing to take up as his own what he himself nevertheless explicitly acknowledged to be the sign of his time, the crisis of the sign. In refusing to lend it his voice, he decided that the crisis was precisely no more than a sign of the times and that, as a result, the temporal mode of signs could be reduced to the contingency of a date.

There is, however, a Sartrean semiology; it is resolutely antilinguistic. The three pages in the course of which *L'Etre et le néant* (which contains 720) polishes off the problem do no more than make reference to a phenomenology of the body. The experience of language is no more than a local, belated, and secondary modality of a private experience of meaning preceding and encompass-ing it. Like Barthes's prototypal man, Sartre's can be called *Homo significans*. But it is not because he speaks; it is because he exists. Meaning is the characteristic medium of his life, not the effect of his speech. The experience of meaning is consequently prior to and independent of the practice of signs, especially of linguistic signs. Linguistics will not be the pilot-science sought by structuralism. I myself am the signifier, says Sartre in all simplicity. Let us not argue about words. Contrary to Paulhan's insinuation accusing him of being "on bad terms with words," it appears that few writers will have felt as comfortable in their language.

DO NOT INSERT (*LANGUAGE*). I am not like everyone, Sartre told Verstraeten. Most people think "that they have words in their head." Genet, for example, for whom words are "like foreign bodies" (*Saint Genet*), Every language is foreign to such silent victims of parasites. Sartre understands them and pities them. But it's not his problem: "I don't have words in me; they are outside" (*Situations* IX).

Language for Sartre does not make a crease: it speaks, but that goes without saying. I no more hear myself speaking than I see myself seeing. Consciousness is meaningful only to the extent that it is unreflected. Whoever listens to himself speaking has nothing to say: the florid quickly turns inflated. In listening to oneself, one loses the meaning. Lack of reflection and spontaneity go together: they define commitment. A committed writer does not go back on what he says. The ban he imposes on self-affection forbids him from leaning over himself: even in its intellectual form (word on word, crease on crease), masturbation de-realizes. The condemnation of reflexivity ends up merging with that of the exorbitant pretentions to priority of the imaginary.

Sartre's entire literary program is thus in solidarity with a restoration of the primacy of perception and the reaffirmation of the transcendence of the object. At the end of *La Part du feu*, Blanchot quotes Hegel: "The first act by which Adam gained mastery over the animals was imposing a name; that is, he annihilated them in their existence." Sartre's Hegel says precisely the opposite. We read in *Qu'est-ce que la littérature?*, in fact, that "naming implies a perceptual sacrifice of the name to the object named. Or, to speak as Hegel does, names are thereby seen to be inessential when confronted with things, which are essential." The political economy of the sign thus would have it that every crisis is but language's entry into a critical phase — a period of inflationary fluctuation in the course of which signs, no longer indexed to the exchange rate of *things*, lose all referential value. These monetary metaphors are Sartre's. It was in 1929, the year of the Wall Street crash, that Roquentin withdrew to Bouville. The interwar years (surrealist or other) are often accused of having overvalued mere words. They were years of madness: *les années folles*. In introducing *Les Temps modernes*, Sartre asserts that they witnessed the process of "words being depreciated increasingly by the day." "We have the firm intention of helping literary deflation along," the article concludes. *Qu'est-ce que la littérature?* takes up the theme again. The risks of clandestinity, while we were publishing the journals of the Resistance, "have taught us to practice a kind of literary deflation." We had to weigh our words, because they were followed by effects. "The 1914 war precipitated the crisis of language. I would posit that the war of 1940 revalued it." Once it has undergone the experience of bellicose reality, literature can no longer pretend to the status of a luxury item. War put things back in their proper place. It reinstated the difference. A book is not a curio or a jewel, but a tool. A weapon. The words which criticism had depreciated by speculating on them are once again revalued now that they are being put to work. Their worth is inversely related to their preciousness. But in the last analysis critical inflation was less a crisis of language itself than a crisis of the object, a retreat of transcendence. Capitalism is an unrealistic economy.

A LITTLE HISTORY. Along with the denunciation of capitalism, the 1930s witnessed the unleashing of a crusade in favor of the object. Nizan's writings (before Sartre's) offer particularly eloquent testimony in this regard. The return from *Aden Arabie* is thus above all a return to the real, a renunciation of flight to the nomadic imaginary of traveling. "Travelers are like those others who are torn in every direction by forces that no object can satisfy, by love stripped of a lover, friendship without a friend, racing without a track, motors without movement, energy without presence." Life at present, he continues, "does not include the presence of a single material or human object: an object of thought is as much the love of a woman as a tree." "Something must be done for objects."

It was at that period that Nizan collaborated on *La Revue marxiste* with Lefebvre, Politzer, Guterman, and Friedmann. In a brief polemical work (aimed, moreover, at Sartre and Nizan), *L'Existentialisme* (1946), Lefebvre recalls their program: "Retrieve the object." He enumerates the era's shortcomings against which they were planning to intervene: "literary interiority, impressionism, femininity, narcissism, lack of energy, insipidity, half-heartedness, in a word: decadence."

Emmanuel Berl's polemical *Mort de la morale bourgeoise* appeared in 1929. It denounced the "interior monologue" through which a class lacking any grasp of reality abandoned itself to "excesses of intimacy": Joyce and Proust both placed on the index. The chapter "Intérieur bourgeois" begins by stating: "The bourgeois, as no one can fail to realize, is a man of interiority." He quotes: "I saw myself seeing myself." And comments: "I heard myself speaking. In positing itself, the ego opposes itself. How might that metaphysical gap be reduced to a minimum? What can I say to myself that would be still more intimate?" The great discovery of bourgeois thought: "There is no reality." "As a result of drawing up so many recapitulatory versions, he concludes that what counts are not things but the versions of them one draws up." Nizan approved of the book and commented on it in a review published in *Europe*: "Nothing exists, but everything is named. Things are not, but words are real. The bourgeois, temporarily sheltered by the walls of his bedroom, can believe himself to be blessed and protected by the inventions, myths, and promises of his vocabulary." The same motif recurs in *Les Chiens de garde*. The bourgeois "does not have any contact with real objects, any direct relations with men. He is there in his office, in his bedroom, with the small troop of his consumer delights, his wife, his bed, his table, his papers." Words are perhaps not necessarily bourgeois. But the proletariat has a monopoly on things. Since the bourgeoisie is an imaginary class, there is no bourgeois class consciousness. But the proletariat is a real class: it is the class of the real.

It was also in 1929, coincidentally, that Heidegger's *Was ist Metaphysik?* appeared — to be published in translation two years later in *Bifur*, a journal for which Nizan worked — a book in which fear (which is always fear of an object) is opposed to anxiety (which is induced precisely by the absence of an object). In anxiety, one is afraid of nothing. 1929: year of anxiety, an unbinding trauma following on the loss of the object. It was also the year of the death of Nizan's father, whom his son somberly eulogized in 1932 in a novel entitled *Antoine Bloyé*. A man disintegrates, prey to primary processes, in the realization that his life has no meaning. "He knew the anxiety of death," according to Nizan, "because of this radical void." *This* railwayman [*cheminot*] did not miss the rendezvous. But there is nothing exceptional about his case. In a pedagogical aside, the author informs us that the entire bourgeoisie these days reads the newspapers with anxiety. It had dared (in French) to give the name "*actions*" (stocks) to mere paper certificates. The novel proposes an antidote to such solitude without object[s]: "the grouping [*liaison*] of the workers' neighborhoods." (Freud had already entrusted to a different P.C. apparatus the task of reestablishing perceptual cohesion.)

1. *Zur Sache selbst.* One would do well to reread in the light of Sartre's attack against critical reflexivity his article (written in 1933 but published in 1939) on Husserlian intentionality. It illuminates in certain respects the relatively unexpected declaration of liberation affirmed in its conclusion: "And there we are, delivered from Proust." The *Recherche* is, of course, the very example of a literature of analysis, a reflexive literature referring back only to itself: "[Proust] indulges himself [*se complaît*] in analysis, whereas I tend toward synthesis." The formula can be simplified. Nothing is lost if we say without redundancy: he indulges himself (a reflexive verb) and I tend . . . *To tend* is the verb used by whoever would touch something. No one pressed further than Proust the analytical dissolution of the reality of objects. Albertine, a new Eurydice, is distended into a myriad of pointillist brush strokes ("flickerings, filtered tremors, confetti of light") when the narrator approaches her face for a kiss. In *L'Imaginaire*, Sartre will again reproach him for his solipsistic conception of affective life. "The link between my love and the person loved is at bottom, for Proust and his disciples, no more than a link of contiguity." *Amabam amare*: the egotism of Eros would have it that love be love of love before being so for whatever object it may alight upon. Which is a randomly encountered object. A pure metonymical contiguity, it does no more than make contact with it, *partes extra*

partes. As the laws of associationism would have it. But Husserlian intentionality reintroduces the transcendence of the object into the narcissistic hermeticism of the lover's state. "If we love a woman, it is because she is lovable." That is, it is not because we are in love. But Proust did not love women. The article continues: There we are, "delivered simultaneously from 'inner life.' We would search in vain like Amiel, like a child kissing her own shoulder, for the caresses and cuddles of our most private selves." A literature of exteriority (on the model of journalistic reporting) is opposed, through the graces of Husserl's concepts, to the hazy intimacy of chamber reading. Note how the child is effeminized as he leans down over himself. Men have other objects. At the very beginning of *La Nausée,* Roquentin's virility bridles at the thought of autobiographical self-indulgence. He hesitates to lean over himself, "day by day, like little girls, in a splendid new notebook." "I am neither a virgin nor a priest," he notes a bit later, "playing at the inner life." The sexual topography is clear. By male, as Aristotle already said, we are to understand a being which engenders in an other; by female, a being which engenders in itself. The lecture in intentionality did not say anything different. I explode (myself) toward, therefore I am a man. Pierre, in "La Chambre," does not go out. Eve watches him sleep: "One might have said that he wanted to caress his cheek with his shoulder." And when little Lucien, at the beginning of "L'Enfance d'un chef," imagines himself as a little girl, a reflexive verb captures him from within: "He felt himself [*se sentait*] so gentle inside," and his body dreams itself forthwith enfolded in self-love: "He felt like kissing himself at the bend of his arm." The opposition between words and things is important. But it presupposes as its enabling condition a far more essential opposition between words referring to things and words referring to words. One reads in "Matérialisme et révolution" that freedom "never derives enjoyment from itself." Revolution is not an autoerotic adventure. We find in the articulation of that opposition, staked in a single wager, both class struggle and sexual difference.

2. Sartre in *Qu'est-ce que la littérature?* defines modern literature (which he dates from the time it sought to promote its own modernity as a value) as a literature that is "its own value unto itself. It has moved into a reflexive phase." Such reflexivity is systematically related to the crisis of language discussed by Sartre elsewhere; it is, in point of fact, a critical position. Every reflection on language, every reflection of language on itself, is by definition critical. And it is precisely that which the Sartrean program of a committed literature proposes to bring to an end. To rid writing of that unfortunate crease it has picked up. It is a matter of urgency that literature stop thinking about itself. That writers busy themselves with something besides their writing. That they even succeed in forgetting that they write. Commitment would put an end to self-referentiality. "If literature were to discover a specific content, it would be obliged to tear itself

away from its meditation on itself." *Les Faux-monnayeurs*, more than a novel, would be the very example of the novel of a novel. In order to devalue the inflationary counterfeit currency of modern formalism, Sartre, in the name of intentionality, calls on literature to commit itself to being the literature of something other than itself.

Chapter 5
The Infelicities of the Present Tense

Qu'est-ce que la littérature? calls on the writer to conquer the mass media (radio, film, editorial and reportorial journalism). He must not allow himself any susceptibility to the interference of propaganda. He is to oversee the transmission of his messages to the point of their reception, making sure that his voice is heard. And it is undoubtedly nothing more than wholesome to refuse to allow power to inform you. And yet there is the matter, more fundamental than any propaganda, of a (not necessarily limpid) medium, the interminable murmur of a garrulous specter that Sartre early discovered himself to be haunted by: "It used to begin with an anonymous chatter in my head," he recounts in *Les Mots*, "someone saying 'I am walking, I am sitting down, I am drinking a glass of water, I am eating a praline.' I used to repeat out loud that perpetual commentary: 'I am walking, Maman, I am drinking a glass of water, I am sitting down.' I thought I had two voices of which one — which barely belonged to me and was not controlled by my will — dictated its words to the other." His own voice is the one that repeats. And it repeats for his mother. A neutral ectoplasm that he occasionally calls his chatterbox [*babillarde*] will have always already interfered with the Sartrean present and condemned perception, to begin with, to double up into its perpetual commentary.

For whom does one write? A prior passage in *Les Mots* had proposed the Sartrean version of the primal narrative. The narrator of *A la recherche du temps perdu*, in the pages opening the novel, tells us that he could not fall asleep until his mother came to his bedside to dispense to him a few moments of marvelously soporific reading. The equivalent scene in Sartre is governed by the opposite imperative. He tells, in effect, how it was he himself who at day's end — snuggled in his sheets and under his covers, his prayers already over — in order to fall asleep would tell a story to his mother. "At that moment, I pronounced the fateful words: 'The rest will be found in the next issue.' 'What did you say?' asked my mother. 'I'm leaving myself in suspense.' And the fact is that I would fall asleep amid the dangers in a state of delectable insecurity." Sartre did not wait for *Les Chemins de la liberté* in order not to finish his stories. There is, however, between this childlike primal narrative and the novelistic endeavor of his maturity a notable series of differences.

It is not enough to switch from passive to active to escape from the Proustian economy of narration. Whether the little boy listens (as in Proust) or tells (as in Sartre), in both cases we are confronted with a narrative of hypnagogic aspiration — told while prone in bed. Sartre's opposition between imagination and perception is developed in accordance with the body's axes. One perceives standing up; one imagines lying down. The bed is the common site of all the cases grouped by *L'Imagination* in its effort to elaborate a pathology of the imagination. *S'endormir* [to fall asleep] is perhaps, along with *s'evanouir* [to faint], the reflexive verb par excellence. As a result, the primacy of the imaginary has clinical origins. From which it follows that the "Tape Recorder Man" was engaging in the most orthodox of Sartreanisms when he pointed to the couch and said to his psychoanalyst: "You can't get cured on that." No need to belabor the point. Clinical immobilizers are analytical machines for engendering unconsciousness. *Tendre* (to tend) is the word, but it's a verb. It should be understood as lying at the heart of intentionality.

For both Marcel and Poulou, the primal narrative arrogated to itself no more than the power to induce sleep. Thirty years later, for Jean-Paul Sartre, a committed writer, the novel will be the expression of a diametrically opposite aspiration. Its task is to awaken its readers, to force them to open their eyes and focus on reality. *L'Imaginaire* described quite effectively how image-producing consciousness captivated itself, entirely on its own, in a kind of autoerotic capture or grasp in which it was at once jailer and prisoner. The committed novel was to aspire precisely to cut short such narrative arabesques that seemed to know no end. *Les Chemins de la liberté* are the paths blazed by an aroused consciousness. After the hypnagogic tale comes the narrative of vigilance. No doubt such a conversion ("There we are, delivered from Proust") implies that the subject changes positions and now turns into the narrator of the tale, whose addressee he had previously been. But that necessary condition is not sufficient. Drowsiness will prevail as long as one is still talking to one's mother. That is why, even after assuming the right to speak, one still has to change one's audience. The study of *Baudelaire* and *Qu'est-ce que la littérature?* illustrate with the requisite clarity the equivalence of the two propositions: to write for the men of one's day is literally the same as no longer speaking to one's mother. Which, moreover, does not prevent the public from being described as "an immense feminine interrogation."

In the beginning was a preverbal osmosis, a symbiotic transparency, unreserved empathy. "I told her everything. More than everything." But in 1917, Anne-Marie remarried. The terms used by Sartre to describe the irreversible break in the intimacy that had until then bound him to his mother are not lacking in interest. "My mother's remarriage," he declared to an interviewer, "brought on a break on my part, a very clear break; I experienced it as a betrayal, even if I never told her so." The break, one might then say, concerned less what happened as such than a certain verbal paralysis issuing from it for him, who as a result could live it only in solitude. If there was a break, in other words, it was strictly speaking because it was unspeakable. A break in communication before being an existential break. Had I been able to tell her that it happened, then it would have been possible for it not to happen. But I could not convey to her that inarticulable break. Broken-hearted, I had lost my voice; I couldn't find my words. The break will have been so deep that she never had the slightest suspicion of it. I broke with her all by myself, without her knowing. I kept it all for myself. For the first time, he doesn't tell her everything. For the first time, he has something to say but no one to say it to. He finds himself alone with a secret buried in his melancholic crypt. Something that doesn't manage to get out. He could not, after all, sing to her, "I miss you, honey." Was the only thing left to sulk? That is: to write? Writing, precisely, in order to punish her for the fact that he could no longer speak to her. Not writing to her — Maman. I'm not speaking to you. But to the men of my day. Outside.

Presenting . . .

Roquentin is not yet at that stage. Sulky, not particularly talkative, he grows irritated in his corner when the Self-Taught Man tries to get him to say that one always writes for someone. *Solitude oblige*. As for him, he never talks to anyone, ever. But the question nonetheless remains: why does he write? For whom does one write, since such is the Sartrean question, a sentence such as "I never speak to anyone, ever"? Are we to understand, as in *Les Mots*: "I'm not speaking to anyone, Maman." To whom is one speaking when one is speaking by oneself? Can we posit as a rule that one is always speaking to one's mother when one isn't speaking to anyone? For whose benefit, moreover, does one fail to perceive that one is writing? Does one write "I am writing" without realizing it, for example? For whose benefit does one sing or, for that matter, even listen to "Some of these days, you'll miss me, honey"? *L'Etre et le néant* as well as the article on Brice Parain, "Aller et retour," will make of language an experience coextensive with that dubbed as "for others." Roquentin thinks he can escape it by making of writing a practice construable as against others. "I don't speak to anyone," he says to we know not whom; "I don't receive anything; I don't give anything." Like incest, of which Bataille said that it is linked to a fear of exchange, the pseudogratuitousness of Roquentin's journal quickly degenerates into a form of greed. If his writing suffers from a lack of presence, it is first of all because it refuses at whatever price to have a dedicatee. It takes care not to give itself. It is not of the same type as those that would make a present of themselves. But language receives its present only in return once it has made a present of itself. That presupposes that one not pretend to be writing without any address. On this unfortunate path, Roquentin, however, will advance still further. He manages to pretend to be writing without paper and without a pencil, even not to be writing at all. *La Nausée*, in fact, systematically passes over in total silence the entirety of its enabling conditions, the processes according to which the text was all the same forced to end up giving itself, be it only to read: what might be called its presentation.

Habent sua fati libelli. Where do books come from? A text is not necessarily informative about where it comes from, it will be granted. Nor is it particularly defensive on the subject. But *La Nausée* is oddly distracted as soon as it is a matter of anything touching on the scene of its engendering. Timid, hesitant — in a word, inconsistent.

Who, for instance, are the publishers who sign the preliminary note in a plural conveying neither royalty nor ceremoniousness but who, a few pages later, forget themselves to the point of lapsing into the singular in signing an "editor's note"? The questions are multiple. Who was it that found Roquentin's papers? What did they contain aside from his journal of February 1932? What did he do, for instance, with the twelve chapters (three years of work) already completed for his book on Rollebon? The fact that one has abandoned the composition of a work does not imply that one has destroyed what was already written. And why "found"? Did Roquentin die (like Bataille's Dianus: "An individual named Roquentin wrote these notes and died")? If that was true, did he die like a hero, in Spain, for example — but in that case, on which side? — or like a neurotic intellectual, by committing suicide? Did he take off in quest of new adventures? Where exactly did he leave his papers: in Paris, Bouville, Barcelona? And when: in 1932, in 1937 (the copyright date is 1938)? And what, moreover, was Roquentin carrying in his luggage when he left Bouville? He mentions only two suits.

Two trunks is rather much, all the same. "The past is a property holder's luxury," says Roquentin, waxing ironic on bourgeois closets stuffed with fabrics, old garments, newspapers. "They kept everything." But he, too, has a chest full of memories, all those travel photos that he showed to the Self-Taught Man one afternoon, with a display of contempt that is ultimately rather difficult to explain.

The last pages of *La Nausée*, entitled "My Last Day at Bouville," fail to whisper a single word concerning his departure from the Hôtel Printania, in which he will nevertheless have lived for three years. His bags are closed and sent off, his bill paid, and his key returned by the time the long series of farewells whose narration constitutes the subject of the final day begins: farewell to the library and to the Self-Taught Man, farewell to the Café Mably, to the Rendez-vous des cheminots, to its owner, to "Some of These Days," and so on. He enumerates everything he is leaving but makes no allusion to what he is keeping. To what he continues to feel sufficiently attached to not to leave it behind in Bouville. His luggage leaves the hotel incognito, almost as contraband. Nothing to declare.

The first part of the account of the day is written in the Café Mably. Roquentin notes, "I then asked for some paper, and I'm going to write down what happened." For whom does one write "I asked for some paper"? And in order to tell him what? The observation, all the same, has its importance. Better late than never. This is the first time that Roquentin realizes he needs paper in order to write. The first time he lowers himself to take cognizance of the support on which he writes. "Does one speak of bread if it is not lacking?" If, on this last day of his stay in Bouville, returning from the station, Roquentin finds himself obliged to ask for the paper to which he will commit his monologue, it is quite probably because he has already packed his journal in one of the two trunks and con-sequently shipped it to Paris. He has no intention of doing away with it but plans, rather, to keep it, perhaps in order to continue it, perhaps in order to reread it, perhaps in order to cleanse himself of the sin of existing and to publish it. But he does not mention a word of all this. He never says what he has in the back of his mind.

These insistent stretches of silence on which the text seems to skid, this systematic blindness that it keeps up concerning anything relating to its produc-tion, might incline one to favor those readings according to which the novel that Roquentin decides to write at the end of his journal would be *La Nausée* itself — that he decides, in other words, to write the novel one has just read, a novel which would simultaneously be (in its past) and not be (in its future) Roquentin's journal. If Roquentin takes his papers off to Paris, it is in order to turn the journal into a novel, to cleanse it — and himself along with it — of the sin of existing. Blanchot suggests a reading of this type when he speaks of a narrative whose conclusion refers us back to its beginning. It is a plausible reading, one among others. But it should not be excluded.

Blanchot ("Les romans de Sartre" in *La part du feu*) contrasts *La Nausée* and the first volumes of *Les Chemins de la liberté*: In *L'Age de raison* and *Le Sursis*, he writes, "the paths down which Sartre takes us lead toward an end he recommends or a definitive goal he points out, and they consequently risk being unable to refer us back from their conclusion to their beginning."

The status of the ending of *La Nausée* is undecidable. Sartre himself oscillates on the subject. He says inside the novel (in accordance with Roquentin's aesthetic, which would have a work of art bear its own end within itself) that it is completed. Outside, he says that it is not. Officially, such uncertainty would be linked to an evolution of Sartre's thought concerning the ends of art. Upon completing his work, the author no longer adhered to the aesthetic he had professed five years earlier at its inception. "When Roquentin thinks he will be saved in the end by a work of art, he buries himself in it. He will go off to Paris and then may do absolutely anything, but he will not be saved." But chronology does not explain everything: the conclusion to *L'Imaginaire*, added to the manuscript at Groethuysen's request and, consequently, posterior to the composition and publication of *La Nausée*, develops an aesthetic position rigorously identical to that professed by Roquentin in the novel.

Among several versions of this ending: (1) Claude-Edmonde Magny's (in *Les Sandales d'Empédocle*), which would see in *La Nausée* a posthumous publication. Roquentin would have delivered himself of the sin of existing but would nonetheless not have produced a work of art. The book would be something on the order of an existential document. The publishers of *La Nausée* would be like Charles Bovary, who after finding it would have brought out an edition of the correspondence of Léon and his wife. They take it upon themselves to read and allow to be read what was not written for them. (2) Nizan's: In an article in *Ce soir*, he gives the opinion that "because of its last pages, *La Nausée* is not a book without issue." This conclusion is not far from Sartre's own. It situates the novel in a dialectical perspective in which its transcendence is programmed toward either a new conception of the novel (such as that which was to govern the elaboration of *Les Chemins de la liberté*) or a transition from literature to political action. In the first case, it is understood that the novel that Roquentin would write after leaving Bouville would not be *La Nausée*. (3) Blanchot's, which might be qualified as Proustian, since at the end of the *Recherche*, the narrator decides to write the novel one has just read and whose hero he would thus have been before becoming its author. A new form of temporal distortion, of usurpation by the secondary of the initiative reserved for the primary: it is the reading, in this case, that precedes the writing. Right after the publication of *La Nausée*, Sartre published the article on Husserl: "There we are, delivered from Proust." But with the same stroke, he was delivered from *La Nausée*, from which it is impossible to exclude this folding back at the end.

The Sandwich and the Pipe

The first pages of *La Nausée* are introduced under the rubric "Undated sheet." Except for an imperative, the beginning is identical to that of *L'Imagination*. There we had "I look at this blank sheet . . . " Here we have "I have to tell how I see this table, the street, the people, my cigarette pack . . . " Later on: "For example, here is a cardboard box containing my ink bottle." These first lines, as plausible as the example of perception in the previous work, are impeccable from the realist's point of view. There is no incompatibility between the statement and the circumstances of its utterance. Roquentin is at his desk in his room at the Hôtel Printania, rue des Mutilés, in Bouville (which shares with Le Havre the title of "seventh city of France"). He writes with the panoply of objects from which he will draw support for the example of writing: ink, paper, tobacco, and, if need be, his hand. And so forth.

The "Undated Sheet" is entirely composed while he is in that posture, as is also the first sequence of the journal itself, which is dated "Monday, 29 January 1932." A portrait of the artist in his studio: he is at his work table, seated before his instrument panel.

The following remarks do not imply that a text bears a relation to the place of its writing. A text takes place only on condition of detaching itself from that place.

And specifically, quite early on 30 January, Roquentin's journal lets itself be carried away by a gesture heavy with consequences and crosses a threshold from which it will not return. What it does is quite simply leave its place of writing. It steps out of Roquentin's room and goes outside into the world to breathe some fresh air. Resolved to no longer rest on anything. From this moment on, it will experience the greatest difficulties in staying in place. Which is not an evil in itself. But it happens that Roquentin, once he himself is outside, is far too occupied with his own limited affairs to have time to see what his journal is becoming and to keep the example of writing in a functional state. One is inclined to tell him not to do so many things at once. One shouldn't write while eating. Or speaking. Or walking. One doesn't have thirty-six hands. No sooner are the desk and the sitting position abandoned, no sooner is writing detached from its support than it is set afloat, hovering, with something of the somnambulist about it. One does not ask a writer for his papers. Roquentin does not even realize that his own are accompanying him. It is only at home that writing is capable of raising anew its writing surface.

1. On 30 January, then, his journal notes: "I am at the Café Mably. I'm eating a sandwich. Everything is more or less normal." More or less, he says. The sandwich in one hand and the pen in the other? But which one in which? With which hand does he eat and with which does he think? Try it . . .

2. On 8 February, things get even more complicated. The sequence is dated "Thursday, 11:30." I won't insist on the fact (although it has its importance) that there has never been in human memory a Thursday, 8 February 1932. Like all the other dates in the journal, this indication is false. But perhaps he couldn't care less. We continue. On 8 February, then, Roquentin performs again. His journal begins by noting in the past that he worked for two hours at the library.

Then that he went down to the courtyard to smoke a pipe beside the statue of Impétraz. None of this causes any problem, since it is not recounted at the same time as it is accomplished: it is told as something already accomplished. But abruptly, a powerful gust of presence arrives and upsets everything. "I leaned against the front of the library. I draw on my pipe, which threatens to die on me." All the rest of the sequence will continue in the present. It is Sartre's preferred tense, but he could have prepared for it. What is the reason for this abrupt shift? Why did the narrative not stay in the past? Who is writing, where, from where, and how?

This present, which seems to hover sufficiently afloat to be called artificial (in the sense of Baudelaire's paradises) is a mere distraction, a slip-up, a case of absentmindedness. What kind of tobacco is Roquentin putting in his pipe? He is no longer paying attention to what he is doing. This false appearance of a present is as inconsistent — as spectral and unreal — as the imaginary present of the first pages of L'Imagination ("I turn my head away . . . "). There is no hand [main] maintaining this present stripped of its now [maintenant]; it rests on nothing. Linguistically it cannot be sustained, perhaps not even tolerated . .

3. And yet on the following day, Roquentin does even better. It is the afternoon. He hasn't gone out. He is keeping to his room. But he is not at his table. From his window he looks at the street. At this point the journal observes imperturbably: "I am holding my pipe in my right hand and my tobacco pouch in my left hand." He continues: "This pipe needs filling." When one has a hammer in one hand and a nail in the other, one doesn't say so (and one writes so even less); one drives the nail in with the hammer. When one has a tobacco pouch in one hand and a pipe in the other, there is no feat of wizardry involved in filling the pipe. And yet Roquentin doesn't manage to. One might, of course, conclude that what prevents him from doing it is precisely the fact that he is writing that he wants and ought to do it. The act of deliberating parasitically feeds off the accomplishment. He prefers to write "This pipe needs filling" rather than putting down his pen a moment, putting aside his writing long enough to take the time to fill it. But that is not what is involved here. "I don't have the courage to," he notes.

With which hand is Roquentin writing? The left or the right? The clean or the dirty? And need one wash one's hands before writing? If one writes with one's mouth full, does that exclude one from writing for people who are hungry? Literature does not fill any stomachs — it is even not beyond flaunting the fact. A hand that writes is condemned to remain desperately clean, immaculately detached. Contrary to Lady Macbeth, but with as little success, committed literature would have given up everything in order to have dirty hands [les mains sales]. Roquentin is not yet at that stage. His problem would be, rather, that he doesn't write with his two hands but with the third — that of Sartre's phantom. A true distinction of substances: the body smokes, the soul keeps its journal. Like the work of art of which Roquentin dreams, the hand with which he writes it has become detached from his body. It cleanses itself with writing of the sin of existing. At the Hôtel Printania, on the rue des Mutilés, the phantom shifts into action.

Defense and Illustration of the Perceiver

Blanchot, even more than Proust, makes of literary writing an experience of lost time, a lost time that no time regained will ever redeem. "Writing," we read in *L'Espace littéraire*, lies in giving oneself over to the fascination of the absence of time." And the author adds: "The tense of the absence of time is without present." Time is out of joint. Literature can be defined, in the strongest sense of the word, as a chronic illness. It draws its inspiration from what Bataille called "the infelicities of the present tense." Between negligence and impatience, one writes without ever taking the time to. The wrong moment? Lost moments? It is not on my schedule that I write. The time to write is not taken; it comes when there is no longer anyone to take it. For such is the second characteristic of the experience of writing that what comes undone, along with temporality, is the structures of subjectivity. The absence of time [tense (*temps*)] is also that of an impersonal nonintimacy. Blanchot: "The poet's words are no longer the words of anyone."

Sartre himself, moreover, did not say anything different at the beginning of *Qu'est-ce que la littérature?* when, while describing — with hopes of exorcising it — the crisis of language into which he accuses modern literature of self-indulgently sinking (which is, he opines, a "poetic" crisis and consequently not fundamentally alien to what Mallarmé had called a "*crise de vers*"), he, too, diagnosed a "seizure of depersonalization of the writer in the face of words." This is the clinical argument of neurasthenia: the poet does not want to say anything, because he is not there. Prose will set him aright. But the agreement between Sartre and Blanchot goes no further than that definition, which they offer with divergent intentions. Whereas Blanchot will extend to literature in its entirety the impersonal — or depersonalizing — experience of poetic language, Sartre, on the contrary, invoking the pathological propensity to depersonalization, will exclude poets from the republic of words. He is particularly severe toward collaborators who accept the compromise of "poetic prose." "The art of prose is interdependent with the only regime in which prose retains meaning: democracy."

Blanchot opposes to the definition of writing as an experience of the absence of time the practice of the journal. His reference is to the private diary, but what he says of it, we shall see, holds no less true for writing that submits to the conventions of journalism. In the case of most writers, he suggests, recourse to a private diary or journal would respond to a need to find for themselves a zone in which they would be removed from the impersonal solitude in which the work possessing them asks them to lose themselves. Rather than a receptacle of unpub-lishable secrets, it should be seen as something of an antidote, an exercise necessary for the mental hygiene of a writer who wants to reserve a base outside literary space for himself, to regain his footing in common time, to remove himself from the absence of time. By reinstating language's referential function, journal writing would resist the dangers entailed in the exercise of literature. Its essence lies not in the facts, thoughts, or comments it relates, but in the places and dates under which they are registered. On such and such a day, such and such a thing took place at such and such a spot. "A diary [*journal*]," according to Blanchot, "roots the movement of writing in time, in the humility of the daily — dated and preserved by its date." "The date one inscribes in a diary," he says further, "is that of a common time in which what happens truly happens." Whomever the passion for writing alienates from the world of the living remains, by dint of his journal, able to recall that he is alive, able to call himself back to life. Certain things, for example, happen to him even though he writes — even while he is not writing. A journal, for that reason, is never that of the writer properly speaking, but the journal of "the one he is when he doesn't write." As though writing were making an appeal to life to protect itself from writing itself, were escaping from itself and taking foot in the world. It attempts to convince itself that it can support itself on something other than itself. Claims to have succeeded in finding repose, unburdening itself of itself . . . To have found a firm basis. On solid ground.

Roquentin is not a writer when he begins composing the private journal that will become *La Nausée*. He writes, to be sure, but the study of Rollebon on which he is working is based, in Ranke's phrase, on the solid ground of facts. The historian's craft is not subject to the same uncertainties as literary experience. As for the journal itself, the "Undated Sheet" which begins it places it explicitly in an analogous perspective. Once again, it is a matter (but concerning the present and no longer the past) of sticking to what is actually given. Not of forming sentences, but of seeing things clearly. The journal indeed comes to the assistance of perception, once that activity suddenly sees itself as threatened. Roquentin does not speak of neurasthenia (and may not have read Janet), but on more than one occasion he wonders if he is not going mad. The experience that brings him to resort to his pen and keep a journal (the experience, rather, from which he asks his journal to protect him), although it does not fall officially under the rubric of literature, is also linked to a threat of depersonalization, to a defective grip on the world. Blanchot would say that Roquentin decides to keep his journal in order to escape the temptation of writing. To regain, while consolidating his ego through intensive exercises of the first person, control of the present, mastery of presence.

Roquentin's journal does indeed open by giving itself over to perception. A humbly referential discourse proposes to take inventory of what it has under its eyes. To say what it sees. Like a journalist.

"I relate only what I saw." Such is the sentence inaugurating Sartre's journalistic career. It opens the first article of the series he contributed to *Combat* in August 1944 to convey and celebrate the present Parisian insurrection and what might be called, after the poetry of the Resistance, after the poetic prose of the collaboration, the return of prosaic prose.

"The best would be to write up events day by day. To keep a journal in order to see things clearly. I have to say how I see this table, the street, the people, my tobacco pouch."

The Present, Reporting

Perception is a defense mechanism resistant to the free association (that is, the free dissociation) of the primary processes. It takes in hand a present falling mechanically apart, running off at the mouth. Roquentin, expert overseer, decides to keep his journal in order to mend the unraveling of a word that failed to come. Confronting that abyss, he wants to certify his presence and once again be plugged into a consistent temporality: to set the machine aright and stave off the generalized rout.

But even if Sartre took himself for Roquentin, Roquentin differs from his author at least in that he has from the beginning been cleansed of the sin of existing, from which the latter (not very cognizant of the duplication) would nevertheless like to cleanse him at the end of *La Nausée*.

To what extent is an imaginary character in a position to actually refuse the imaginary? By being registered under a date borrowed from the social context of chronology, that which is related in a journal belongs, as Blanchot says, to the world in which "what happens truly happens." Sartre himself also speaks of the imaginary world as a world where "nothing happens." What is strangest in *La Nausée* is no doubt that this imaginary journal does not even make the minimal effort to resemble what it nevertheless claims to pass itself off as. In spite of the dates (or rather because of them), it drifts from the very beginning into a world into which nothing will ever happen. The inconsistency of Roquentin's temporality is in no wise inferior to that of Faulkner's narrative.

It would appear that this is because space offers better support to the imaginary than time. It offers firmer resistance to its contagion. One has no objection, for instance, when Roquentin in Bouville (an urban area found on no map) takes a train that nonetheless is to take him to an eminently real city, Paris. The crossing of the border between imagination and perception takes place wthout difficulties. Just as there is no problem occasioned by Bouville's competition with Le Havre for the title of the "seventh city of France." It is far more difficult, by contrast, to fix the limit of the damages engendered by chronic unreality. A private journal that begins "Monday, 29 January 1932" would seem to have made a very poor start if it has serious hopes of escaping from the absence of time. By virtue of the fact that such a date does not appear on any calendar (in 1932, 29 January fell on a Friday, and it was in 1934 that it was a Monday), an imperceptible problem in "*maintenance*" will undermine his writing. And it will condemn it to a purely idio(syncra)tic chronology, without the slightest referential value, incapable of going beyond the margins of the novel enumerating it. Roquentin, without a watch or an appointment book, writes without counting. He has turned off his meter. For that matter, what is a date? In 1932, he couldn't care less. Nothing counts for a man alone.

It was in 1932 that Sartre began composing the adventures of Roquentin (which also take place in 1932 as their author relates them in the first person of the present tense). But it was no doubt in 1934 that he decided, in order to make things more life-like (less literary), to transform into a private journal reflections that until then were more or less similar to Rilke's *Notebooks of Malte Laurids Brigge*. He thus mixed the year of departure (1932) with the days of the current year (1934), welding — but out of negligence — the time of narration and the time of the narrated. Managing to proceed as though there were no gap between the two. Imagining a time in which the moment evoked and the moment of the evocation would fuse. Acting, then, as though the time needed for writing counted for nothing. The writer, according to Blanchot, when he keeps his journal, remembers "the one he is when he isn't writing." More bizarrely, when Roquentin writes his journal, he does not even perceive that he is writing it. He succeeds in being the one not writing even in the course of writing it. In 1921, Paulhan published a short narrative, *Aytré qui perd l'habitude*, at whose center is found a ship's log which — forgetful of the genre's sobriety — abruptly veers into literature. It begins to expand, says the fictive publisher, "as though it had not been written." More than one passage of *La Nausée* would give an attentive reader the same strange feeling that he is in the process of reading a text which has not had time to be written. Roquentin in this sense is the exact antithesis of Nabokov, who (according to Sartre) never wrote "without *seeing himself* writing"; he does it without ever seeing himself doing it.

ERRATA. — Sartre was in all probability never worried by these minutia. He is not alone, since a good million readers (if we admit that each copy of the book sold in France was read at least once) appear not to have been troubled. We shall nevertheless point out — without claiming to be exhaustive — several points indicative of a certain lack in the finish of a book pretending to bear its own end within itself. I quote from the Folio edition (number 46 of the collection), printed on 5 March 1974 (a Tuesday).

— Page 13: 10:30 P.M. Beneath Roquentin's window, a series: people are lined up waiting for "the last trolley." They are early, since it is not scheduled to come through until "10:45." A quarter of an hour later, the trolley comes through. But this time Roquentin says it is the "next to the last one." He even specifies that the last one should come through "in an hour." All this, of course, with utter informality. Without erratum.

N.B.: page 221, among the contingent but immutable laws of nature, Roquentin mentions the departure time of the last trolley: it leaves City Hall at 11:05 P.M.

— Page 16: Roquentin remembers how his six years of adventure in Indochina came to an end four years earlier (consequently, in 1928). It was in the office of one Mercier, who asked him to accompany him to Bengal. At those words, he says, he awakened from a dream that had lasted six years. Another allusion to the scene specifies on page 58 the Indochinese city where it took place: Hanoi. On page 95, it is Saigon. But on page 140, Mercier's office is said to be in Shanghai.

— Page 74: On "Sunday" (11 February), Roquentin is going to read *Eugénie Grandet* at the Brasserie Vézelize. The entire episode is composed in the present ("I recognize my neighbors. . . . I open up the book at a random page. . . .") But it is a rather distracted present which caves in at the slightest outburst: "The husband's voice drew [*tira*] me out of my reading," as Roquentin indeed notes with a *passé simple* that appears to have survived all the editions of the novel.

— There is also the meeting with Anny. On 13 February ("Mardi Gras"), Roquentin receives a note from the woman he loves, which rather imperiously summons him to Paris on the 20th, a week to the day later (p. 91). Two days afterward (the 15th, "Thursday"), however, after a few melancholy lines, Roquentin notes: "A week from today I'm going to see Anny" (p. 104). Would their meeting have been postponed to the 22nd? There is no mention of it. On the 21st, in any event, he still hasn't gone to Paris and can be found at the restaurant waiting to be joined by the Self-Taught Man and anticipating again the pleasure promised by his forthcoming reunion with Anny: "In four days, I'll see Anny again. That, for the moment, is my only reason for living" (p. 147). And yet, without the slightest explanation, it is neither on the 20th (as she had ordered him) nor on the 22nd or the 25th (as he had announced respectively on the 15th and the 21st), but on the 24th that he goes to knock at the door of her hotel in Paris. What is a date?

The past of his relations with Anny is not governed by a chronology any more rigorous. When he receives the letter, he notes (p. 90): "It's been five years since I've had any news of her." From recollections mentioned two pages later, however, it follows that their separation occurred six years before and that at that time Anny asked him not to "call her" anymore (p. 93). The span of six years is confirmed a bit later when Roquentin wonders (p. 118): "What has she been doing for six years?"

But when he sees her in Paris, he asks her if she needed him "during those four years she hadn't seen him" (p. 193). That duration is confirmed by the author's blurb: "Anny, the woman he loves, disappeared four years ago." Five years earlier, moreover, it appears to have been the case that they were both in Portsmouth (although, according to other versions, he should have been in the Far East — Indochina or Japan — at the time). He has in his trunk a signed and dated photo ("Anny. Portsmouth, 7 April 1927") that he thinks of (p. 54) just before the Self-Taught Man knocks at the door of his room.

— We have already noted that Roquentin (but also Sartre) imagines that 21 February ("Wednesday"), the day of his lunch with the Self-Taught Man and his visit to the Public Garden, is the first day of spring.

— At the Rendez-vous des Cheminots, Roquentin asks Madeleine, the waitress, to play his favorite record ("Some of These Days") on the phonograph. But when he mentions it to Anny (p. 212), the instrument changes. He tells her that he had it played on the piano. In his memory, it is not a copy.

— On 29 February, before packing his bags for good, Roquentin stops at the library, where he reads the *Journal de Bouville*. He comes upon a summary of accomplishments in the year 1932 even more precocious than the arrival of its spring: "It can hardly be said that MM. Lagoutte, Nizan, Pierpont, and Ghil have been idle during the year 1932," announces the local editor, whose precipitousness is not about to be inhibited by a single anachronism.

— There is, finally, on this same last day of February (the 29th), one of the most spectacular sunsets in the history of literature.

It is mentioned for the first time at the beginning of the sequence composed at the Café Mably, when Roquentin relates his entry into the Municipal Library, "toward two o'clock in the afternoon." The "setting sun," rather premature as is the tendency in Bouville, is already there tinging the table, the door, the leather of the bindings in its reddish light (p. 25). Two and a half hours later ("at 4:30," p. 226) the Self-Taught Man enters. Several temporal references ("a few minutes elapsed," p. 228; "a quarter of an hour passed," p. 229) help to pass the time in preparation for the onset of the great scene: the librarian discovers the furtive pederastic moves of the Self-Taught Man's hands, and he is expelled from the bookish paradise. Upon following him out, Roquentin is able to observe *de visu* that the sun is still every bit as much involved in setting, now that is almost five o'clock (p. 235), as it had been three hours earlier.

But the immobility does not stop there. The Self-Taught Man takes flight. Roquentin searches "the whole city in order to find him" (p. 224), then goes to the Café Mably, where he manages to get some paper (his journal is in the trunk that has already been registered for shipment to Paris) to note down the series of the afternoon's events. Upon entering the library, he had mentioned along with the time (two o'clock), the timetable of his train ("In six hours, I will have left Bouville": it leaves at 8:00 P.M. The second sequence of his journal (written — "written"? — after leaving the Café Mably) thus begins around six o'clock, since it notes that his train will leave "in two hours" (p. 235). Roquentin, in passing, glances at the sky. Everything is in place; nothing has moved: "it's gray and the sun is setting." Everything is in order. No need to introduce anything strange where there isn't anything.

In a West perpetuating itself out of weakness, Sartre's novels are not alone in being interminable. Rarely will a sun have been as still — without even [Valéry's] great strides. It is not *La Nausée* that will extricate us from heliotropism. The novel's conclusion is undoubtedly endowed with an axis as unmoving as, according to Girard, the antiromantic revolution demands.

Roquentin spends the two hours remaining to him at the Rendez-vous des Cheminots, where he meditates a bit, listens one more time to a scratched recording of his favorite ragtime ("the train is leaving in three-quarters of an hour," p. 240), listens to it again ("I have to go now," p. 246), rises, reflects for a moment, and leaves ("I'm leaving," p. 247). One last glance at the Bouville sky. Night has still not fallen: it "is falling" (p. 248).

And then?

Maybe the sun has an alibi? Perhaps there is also one for the author's ragtime — and his ragged time. "The prewar period," Sartre would say after 1940, "had no knowledge of time." Which is the least that can be said of the botched and dislocated chronology of *La Nausée*.

On 21 February, Roquentin no longer holds back. He writes without counting. Won over by the "rapturous abundance" into which springtime plunges the cosmos, he loses all restraint and covers his journal with the equivalent of forty-three printed pages in the Folio edition. Such a performance makes the day the most prolix in his journal. Far behind, trailing in second place, will come the 24th, with twenty-seven pages, then the 29th, with twenty-four, and so on.

And yet on the 12th ("Monday," "7 P.M.") Roquentin gave us an indication of his rhythm of production: "A working day," he notes. "Didn't go too badly; I wrote six pages." Plainly he is referring to pages written by hand. But on "Tuesday, 30 January," an observation allows for their conversion into printed pages: Roquentin, in referring to a sequence that occupies four pages of the book, notes that he has just "written ten pages." The forty-three printed pages from 21 February should thus — if they are similarly proportioned — correspond to more than a hundred written by hand. It may be granted that inspiration was no longer there in February 1932, when Roquentin was working on Rollebon. But from six — or ten — pages per day to more than a hundred, there is a margin of difference one is hard put to attribute entirely to a shift in the subject of his reflections. It's the spring. Roquentin feels less self-conscious. He takes off. And unbound, begins to write fluently, without even taking the time to do it.

The forty-three (printed) pages that Roquentin fills with his reflections on 21 February are divided into two sequences. The second relates the visit to the Public Garden that taught him so many things about existence. But I shall restrict myself in this context to the first. With the narrative bad faith governing all the passages in the present tense, it relates without apparent mediation Roquentin's lunch with the Self-Taught Man, the ensuing flight, and the trolley ride that takes him to the gate of the Public Garden (where, in a different tempo — reminiscence — the second sequence will take over). The first sequence occupies thirty pages covering a period of between two and two and a half hours. Which does not imply a particularly slow rhythm of narration. Genette, clocking *A la recherche du temps perdu*, had no trouble finding better. The description of the Guermantes *matinée*, for example, for a duration of the same order, is stretched out over 190 pages. But such slowness is not in itself the source of any oddity, since the pages are composed in the past tense, a circumstance allowing the narrator all the time he likes to make the pleasure of remembrance last. In contrast, in the case of the lunch with the Self-Taught Man, which is written in the present, such a swelling of time, however unworthy of mention in itself, loses all credibility. The two hours in thirty pages become simultaneously, because of the present tense of their utterance, thirty pages in two hours. Which gives us an average of fifteen pages an hour, a positively infernal rhythm that might have been the envy of Sartre himself.

One does not choose one's time. There are no grounds for holding Roquentin personally responsible for the anachronisms he perpetrates en route. Sartre would later name the true culprit. "The prewar period had no knowledge of time." The present of *La Nausée* is the tense of time's absence.

The written statement of the lunch with the Self-Taught Man cannot be sustained according to criteria of plausibility, for reasons that are no longer a function merely, as in the case of the sandwich, of questions of propriety ("One doesn't write with one's mouth full") or, as in the case of the pipe, of technico-anatomical exploits ("One doesn't write with one's hands full"), but that are tied more fundamentally to problems relating to the time of writing, to the relation between writing and time. Roquentin plainly does not have the actual time to write the thirty pages during the time they refer to. Should one want to find a plausible equivalent, those two hours might conceivably be adequate to their oral utterance. They constitute about the time taken to read the pages out loud or to hear a recording of them.

The recounting of the lunch clings rigorously like a narrative film, without gap and without addition, to the duration of the lunch itself. It duplicates it without exceeding it. Things are immediately accompanied by their verbal counterpart as though they were recorded at the precise instant of their occurrence, without the shadow of a delay or hiatus. Exactly synchronized, the narrative begins and ends at the same time as the facts it reports but without ever affecting them, infringing on the lunch itself, leaving its imprint on it. It takes place at the same time as the lunch but does not count itself among the things transpiring during the lunch. To put it differently: it takes place during the lunch, but it does not take place; it has no place in that which takes place at the same time as itself. Atopical and without extension, the narration is also instantaneous: it takes neither time nor place. Costs nothing. Its writing, utterly gratuitous, claims not to enter into account. Gratuity not included: Roquentin does not even have time to see that he does not have time to write. "For example, at this moment, I am writing, but I do not realize that I am writing." The check is not to be seen. The inscription is gratuitous. I weigh my words. But what can be the weight of writing so unburdened?

It should be possible to sketch out a gestuary of speech acts. Prayer, for example, is said on one's knees, with one's head inclined and hands folded. Oaths are taken standing up, with the right hand raised. A — gymnastic — ritualism allows words to become embodied. A writer who promises must first get up. The same holds for a writer about to commit himself. He has to leave his chair, his table, his ink bottle, this sheet of paper, and so forth. But writing is a hopelessly sedentary activity. No doubt that's a little better than the bed, but it all the same remains only halfway toward verticality.

There have, in fact, been several dictators in the annals of literature. Montaigne used to walk about as his scribe took his words down. When a writer rises, it means he is not alone. His vertical effects always rest on other people's backs. For the rest, if Roquentin had had a secretary or a script girl, word would have leaked out. Scribes are paid at a fixed rate. Nor can the solution of a tape recording that he would have recopied himself upon returning to the hotel have any more validity in 1932. One does not choose one's time, and the recluse of Bouville could well have been the father of the Tape Recorder Man. Interviews at the time were still done by hand or by memory.

The fact is that he did not have to wait for technological progress in order to record himself. He, too, had his chatterbox that followed his every gesture like an omnipresent writer: "Maman, things have been freed of their names. . . . The word stays on my lips, Maman."

Roquentin, a journalist of himself, does not depart from himself in the slightest. As soon as it passes to the present, the writing of *La Nausée* no longer has anything to do with a private journal or diary. What might be called its "free direct style" — its mixture of descriptions, more or less interior monologues, and dialogues — makes of it, instead of the written journal it would like to pass itself off as, the transcript of an oral diary. You are plugged into the subject. Even before the intervention of the media (Roquentin never listens to the radio), spoken autobiography suffers interference from the immediate.

Sartre, during the war, published his own journal, of which several pages were published under the title "La Mort dans l'âme." (They cover approximately the same period as the volume of *Les Chemins de la liberté* that would bear the same title eight years later.) Those pages from his journal constitute his sole publication during the somber year 1942. Contat and Rybalka include them in their *Les Ecrits de Sartre*, where one has little difficulty realizing that when it is his own diary he is keeping, Sartre emerges far better than he had with Roquentin's. There would, of course, be grounds — were one to seek an explanation for such progress — for entertaining the hypothesis that the sense of the present would have been revealed to him quite abruptly, precisely during those June days in 1940 during which the journal was written. It would thus be the journal of a neophyte of reality — better still, the journal of his conversion to the present. But that interpretation suffers from a serious weakness: it sticks too closely to Sartre's version of events . . .

What is a private diary when the sphere of telecommunications has infiltrated the space of domesticity, and daily life offers to the distractedness of everyone a familiarity with what is most distant? What is a private journal when the technology of the media has insinuated its way into the innermost recesses of privacy, thus dispossessing it of its presence to self? when the telephonic proliferation of that external noise screens out with its buzz the retreat of writing?

Mallarmé excepted (to use his word) literature from what he called "universal reporting." In an inverse move, Sartre will militate in favor of the literary status of journalism — better still, in favor of reporting being acknowleged as the "pilot" genre of present literature. "Reporting," he writes in his "Présentation des *Temps modernes*," "is one of the genres of literature and can become one of the most important of them." The writer as correspondent: he corresponds to his time because he corresponds with it, because, through him, it corresponds to — or with — itself. The American model was Hemingway. The French rival: Camus. A writing both purposeful and effective; the proximity of the rotary press; the fraternity of the printers: a newspaper is a minigroup in fusion which dismantles the haughty myths of the ivory tower or the sixth floor. It has to appear on time, as punctual as a train or airplane. We have seen Sartre on the morrow of the war investing his person and his pen in the promotion of the genre. Beyond such anecdotal tribute, the structure of journalistic reporting joins up with the most persistent Sartrean fantasy — that of a writing without difference, stripped of any time gap and clinging to the present, a writing rigorously contemporary with whatever it would speak about. From our special envoy: bananas are better on the spot. And when I say "a banana," I do not mean one absent from every diet.

As a good journalist, Sartre the novelist always began by using what he had before his eyes.

One recalls the scene in *Les Mots*: "I am walking, Maman, I am drinking a glass of water." It has found its title: *Poulou reporter*. "I described what I saw, what Anne-Marie saw as well as I did, the houses, trees, people." In *Qu'est-ce que la littérature?* that will be called "unveiling." But it is exactly the same running off at the mouth that was heard in Roquentin's perpetual commentary: "I have to say how I see this table, the street, the people, my tobacco pouch." We have seen the present lose itself and writing lose time in the process. Which says everything about the quantity of reality programmed into Sartre's journalistic aspiration. By clinging too closely to the present, words come to take its place. The triumph of directness is the closed circuit; the media begin turning in a circle, have no other object than themselves, find their end in themselves. Reporting is no longer the relating of an event, but the event itself. Its own report preoccupies the present like a parasite that would replicate it before it even occurs. Nothing will have taken place but the reporting. The news of the day is reduced to its coverage. And yet, if a present allows itself to be reported [*reporter*; also: carried over, postponed], no one is in a position to say until when. Who spoke of writing without difference? of a writing that would not take time? of a world in which words and things would be contemporaneous? Roquentin, to be sure, did not have the actual time to write his thirty pages. But actual time is not made for writing. Its narrative, with its appearance of a present, pretends to be written at the same time as the events it reports. But it is written at the same time in a different time. That's it: at the same time and in a different time at the same time: reporting simulates.

It can be imagined without undue risk that it was in February 1932 that Sartre and Roquentin together began writing, the latter his journal and the former *La Nausée*. Author and character, like a single man, begin writing a single and double text, their two hands holding a single pen together. That impeccable harmony will not, however, survive their joint start. Sartre and Roquentin begin by together keeping the latter's journal, but it is precisely the latter who wastes no time in breaking away, moves out in front, and leaves his author behind in a few days. In just a month he will reach the end point that it will take his partner six years to catch up to. Sartre, like a good novelist, was already beginning in all directness with what he had before his eyes. Until he lost sight of it. It is, moreover, still not known what Roquentin may have done while waiting for Sartre to get over his nausea. Between 29 February 1932 and the spring of 1938.

From Where Are You Speaking?

The eighteenth century remains the unique historical opportunity and the soon to be lost paradise of French writers.

Sartre, *Qu'est-ce que la littérature?*

One further remark on the two sequences in Roquentin's journal dated "Wednesday," 21 February. In the first, as we have seen, Roquentin recounts his lunch with the Self-Taught Man in the first person indicative. The second sequence is undoubtedly more significant in terms of the philosophical and ideological themes it calls into play (existence, contingency, and the like), and yet its composition is governed by a far more customary narrative technique: Roquentin relates in the past tense the events and discoveries for which the Public Garden had been a theater in the course of the afternoon. The narrative begins in the present, but it is a present intended only to establish the scene within which the evocation of prior events will be adduced and framed: "I have achieved my goal: I know what I wanted to know." Whereupon there follows the narrative of the revelation, ending with the words "I went out, I came back to the hotel, and there it is, I wrote." In terms of Blanchot's formula, Roquentin (for once) remembers while writing these pages what was happening to him while he wasn't writing them.

The narrative formula of the first sequence might be expressed: (I am writing that) I am not writing. That of the second: (I am writing that) I wasn't writing. The juxtaposition of these two narrative modes can be found in reverse on 29 February, the last day Roquentin spends in Bouville. The first of the two passages composed on that date (like the second sequence on 21 February) relates in the past an event prior to its composition and (it, too) manages to mention in passing the conditions of its production. Roquentin notes, in the present, "I am writing this in the Café Mably." But that is in order to make clear that what he is recounting preceded the narration he is giving of it; that present is not part of the account he is presenting. Even more: what it is he is telling comes to an end with the decision to tell it: "Whereupon I asked for some paper, and I am going to relate what happened to him." There follows the tale of the Self-Taught Man's misfortunes.

But the second sequence of 29 February, like the first passage from the 21st, is (on the contrary) written in a present that is indistinguishably the time of both the utterance and its contents ("It's cloudy, the sun is setting; in two hours the train leaves. . . . I am walking on Rue Boulibet"). But it is an act — of utterance — which as a result is no longer noticed. Once again, in the temporal modification of the narrative shift, time gets lost and, in particular, the time of writing. Such passages in the present, in fact, invariably induce effects of the greatest strangeness. It is enough for the text to shift into the present for us no longer to know where it is coming from. As soon as the text approaches its source, it comes from nowhere. Its act of utterance suffers a dislocation and is encrypted. Origin is lost in a present tense which is anything but the temporality of self-presence — the least realistic of temporal instances, the most devoid of referentiality.

Sartre's interest in techniques of simultaneity thus existed considerably before his attempts in *Le Sursis*. But the simultaneity activated by *La Nausée* is not only, as will be the case for the second volume of *Les Chemins de la liberté*, the dispersion of a story whose events take place simultaneously in several distinct points of the globe (like the so-called Munich events of September 1938, which occur in Paris, Prague, Berlin, London, or Marseille just as much as in Munich itself). It is the more troubling simultaneity — implying no transfer of information from one point to the other — of two events (the event itself and its narration) that take place, without interfering with each other, at the same time in the same place. I am writing something instead of doing it but without the writing taking the place of the accomplishment. It is precisely where I write it that it should be done. I write it not only in the very moment but also in the very place of doing it. (As though absolutely any verb could become a performative.) At stake is an entirely positive topographical indication and not an adverbial expression indicating replacement or opposition. One and the other (I accomplish it in the place where I write it) and not one or the other (I accomplish it in place of writing it). But can such an unrestricted arrogation of place constitute anything other than a usurpation?

In *Qu'est-ce que la littérature?* Sartre severely condemns the narrative technique of the bourgeois novel, which he reduces in its entirety to the formula of retrospective narration: a "primal subjectivity" expresses, *sub specie aeternitatis*, now that they are over, the disturbances which had formerly wracked a number of "secondary subjectivities." The retelling of those disorders is part of the ritual of their reabsorption. The return to order requires nothing more; such wounds are healed by being narrated. "In the stable world of the prewar French novel," writes Sartre, "the author, situated in a point *gamma* representing absolute repose, had at his disposition contextual bearings allowing him to determine the moves of his characters." And while preaching in favor of the narrator's mobilization, Sartre formulates precisely the opposite ambition, that of speaking only of what has not yet come to an end. Were it over, what interest would there be in talking about it? To tell a story is to intervene in what it relates, not in the manner of Sterne in *Tristram Shandy*, but rather in that of Zola in *J'accuse!* As the word indicates, the committed [*engagé*] novelist is engaged in what he speaks about. Which implies, in particular, that he has not yet emerged from it. (Knowing whether he will ever emerge from it is a completely different question.) Contemporary physics has taught us that the observer is part of the observation.

The sequences from 21 and 29 February, composed by Roquentin after the event and making use of the completed past, thus fall subject to the condemnation of pre-Einsteinian narration. Roquentin doesn't write them only for the pleasure of the telling but also to ensure that they took place: it's really over. As though he were Mauriac. But after the war, Sartre corrected his aim. One must speak both of and from the present [*du présent*]. A present that is both discourse's referent and the source of its emission. Committed fiction should thus neither condemn (or pine for) the past in the name of the present nor judge the present in the name of the future or the eternal; it should present the present, become "the reflexive self-presence of a classless society," "the world become present to itself." It remains to determine wherein such self-presence is to be distinguished from the absences that took hold of Roquentin every time he undertook to write in the present tense. We have seen that it sufficed for him to revert to that tense for him — far from manifesting any commitment — no longer to know what he was doing. But Saint-Exupéry did not write a *Journal du volant* [the flier's or steering wheel's journal], and it is thus Roquentin who must be considered the true prototype of the mobilized narrator; this is because, as soon as he shifts to the present, he cannot be kept in a single place. He moves, as the Greeks say, by metaphor. And as for me, I have no wish to stop him. Quite the opposite. Metaphors, moreover, don't stop. Sartrean shifters, Barthes would have said, are intensely atopian.

Beaufret notes that Sartre accords the present a privilege reserved by Heidegger for the future. Which is quite accurate. But it should be specified that only a certain kind of present benefits from that privilege and that it does so precisely because of its complicity with the future — a present with a future in store for itself, a kind of revenue accruing from the future; its presence comes to it from the future it (already) possesses. To be present is to have a future. It was for that reason that the article "La Temporalité chez Faulkner" was able to play off the American novelist's "unspeakable" present, "leaking at every seam" (what a first article a few years before had called his "superpresent"), against Heidegger's preoccupation with the future. Faulkner's present "is cut off from itself"; it needs a future in order to catch up with itself. For Sartre, to catch up means to go beyond. What is needed is thus the divided structure of the coupé without which the present's presence would fail to cut a figure and not manage to emerge.

For the present is not up to presenting — or introducing — itself. A fundamental nonpresence of the present cuts it off from itself. And the experience of nausea is first of all that of the nonpresence of an unpresentable present: an excess of the present which is simultaneously a lack of presence, a desire for presence which veers into a disgust with the present. After renouncing the completion of his book on Rollebon, Roquentin perceives the error on which that historiographic project was based: the past does not exist; only the present does. He returns to that motif after the Apocalypse in the Public Garden: existence, he says, is an "enormous presence," but a presence without presence (things having lost their diversity, their individuality) which it is impossible to escape ("The world was everywhere present, in front, behind . . . "). *No exit*: Roquentin observes that his death would not change anything. Nothing eludes the present, and nothing resists it. It absorbs everything. It suffices for it to approach for things to melt. A temporality without solidity, without reality or objectivity. A viscous temporality — or tense. The time of time's absence. Roquentin notes: "Time had stopped."

What is a date? "I have often been told," concerning bananas and dates," writes Sartre (in "Ecrire pour son époque," a first version of *Qu'est-ce que la littérature?*): " 'No matter what you say, in order to know what they really are, you have to eat them on the spot, when they have just been picked.' And I have always considered bananas as dead fruit whose true, live savor escaped me. Books which pass from one age to another are dead fruit. In a different time they had a different taste, tart and keen. One would have had to read *Emile* and *Les Lettres persanes* when they were just plucked." This impatient campaign on behalf of the present is dated 1946.

Perhaps the quotation should have been read when it was just plucked (but by whom?); in thirty-five years, it would surely have dried out. Sartre frequently quotes a line of Prouhèze in *Le Soulier de satin*: "He will not know the savor that is mine." This time it's our turn to no longer know the taste of what Sartre wrote. And to cultivate a taste for the savor we shall never know.

It affirms the privilege of that temporal ecstasy. It is found again that same year in "Présentation des *Temps modernes*." One doesn't choose one's era, and this one is ours. "It is our wish to miss nothing of our time." I won't miss you, honey: "We have only *this* life to live, in the middle of *this* war, and perhaps of *this* revolution." (One recalls Roquentin: "I have to tell how I see this table," and so on.) But precisely contemporaneous with this promotion of the present, Sartre's text allows us to hear the palinode of its condemnation. For example, in "Matérialisme et révolution," which also dates from 1946, he denies to materialism any revolutionary capacity to the extent that it fails to transcend presence and the contiguity of presents: "The present," he says, "engenders another present and not the future." It is thus of the same — absolute, unsurmountable — present that these two texts at once (simultaneously) speak; but the first does so in order to praise it, whereas the second is concerned with discrediting it. Sartre's doctrine of time will, in fact, never succeed in choosing between a morality of the present and a politics of the future. Between an atomistic (and bourgeois), if not mechanistic, conception of the present — the present engenders the present, and a dialectical (proletarian and progressivist) conception — the future engenders the present.

It will be observed that:

1. this absolute present, as it is described in "Ecrire pour son époque" ("That final slide of the bordeaux over your tongue can be taken away from you by no man"), outlines the unexpected synthesis of two motifs which are generally opposed by Sartre, that of the group in fusion (since in order to miss nothing of

one's era, one would have to plunge into it) and that of seriality (for the data of experience exist side by side in space and time, inimitable and incomparable, renewed indefinitely by an imperturbable and continuous creation). This absolute present thus allows itself to be thought of only — simultaneously — as multiple and unique. Moreover, such uniqueness is itself but the effect of its being taken over by the structures of repetitive secondariness: language or, rather, literature. It is thus that modern times [*les temps modernes*] need be presented. And the present represented. What is literature? It is that through which presence comes into the world. It is that through which the world becomes this very world. The counter on which the present is laid out and presented. Absolutely.

2. this absolute present is no more generative — or productive — of the future than it is generated — or deduced — by the past. And yet it has a future, or (more precisely) its presence is certified only to the extent that it has a future. This present remains without presence as long as it remains deprived of the future, which alone will allow it to catch up with itself, to no longer be cut off from itself. So that the flavor of an era, the unique savor of an absolute present, turns out to be above all its future (an era has the taste of its future), that future which alone imbues (and enhances) present insipidity with a measure of pungency. Without the presence accorded it by the future, the present does indeed have something disgusting about it, which is not unrelated to Roquentin's bouts of nausea. What is most idiosyncratic about an epoch is thus "a future which was *its* future and which dies with it." What defines the Sartrean present most intimately is that vacant zone, a former future which will never have been present. To which we shall return.

The example of dates and bananas concludes by mentioning *Emile* and *Les Lettres persanes*, two works for which the public has lost its taste over the course of time. The reference to the eighteenth century is in perfect harmony with the brief history of literature as an institution proposed in "Pour qui écrit-on?" the third chapter of *Qu'est-ce que la littérature?*. Sartre there attributes to the century of the Enlightenment, as its specific discovery and invention, the present itself. The present has a date: the eighteenth century.

In earlier days as a cleric in the Middle Ages, as an *honnête homme* in the seventeenth century, the writer lived in the unchanging time of eternal truths. He knew nothing of history, which he called the "*siècle*." In its nearness and noisiness, he could only deplore it, but he condescended to take it into consideration when it had accumulated sufficient age to be in need of unearthing. Whereupon there came the eighteenth century, which rang in the death of the eternal. In opposition to the clerics, the "philosophes" allowed themselves to fall prey to what might be called century-sickness (in the same sense as one suffers from homesickness), under cover of which there emerged for the first time (in the history of humanity?) "a new dimension of temporality: the Present." From then on the eternal was a thing of the past. The modern definition of the present says precisely that it is not eternal and will not be present eternally. A frail, fragile, already crumbling present. Yesterday it was not, and tomorrow it will no longer be. It is a mode not of the nominal, but the indicative: "this hour which he is in the process of living and which is already fleeing," this hour concerning which he knows "that it is unique and that it is his." This "impassioned sense of the present," first given voice by the intellectuals of the eighteenth century, will make of them for Sartre the model par excellence of a writing intended for its short-term effects, the kind in favor of which he himself would militate at the time of the Liberation when he formulated the program of committed literature. If we think of the future, he says in "Présentation des *Temps modernes*," let it be "the future of *our* time," "a limited future barely distinguishable from it — for an era, like a man, is above all a future."

"After which, the deluge," ran the similarly oriented conclusion of "Ecrire pour son époque," in which Sartre did not hesitate to divert toward more committed ends the celebrated sigh heaved in his fatigue by the least enlightened monarch of the century of Enlightenment. But what was in the case of Louis XV a more or less waggish aversion for what would transpire once he was no longer around (and was consequently an entirely negative attitude) becomes in *Les Temps modernes* the expression of a positive passion for a present whose richness allows no leisure for the consideration of anything other than itself.

Consequently, when (in *Qu'est-ce que la littérature?*) Sartre says of the writers of the eighteenth century that "concerning the future, they possessed only a confused notion," it is in no way a rebuke. He would, moreover, have some difficulty in reproaching them for it. One does not live an absence, and at the time, the future did not yet exist. Every century must be content with its invention or discovery. The sixteenth had America, the eighteenth the present. In the *Baudelaire* study, the nineteenth is called "the era which had just discovered the future," that future on which, now that it existed, the author of *Les Fleurs du mal* was to be accused of turning his back. For there is a difference between Baudelaire turning away from it in full awareness and Voltaire, Diderot, or D'Alembert looking straight ahead (facing up to the present) but not yet seeing very far (it being necessary to "cultivate one's garden"). This does not prevent the later discovery from casting light, after the fact, on the tarnished reverse side of the preceding century's medallion. The king's "Après-moi-le-déluge" constitutes a double-edged epigraph for a manifesto of commitment. If it is true that an excessive concern with future harmonies risks serving up anew no more than "Some of These Days," enthusiasm for the present nonetheless has its limitations. In particular, for lack of a future, it runs the risk of not lasting. The most serious defect of the eighteenth century's discovery lay precisely in the fact that its present was one without a future.

The bourgeois writers of the nineteenth century, according to Sartre, committed the error of writing against their public because it was bourgeois, instead of taking off to conquer a mass public for which they could have written. The unique opportunity in literary history accorded to the writers of the eighteenth century was to have been able (bourgeois themselves) to write for a bourgeois public. The bourgeoisie in that felicitous era was still an oppressed and revolutionary class. It did not yet know the wrenching division of the modern writer unable to choose between writing against those who read him and for those who don't. The present — and that is its positive side — is the most effective of weapons against the eternity of clerical regimes and the domination of aristocratic regimes by the past. But once the eternal is buried and the past destroyed, its time is up. Entirely devoted to the discovery and struggles of his century, the committed writer of the eighteenth century fails to perceive that the present to which he has given himself is depriving him of a future. A century later, things are no longer the same. His grandsons now are familiar with the future and know that it is escaping them, know even that it belongs to their grave diggers. As is required by the implacable conjugation: the past was aristocratic; the future will be proletarian; the present alone is bourgeois. The bourgeoisie is a class without traditions and without hope, devoid of both past and future. Between two syntheses, that of the Old Regime which it destroyed and that of the future (Sartre calls the proletariat the "synthetic class") which will destroy it, its characteristic moment is that of analysis (for which Sartre's deeply engrained repulsion is known). It is, in fact, not the smallest paradox of this "paradise" that it has always been associated by Sartre with philosophical and political motifs which, from his first book to his last, from *L'Imagination* to *L'Idiot de la famille*, he has never forgone an opportunity to denounce: atomism, associationism, the primacy of contiguity, the abstract egalitarianism of human nature. All that Bachelard before the war had pinpointed, in *Les Intuitions atomistiques*, under the name "metaphysics of dust." In that work, he quotes Father Enfantin: "In order to blow on the dust of the corpse bequeathed by Voltaire, we have but to aspire (toward) the future." Against the dust of materialist wear and tear, Sartre's solution will be the political *aspirateur* — aspirant and vacuum cleaner: one that works on the future. Not toward the future, but on it. As others work on electricity.

And then what?

Chapter 6
A Lecture

(A title, Sartre's Ends, *had initially been announced, to which the contingency of an event, Sartre's end, unfortunately contributed anecdotal and — quite literally — regrettable connotations. About that I can do nothing. On the unswerving roads crossing Normandy, on my way to read these pages, I thus thought of the following as a replacement:*
HUMBLE ADDRESSES
Inasmuch as Sartrean existentialism, along with a humanism, will have long nourished the ambition of being a humilism. We are confronted, once again, with the contradictory aspiration to descend, a desire to come down to earth which at times disheartens, to the point of interment, the pride of the most demanding practitioners of literature. All returns to the earth are not as facilely georgic as Giono would have liked. It was the morning of 31 July. Circumstance had it that for the duration of the trip, chance had given over the airwaves of France-Inter to a singer named Antoine — (though not Roquentin) — who was to call upon his Polynesian experiences in order to celebrate nonstop the legend of the banana. I had nothing to do with it.)

A few years ago, I participated at this very place in a colloquium on Artaud and Bataille, and I recall that after reading my contribution, I was vigorously attacked for having strayed from the program. I had, in fact, introduced before his time the name of Nietzsche. Nietzsche, I was told, is next week. His was, in fact, the next colloquium. It would appear that the *genius loci* charges me with contributions somewhat out of place. I shall persevere today in a certain anachronism. But this year I shall not be in advance, but late. First of all, because, if I can trust the institution's schedule, Sartre was last year. And then because it seems to be generally accepted that the Sartrean problematic has by now been essentially relegated to the past. Smiles are quick to surface whenever anyone is still interested in Sartre or still writes about him, as though the person were all but suspect of still being "with" Sartre, of having stuck with him. A ban on reading can, in fact, take the form of negligence or of haste. I shall limit myself to justifying this apparent belatedness or untimeliness by recalling that Sartrean existentialism constitutes the historical focus of the attack launched by the text that brings us together. "Les Fins de l'homme" is, of all Derrida's texts, the one in which the relation to Sartre is most explicitly gauged. Here go, then, these considerations on the late Jean-Paul Sartre . . .

This lecture, unpublished in English, was delivered at Cerisy-la-Salle in July 1980 on the occasion of a colloquium organized by Philippe Lacoue-Labarthe and Jean-Luc Nancy. The proposed topic was "The Ends of Man: On the Work of Jacques Derrida." ("Les Fins de l'homme" constitutes the fourth or fifth of the texts collected in *Marges de la philosophie* in 1972. Dated 12 May 1968, it is the only piece in the volume dated in the text by Derrida.)

The signer and deliverer of this contribution — myself — was passing through. He was unable to do any more than hear himself speak. The all too brief pleasure of self-affection.

I

His death submits his work to a reading it rejected; it subjects it to a reading against which, in the most literal sense of the term, it *rose*. His work constituted itself with the resolute will, as an inner principle, to resist a reading of the kind we are attempting, a posthumous reading. Survival? There is little reason to take pride in that superstition. Sartre the writer never stopped defining himself in terms of his will to belong to his era, without the slightest reservation. He even defined literature as the surest means for a man to enter into it, to give himself over to it, to espouse his time. Committed literature, at the sign of modern times, had as its motto: write for one's age, for the present. Sartre often quoted, to condemn it, the formula from the *Journal des Faux-monnayeurs* in which Gide announces that he would win his case on appeal. What difference do our great-nephews make? We want a literature of the finite. Committed literature is first of all the will to stick to the present without reservation, without difference. It is the celebration of what will not wait.

One recalls the bananas which Sartre (in *Qu'est-ce que la littérature?*) charged with illustrating that ambition, the bananas which had to be eaten on the spot, because they lose their taste when exported. On the spot and instantaneously because they also lose it a few seconds after having been cut from the tree bearing them. The slightest delay, the slightest displacement, and it is no longer the same thing. The comparison is worth whatever merit it may possess. Sartre uses it to denounce the timeless insipidity of class masterpieces, such deracinated books as *Phèdre*, *Les Lettres persanes*, and the other titles of the curriculum. The example of bananas is introduced by a phrase attributing it to others. Sartre is quoting, no longer speaking in his own name. When it comes to tastes and colors, moreover, argument could go on indefinitely. But on this precise point, Sartre's own are known. He never concealed that, on the spot or elsewhere, he detested bananas and never appreciated the fruits of the earth any other way than canned. There is no restriction on wondering

> 1946: extract from the portrait of Sartre given by Simone de Beauvoir to an American magazine ("Strictly Personal," *Harper's Bazaar*): "He enjoys neither raw vegetables, nor milk fresh from the cow, nor oysters, only cooked foods; and he always asks for canned fruits rather than the natural product" (quoted in *Les Ecrits de Sartre*).
> 1947: extract from the portrait of Baudelaire sketched by Sartre in the study devoted to him: "I would bet that he preferred meats in sauce to grilled meats, and canned to fresh vegetables."

about the consequences the object of the comparison might suffer as a result of the comparer's oft expressed disgust concerning the vehicle of his comparison. What is the status of the literature of the present if it has as its models bananas which provoke in the propagandist himself nothing but nausea? One might also peel the example still further and attempt to determine, given the concrete modalities of the growing of bananas, what portion of the pick is consumable on the spot and what portion is due the plantation workers. The exotic is a product for exportation. The utopian banana republic proposed by *Qu'est-ce que la littérature?* as an ideal to the committed writer in reality produces only dream-bananas, the only kind that don't risk provoking nausea in aficionados of canned foods, because they alone have been carefully cleansed of the sin of existence. Sartre himself, moreover, was to develop a taste, not for the fruit itself, but for the comparison it sustained, and upon returning from America in 1945, he would once again make use of this perennial fruit to speak in praise of jazz that can be picked on the spot, where it grows, between New York and Memphis, but without difference. "Some of These Days" has a different taste in Nick's Bar than in the streets of La Rochelle, not to speak of the pages of *La Nausée*. But man does not live on bananas alone, and their enlistment as an example makes no pretense of conveying to us Sartre's fundamental projects, his most intimate gastric penchants. The strength of the example lies, rather, in the way it proceeds as though bananas were for reading rather than eating. One does devour books, after all! It serves to illustrate the specific ambition of committed literature. Sartre first proposed it in concluding a homage to Vercors's *Le Silence de la mer*, whose humble greatness consisted in not pretending to be a masterpiece, in being bold enough to retain a taste and remain readable only in 1941 — the courage of being dated, of "seizing" the moment. Literature ought to be consumed on the spot, and instantaneously.

ERRATUM. The first time the example appeared was in the German translation of "Ecrire pour son époque" (*Die Umschau*, No. 1, September 1946). *Qu'est-ce que la littérature?* uses it again in an issue of *Les Temps modernes*, in which that text appeared serially (no doubt no. 18 of March 1947). It was the third occurrence which earned it its fame. "Nick's Bar, New York City" (*America*, no. 5, June 1947) begins with a crash of cymbals: "Jazz is like bananas; it has to be consumed on the spot." The example is found again in *Les Temps modernes* of June 1948, which published the French version of "Ecrire pour son époque." The literary references to which that text applies the example of bananas are *Emile* and *Les Lettres persanes*. It was in *Qu'est-ce que la littérature?* that he explained how little taste remained in — and for — *Le Silence de la mer* five years later.

It is inadvisable to touch wet paint, because one will get dirty. In order to have dirty hands [*les mains sales*], there is but one solution, and it is political: read wet print.

His professed taste for the theater, the fascination exercised on him by diverse media techniques should be linked to this wish for something of a closed circuit from which every difference, every delay (between production and consumption) would be eliminated. For in a certain sense, the very definition of theatrical performance demands that it be consumed on the spot, at the same time as it occurs. The author affords himself the pleasure of being present at the consumption of his works. If it is objected that he was nevertheless obliged to write it before it could be staged, it is undoubtedly within that reservation that we must see the origin of those reveries of a theater without text and of happenings, in which Sartre indulged around 1968. As for the art of reporting — in newspapers, initially, but attaining its full scope with radio and television — it underwrites the dream of a transmission requiring no time at all, information received at the very second of its emission. Superman, it should not be forgotten, was a journalist. His exploits presupposed that he be immediately informed of what was, all the same, only beginning to happen.

It is consequently the media — to which, however, he would not abandon himself until after 1968, when blindness would prevent him from continuing to write — that fulfill most precisely the ideal formulated in 1947 in *Qu'est-ce que la littérature?* of a literaturte bearing on the present, describing it even as it speaks to it, allowing it to accede to self-presence immediately and on the spot. It would mediate the present but would do so immediately. The writer would thus write both about his era and for it. Literature must, in fact, treat subjects contemporaneous with itself and be read by readers who are contemporaries of those subjects.

A work must never have the time to become detached from its time — or be able to take flight from it.

It is on the basis of this ideal face-to-face encounter between a writer and his readers that the chapter "Pourquoi écrire?" develops the Sartrean version of the struggle for recognition, a version whose most noteworthy trait is plainly the substitution of the bookish relation between writer and reader for the risk of death that in Hegel is the sole means by which desire can win recognition of its escape from finitude. Literature is here a freedom managing to win recognition for itself without undue risks, sparing itself a relation to death. At which point we find ten pages in which the writer and his reader engage in rituals of deference bordering on the comic; neglecting the paper separating them, they pretend to be present to each other and compete for the recognition of their respective freedoms. Because the specificity of the reader is to be present. The committed writer wants to be read by nothing but [Mallarmé's] "virginal, perennial, and fine *aujourd'hui.*" Sartre repeats this insistently: For a literature managing to fulfill its essence, "audience and subject would be identical." There would be "no difference of any kind between its *subject* and its *audience.*"

It will be noted in this context that in the closed circuit of I-am-speaking-to-you-of-yourselves, no place is allotted for the time of writing. The present, as the book's subject, as what is represented by it, precedes the writing. As the book's addressee, on the other hand, it succeeds it. And yet they are identical and contemporaneous: it is the same present that precedes and follows the intervention of writing. Which implies that that intervention itself takes no time. It is precisely in the light of this eclipse that the failure of *Les Chemins de la liberté* should be read. Sartre wanted the France of the Liberation to be both its subject and its audience. It was to be the reflexive self-consciousness of French society on the morrow of the war. But the time needed for writing and the postwar period had already been left behind. By 1952, 1944 had become history, had freed itself from the present. And the committed novel was, above all, not to be a historical novel.

The most important chapter of *Qu'est-ce que la littérature?* is entitled "Pour qui écrit-on?" The first element in that portrait of the reader, we have seen, is presence. One writes, one ought to write — if one wants literature to "actively" fulfill its "essence" — for one's contemporaries. The second trait can be elicited through remarks touching on the question itself. "For whom does one write?" for one thing, is not synonymous with the question "To whom does one write?" That semantic difference is never thematized by Sartre, but it will be seen that it is an integral and active part of his text, that the very refusal to thematize it is a decisive element in the text's strategic disposition.

> On one occasion, orally, Sartre slipped up and said: "One ought to write to men by addressing their freedom" (*On a raison de se révolter*). Fénelon and La Bruyère, he continues, spoke about the peasants. But today, one

ought to "speak to the peasants." The context of the intervention in the course of which the slip-up occurred helps explain it. Sartre was evoking the kind of militant friendship which implies that, among comrades, people speak to one another. The difference between *for* and *to* is that between writing and speech. The classical intellectual writes for. The new-style (polyvalent Maoist) revolutionary speaks to.

For one can very well write for someone without writing to him. The beneficiary of a text is only rarely its addressee. With letters of recommendation, that distinction is one of principle. And yet Sartre never calls that difference into play. He acts as though literature's addressee were its beneficiary. He will condemn those writers of the nineteenth century who, like Baudelaire or Flaubert, lacking the arrogance to write for an obscene bourgeoisie, would imagine they were writing against it. But in Sartrean economy, there is no sense in wanting to write against those for whom one writes. In all rigor, it should not be possible to write against one's readers. It is at this point that the second characteristic of the Sartrean reader surfaces. The first was presence. This one is quantitative: large numbers. One writes for one's contemporaries, to be sure. But, it should be specified, for the largest number of one's contemporaries. If the question "To whom does one write?" fails to occupy Sartre, it is because its very formulation entails too personal — almost too intimate — a turn for it to be relevant to what we are to understand as literature. It defines the register of private correspondence, demands as an answer the proper name of a unique, exclusive, and jealous addressee. If it is possible for me to write to a person, literature, which writes for, writes, by definition, for always more than one person. It writes for ever more persons. It writes even for the most persons possible. The ideology of elites and coteries confused literature with letter writing. Poets felt free to spit on their era with total serenity once their limited editions reached their destination: a nod from Mallarmé, at times a word or note from his hand. The competition was for who would be read the least — that was the mark of authenticity. The bourgeoisie, although in the minority, still seemed too much of a crowd. Moreover, one belonged to the last aristocracy. One would betray while asking Literature to nourish her servant.

Baudelaire's error lay in having believed that he could write against those who read him, against the pseudoelite in which he recruited his "hypocritical readers." It is at that precise juncture that Sartre effects his dialectical reinstatement. The nineteenth century, up to and including Roquentin, wrote against the small number, against the bourgeois minority. The twentieth century will have to write for the great number, for the crushing proletarian majority. There is nothing accidental about the qualitative criterion: the public is defined by its plurality. When Sartre refers to it, he does not speak of the reader, but of readers. Singularity is, in fact, a trapping of the writer: a Don Juan–like singularity that flourishes as the number of its readers increases. *Mill'e tre*, under such conditions, is a remarkably limited printing. Sartre's sarcasms concerning elites bear witness as much to his taste for the majority as to his hatred for hierarchical heights. Even if he is not hungry, the prose writer in a democratic regime must live from his pen. It happens that, given the royalty system, elites are not profitable.

It is precisely at this point that Sartre's text is marked by an idiosyncratic impasse, an aberration entering into its calculation to the exact extent that he never takes it into account. We just saw him failing to perceive the distinction between a text's addresse and its beneficiary. What is at stake at this juncture concerns the reader. It often happens that one is not read by those for whom one writes. It can also happen that one is not read by those to whom one writes. Because a letter can be lost, or an addressee can change his address, or in certain cases because that same addressee is unable to read. It can also happen that one is read by those for whom one does not write, by those to whom one does not write. And so on. It is for that reason that Sartre, from *Qu'est-ce que la littérature?* on, repeated that he had nothing to say to the bourgeoisie. But it is unclear to what address such announcements are being sent if not to that of a bourgeoisie they reject. The numerous interviews from the time of *L'Idiot de la famille* — that is, contemporaneous with Sartre's Maoist stands — will go rather far into the pathetic impasse in which one finds an author straining to convince those he is addressing that he has nothing to say to them. For the two attributes of the Sartrean reader are not compatible: he is to be present, but he must also be the majority. Now it happens that at present, for numerous reasons of which the most obvious are undoubtedly economic and political, that majority does not read. In 1947, we thus find *Qu'est-ce que la littérature?* answering without flinching the question "For whom does one write?" One writes for "those oppressed classes who have neither the leisure nor the desire to read."

All the appeals proliferating through the manifesto of committed literature and directed to the reader thus end in the surprising contradiction that the reader is a "virtual" one — indeed, a reader who does not read. One might ponder the meaning of this will to write for those who do not read, wonder in what ways, for instance, it can be regarded as specifically Sartrean, and so on. I will limit myself to evoking a single aspect. It implies at some level, in point of fact, that one writes, literally, in order not to be read. A formula that goes further than the simple claim of not writing in order to be read. A letter can always not arrive at its destination. In Sartre's case, that mistaken address — or maladroitness — is part of the system. The specific characteristic of the Sartrean text will always have been to miss its end. Sartre's books, behind their frequently demagogic rhetoric on behalf of a reader they take it upon themselves to set free (but he is precisely a virtual reader because he never has enough free time to read, but also because he couldn't care less), deploy toward such potential readers an extremely effective defensive strategy. The most conscientious critics have already bruited as much by deploring the 2,800 pages without an index of *L'Idiot de la famille*. The table of contents of *Critique de la raison dialectique* is no more than three lines, forewarning to whoever would drown himself in it. Recall as well the portrait of the actual, or professional, reader found at the beginning of *Qu'est-ce que la littérature?*. All that Sartre retains of his case is his marital problems and difficulties in paying bills. Such empathy shows the measure of confidence he had in his nonvirtual readers, those to whom he exposed himself by writing. If Sartre writes for those who have neither the leisure nor the taste to indulge in reading, it is because he distrusts those who lack the leisure not to read. Which brings us back to the first portrait sketched in the chapter "Pour qui écrit-on?" — that of the medieval cleric, prolonged by the *honnête homme* of the classical age. During those eras, according to Sartre, what prevailed was not a closed circuit but a vicious circle. One wrote only for one's peers, among clerics; every reader was a potential writer, which seemed to hint at a horrendous mixing of substances. For the actual distinction between the writer and his readers, a singular and his plurals, remains the fundamental axiom of the entire argument of *Qu'est-ce que la littérature?* and no doubt also of the whole of Sartre's work. *Nulla ars in se versatur.* It entails that one write only for those who don't write, even if that should entail that those who don't write can't read either.

II

"Les Fins de l'homme," against a backdrop of the political and academic disturbances of 1968, takes cognizance of a certain resignation affecting classical humanism. By virtue of its knell, the possibility of a noninfinite end to humanism would be heard. The infinite is the definition that academic philosophers propose as the most characteristic possibility given to man. Or, to put things differently, humanist man has never allowed himself to be defined otherwise than in terms of infinity, the exclusive property of exceeding any definition, surviving it, and rising above it. When the finite ends in man, the infinite emerges through man. Death and survival: man transcends himself without end in an economy articulating the end with the prefix *sur*. The end of life [*la vie*] is survival after life [*la survie*]. What comes to an end when a man dies is but his finite existence, his finitude, so that through his death and his death alone the being born finite encounters an opportunity to realize the infinite, whose vocation he bears as his specific difference, that infinite which is his most characteristic end and makes of him a nonanimal. Humanism is the religion of the autographed corpse. If animal life is terminated with death, human life begins through it. Man is a function only of his end. Around Sartre, first Alain, then Kojève and Hippolyte all repeated it: an animal is life holding fast to life; man is life holding fast to death. An animal is incapable of transcending need. His ends remain finite: a lamb — or a banana. In the experience of desire, on the contrary, man assimilates sheer infinity; that is, he assimilates himself to the infinite. In 1968, consequently, "Les Fins de l'homme" takes cognizance of a scene and symptoms through which surfaced an intuition of the end of the ambiguity about ends, the end of the humanist-existentialist equation according to which man, if he ever succeeded in ending, should do so only in order to meet up with the infinite which defines him. Man's special opportunity is that his fall (his death) is in no way natural.

I would like to quote in the context of those thoughts a brief passage from *Les Mots*. It is found in the last part of the autobiography of his childhood, in which Sartre describes the genesis and structure of what he elsewhere called his writer's neurosis, the metamorphosis of little Poulou into the author of *La Nausée*.

> In order to assure myself that the human species would perpetuate me, it was decided in my head that it would never end. To extinguish myself in it was to come to life and become infinite, but if one were to utter in my presence the hypothesis that a cataclysm might someday destroy the planet, even in 50,000 years, I grew frightened. Today still, although disenchanted, I cannot think without fear of the cooling down of the sun: should my fellow creatures forget me the day after my burial matters little to me; but were humanity to disappear, it would kill its dead for good.

Behind the Barrès-like resonances of that last proposition, what is at stake is, of course, the peril of an atomic destruction of the human species. One must mobilize against the suicidal explosion, because such suicide cannot occur without being simultaneously accompanied by another murder, the most horrible of all, that of the human dead thus abandoned to an inhuman — natural — death. For it matters little that I am forgotten, if I am forgotten by someone. The shiver of horror comes from the idea that a day will come when no one will remember me because there will not even be anyone to forget me. One day I will be dead for no one. Taking up the burden of the question "For whom does one write?" the question "For whom does one die?" pursues a similar economy of death. As long as one is dying for someone, one is not really dying. As long as someone survives me, I survive myself in him. I do not truly die if I die alone. From here to eternity. The page from *Les Mots* could in effect be entitled, as was the American film ending with the disaster of Pearl Harbor, *Tant qu'il y aura des hommes* [so long as there are men]. The primal question of American philosophy classes, taken, I think, from Emerson, asks whether it is possible to say that a tree falling in a forest makes a sound even if there is no one there to hear it. In the light not of Pearl Harbor, but Hiroshima, the Sartrean question bears on the status of literature on an earth without men, that is, without a sun. Can a book that falls to the surface of a cold earth be said to make a sound?

Two brief observations: (1) What is at stake in this entropic cataclysm and what I shall call its eschatophobia is an end to ends, the end of the identity between the end and the infinite, death and afterlife. All the active, and even radioactive, fantasies conglomerating in Sartre around the word and the concept *atomism* fuse therein. They reduce man to no more than dust. (2) In the course of these six or seven lines, there is a change in the status of the event that would put an end to the human species. Perfectly natural in the beginning (that is, physical or astronomical), it becomes by the end of the text just read strangely human. At first it is the sun that cools down. But then it is humanity that kills its dead. A double-edged effect: the atomic bomb allows Sartre to rehumanize the cosmic disappearance of the human species by disguising it as a suicide, as though it were entirely up to the species itself to survive. At once an unleashing of the energies of matter and the final stage in the development of man's technological capacities, it is not subject to the opposition between the human and the natural. Art used to be defined: *homo additus naturae*. Atomic power effects a change of sign: *ars, homo subtractus naturae*.

There are numerous passages in Sartre in which the fantasy of an earth without men, a posthuman world, a planet without survivors is linked to the program of literature without an addressee. A literature which would have, in Sartre's terms, its end within itself would find its place only on the surface of a deserted planet. The atomic bomb and literature, at least a certain literature, occupy within the scheme of evolution a rigorously identical position — that of a definitive dead end. The principal figure in this case is Mallarmé, the poet in whom humanity effaced, rather than transcended, itself, the last man and not the superman. "Not for a second," Sartre writes of him, "did he doubt that if he killed himself, the human race in its entirety would die in him." At the end of *Les Mots*, Sartre through his death ensured the immortality of the species. Mallarmé, through his, took himself for an atomic bomb that would put a definitive period at the end of human history. At the time of his demise, the author of *Un coup de dés* left a message for his wife and daughter: "Rest assured that it was to be something quite beautiful." Sartre comments: "It is man himself, in his entirety, that Mallarmé wants to be: man dying the whole globe over from atomic disintegration or a cooling down of the sun and murmuring at the thought of the society he wanted to build: "Rest assured that it was to be something quite beautiful." Those remarks on Mallarmé are undoubtedly earlier than *Les Mots*. They date from after the war. But it was during the war that this vast necrological dream, as he calls it in a discussion of Ponge, preoccupied Sartre's thought on literature. Its shadow traverses the critical texts of *Situations* I as well as the historico-political studies of *Situations* III.

Ponge, for example, is reproached for not writing in order to be read, or even (more radically) for writing in order not to be read, if being read is always being read by a man. The addressee of *Le Parti pris des choses* would in fact be, according to Sartre, some higher ape, the ludicrous survivor of the next cosmic cataclysm, into whose line of sight an incalculably random bit of luck will one day have cast that French-language Noah's Ark in which I have not had time to verify whether it will have the nostalgic pleasure of biting into a banana. Like Mallarmé, Ponge represents a literature whose ambition is not to proceed so that man might survive and it might survive through man: its program is to survive man. The articles on or against Bataille and Blanchot develop analogous reproaches. The author of *L'Expérience intérieure* is thus accused "of seeing himself through the eyes of an alien species" and consequently of leaving, or wanting to leave, or claiming to have left humanity in order to see himself. The same rebuke is lodged against Blanchot, who would like to "look on himself with inhuman eyes." It would be worthwhile pondering the extent to which that gaze anticipates what Blanchot had yet to call Orpheus's gaze. Sartre mentions it more explicitly at the outset of the article on Brice Parain. He evokes the 1930s. "There was a desire," he writes, "to make contact both in man and outside him with nature bereft of men. One came on tiptoe into the garden to surprise it and at last see it as it was when there was no one to see it." Similarly, in *Les Mains sales*, Jessica hides under Hoederer's desk because, she tells Hugo, "I would like to see how you are when you are by yourselves."

Such pathologico-literary patterns of behavior are classified in Sartrean nosology among the vast array of deficiencies labeled depersonalization. It is that term, it will be recalled, which defines (in *Qu'est-ce que la littérature?*) the linguistic debility honored under the name of poetry. The texts of *Situations* III propose to subject it to a political reading. "Paris sous l'occupation," for example, in order to describe the spectacle of the deserted boulevards of the capital, will evoke the fits of depersonalization and loss of a sense of reality experienced by the mentally ill on whom "it suddenly dawns that 'all humanity has died.'" The following text, "Qu'est-ce qu'un collaborateur?" in an important parallel between Drieu and Roquentin, will make of the erratic editor of the collaborationist *N.R.F.* a man who feels himself to be "superfluous," who in a certain way feels man to be superfluous, and who, on the basis of such ill-humored sentiments, invests in fascism the suicidal dream of humanity's self-destruction. Fascism, like Mallarmé's art, is nature minus man, man removed from nature and cleansed of the sin of existing.

I shall conclude this series of examples by mentioning an article published in *Combat* to celebrate the first anniversary of the Liberation of Paris. Contat and Rybalka have included it in *Les Ecrits de Sartre*. The celebration is not entirely euphoric. In an initial antithesis, the victorious insurgents of the previous year are contrasted with the armies of the defeated. Man, the vertical rebel, rose up against the mechanical inhumanity of what Sartre calls the German "divisions." That, however, was a year ago, when Paris in a state of fusion allowed the virile insurrection to win out over the divisible substance of the Wehrmacht. But today,

Sartre continues, that victory is, in turn, threatened and by an even more formidable agent of division than Germanic substance: the Anglo-Saxon atomism which, from Hume to Hiroshima, threatens to make of our earth a planet without men.

It is in the light of this series of examples, which I cut short here, that I would like to read the last lines of *Qu'est-ce que la littérature?* "Nothing assures us," writes Sartre, "that literature is immortal; its chance today, its only chance, is the chance of Europe, of socialism, and of peace. We have to bet on it. And if we writers lose in the process, so much the worse for us. But also, so much the worse for society." One senses in these lines the same movement as was found in the passage from *Les Mots* just quoted. I do not truly die if it is I alone who die. So much the worse for me, that is, so much the better. But things are not that simple. For literature cannot die alone. It's too much for literature, which just can't do it. It happens that the end of literature is always at the same time the end of everything. Don't expect absolutely anything to survive it — neither Europe nor peace nor socialism. *From Here to Eternity* translates this time as *Tant qu'il y aura des écrivains* — so long as there are writers. Sartre continues: "All this, to be sure, is not very important. The world can make do quite well without literature. But it can make do even better without humanity." One ought not to take that last line literally. And yet it is deserving of our attention. One might, for instance, rephrase it as a riddle: Given the world, which one — man or literature — is more necessary to it? Against all expectation, Sartre answers: literature. A world without men is a bearable thought as long as there will be books. That comes after a 350-page discussion of the presence of the reader as essential to any definition of literature, of the utilitarian or instrumental nature of prose, and so on. It should be understood, to be sure, with a grain of salt, but it is a bit as in the case of Carthage: there is a sharp risk that the grass will not grow back. This is not a unique case. It should be recalled, in this context, that not a word is said to us during the whole of *La Nausée* concerning the recipient or addressee of Roquentin's journal (for whom does he write?). Roquentin, as we are reminded in a footnote in "Les fins de l'homme," does not fail to manifest his scorn and impatience when the Self-Taught Man tries to get him to admit that one always writes for someone. Despite the elaborations on the theme "For whom does one write?" despite all that is said concerning reading as the moment in which the written is objectified, if the reader's place were to remain vacant, it is not entirely clear that Sartrean literature would run a fatal risk as a result. Rest assured that it was to be something quite beautiful.

III

In a famous passage of his *Three Essays on the Theory of Sexuality*, Freud describes the genesis of the sexual drive through its "propping" on the biological function of nutrition. Autoerotic sexual pleasure is derived from behavioral patterns whose aim is the satisfaction of hunger. In a first phase, the exercise of a bodily function linked to the self-preservation of the individual, hunger, brings the infant to suck at his mother's breast. That activity has an object: the milk he draws from it. But already, in the margin of that functional pleasure, a pleasure-laden aureola breaks free from mere nutrition. At the same time that he absorbs the nourishing milk, the infant uses his lips to suck on the breast, play with it, do no more than touch it. It is this phenomenon of marginal sucking, according to Freud, that becomes the underpinning of sexuality properly speaking, the pleasure procured by the infant in continuing to suck but without ingesting anything, to suck, moreover, nothing or anything, the mother's breast, his thumb, his own lips, it matters little. Such sensual sucking is sexual to the precise extent that it is without object.

I would like to play that famous Freudian description off against the final pages of *L'Etre et le néant*, those preceding the work's conclusion. One finds in them, in fact, a suggested sequence of the earliest infantile experiences covering the same period as that proposed by Freud, but differing on several crucial points. It is in the light of those divergences that I shall attempt to evaluate the importance, in the economy of Sartre's text, of a theme which began cropping up in it during the 1950s and 1960s, that of man's hunger [*la faim de l'homme*]. If the *a*, silent once again, risks degenerating into a deplorable pun, it is because bad taste, for its part, is part and parcel of the fate of homonyms. After war, and above all after the Korean War, the ultimate threat — which risks dehumanizing the planet in its entirety — is no longer the atomic bomb, but malnutrition. Two quotations can be invoked here as epigraphs. The first is from *Les Mots*. In it Sartre evokes his gorged childhood and those meals during which it occurred to God to dispense to him "on occasion — rarely — that grace which allows one to eat without disgust — appetite." Give us this day our daily hunger. The second quotation will be borrowed from the interview Sartre gave Jacqueline Piatier after the publication, precisely, of *Les Mots*. That interview articulates in a forceful but obscure manner the condemnation of *La Nausée* and the decisive character for modern literature of the malnutrition suffered by the Third World. "I have undergone a slow apprenticeship of the real," he says. "I have seen children die of hunger. In the face of a dying child *La Nausée* is quite simply lacking in weight." He continues: "Such is, in fact, the writer's problem. What is the meaning of literature in a hungry world? The writer must thus line up on the side of the greatest number, the two billion of the starving, if he wants to be able to speak to all, to be read by all." The new answer to the question "For whom does one write?" is distinguished from the previous one only by its rise above a new quantitative threshold. The European or French proletarian of *Qu'est-ce que la littérature?* had neither the inclination nor the leisure to read. The undernourished are subject to a more radical obstacle: they don't know how to read. Malnutrition and illiteracy are twin tragedies. Sartre, however, returns to the subject: "For so long as a writer cannot write for the two billion who are hungry, a malaise will weigh upon him."

Freud, as we have seen, would have sexuality derive from feeding. The infant begins by eating, then pretends to be eating, and mimics the feeding process — as in a jest, he sucks on his thumb. At the end of *L'Etre et le néant*, the Sartrean sequence reverses the Freudian order. The passage begins with a description, in terms of existential psychoanalysis, of the experience of a hole, or orifice, an experience, Sartre is intent on showing, that is itself in no way sexual. "The infant recognizes," he writes, "from his earliest experiences that he is himself studded with orifices. When he puts his fingers in his mouth, he is attempting to close up the holes of his face." The text continues: "That tendency is assuredly one of the most fundamental among those underlying the act of eating: food is 'putty' that will seal the mouth." If the infant starts out by putting his finger in his mouth, the gesture owes nothing to an experience of need. That primal infantile experience is part of a rudimentary epistemophilic exploration carried out over the body's surface. An infant does not eat impelled by hunger, but because his body has holes in it. As for sexuality, it appears in the Sartrean scheme only in a third phase. The infant began by sucking his thumb. Eating derives from that stopping-up of the self: the subject seals up his mouth with an object alien to his own body. Sexualization surfaces when the drive to seal up brings him to stop up other people's holes with his own body.

The experience of hunger is in no way fundamental for phenomenological ontology. On the contrary, it has a rather supplementary character. It is, according to the author of *Les Mots*, a grace allowing one occasionally to eat without nausea. Whereas autoerotism in Freud came to prop itself derivatively on the function of nourishment, in Sartre things are bizarrely the reverse. The subsequent analyses in *L'Etre et le néant* only confirm the secondary status of hunger in the oral theater. After the stopping-up of orifices, we encounter an analysis of tastes — that is, of a relation not to the calories but to the flavors of various nutriments. It is, in fact, through his tastes that the subject would reveal most directly his fundamental existential choices. If he eats, in the last analysis, it is less in order to nourish than to express himself. "It will be understood," Sartre then says, "that flavor has a complex architecture and differentiated matter: it is this structured matter that we can assimilate or can reject with bouts of nausea, according to our original project. It is by no means inconsequential to like oysters or clams, shrimp or snails, insofar as we are able to tease out the existential meanings of those foods." Existential psychoanalysis does not ask its analysand to stretch out on a couch; it asks no more than that he sit down to table. It is of no use, but it produces a signature. Man is a useless mouth that eats out of a taste for self-expression.

How might literature answer for undernourishment? measure up to it? conjure up some weight to throw into the balance in its presence? How in particular, in Sartre's case, might it be converted to an oral status which the author's own body (with several felicitous exceptions) never managed to recognize in his own case? Sartre was particularly severe toward the elitism inclined to pout at the mere idea that literature might be a source of nourishment. If one sells oneself, let it be out of a perverse taste for prostitution but not out of need, please. So be it. But what becomes of that condemnation if, at his *Banquet*, Sartre serves his guests, on the spot, nothing but the word *banana*? It is not enough to earn one's bread: one also has to eat it. A common hatred may unite those who don't eat against the well nourished, and yet there is no great bond between those who don't eat for lack of food and those who don't eat for lack of appetite. There is a play on this subject in the writings of the same author. In it, one learns that unless one is hungry, one will have but little chance to sully one's hands.

The entirety of Sartre's work is shot through, in this same vein, with a blind and Platonic passion for the real, harsh world, the world of necessity, need, machines, and even arms. He opposed Halbwachs, for instance, who would have it that if a worker eats, it is not solely in order to survive. And yet that urgency seems always to be the evanescent object of an almost childish whim, the experience concerning which he — to whom nothing is refused — cannot fathom that it has not been granted him. A strange jealousy toward the have-nots. It regularly accords necessity the status of some luxurious trifle and places the useful in a realm beyond the gratuitous. Carried away by that passion, Sartre wanted to engage literature in its time. But it was not so much for the good of the age as for the good of literature. Hegel defined man as the desire having as its object another desire. There is a violent nostalgia haunting Sartrean literature that I suggest we call the desire for need.

These pages were written — and read — in France, where I found myself for the first time since the death of Sartre, whose silhouette, that summer, I had not seen in the vicinity of Montparnasse.

Certain of those in attendance at my contribution reproached me for insisting only on the negative aspects of his work. That surprised me. Not that I was, on the contrary, intent on insisting on its positive aspects. But is it, in fact, sure that Cézanne "liked" Mont Sainte-Victoire? I will say, still again, quoting Sartre: one doesn't choose one's era. And I did not choose Sartre. It is not my fault if the most stirring texts are governed by an uncontrollable necessity.

In addition, a certain atopia on the writer's part (the fact that he doesn't manage to be where he appears), although playing havoc with those hopes Sartre deemed it valid to place in the concept of *situation*, in no way seems to me to imply anything reprehensible.

P.S. I had forgotten (being without books) the first appearance of bananas in his work. Far more precocious than I had implied, it dates from about 1912, the year the diminutive Poulou writes a second novel, entitled *Le Marchand de bananes*. In vain was his mother to recopy it on glazed paper; grandpa would not deign to even look at it. For whom does one write *Le Marchand de bananes*? But already it is not a matter of eating them but of letting the largest number possible know the taste they don't have on the spot.

Chapter 7
A Study of Hands

Sartre's taste for neat distinctions is well known. Which makes it all the more
surprising to observe the persistence with which he refused that between body
and soul. There is nothing in common between consciousness and its objects,
between the inside and the outside, imagination and perception; there is no third
path either between poetry and prose or between the bourgeoisie and the proletariat. And yet when it comes to the distinction between substances, our en-
thusiast for Descartes recovers his freedom and declares (in "Présentation des
Temps modernes," for example), "Without being materialists, we have never
distinguished the soul from the body and recognize only one indivisible reality:
human reality." A few years before, *L'Etre et le néant* had already let it be
known that there is nothing "*behind* the body," that being-for-itself "cannot be
united with a body" because it must be "in its entirety consciousness and in its
entirety body."

If he does not distinguish between substances, Sartre nevertheless distinguishes
two versions of the indivisible reality constituted by the "fundamentally psychical"
body. The first defines what he calls the body properly speaking, what Merleau-
Ponty was to call the body proper. This is the harsh — at once active, virile, and
transcendent — version of human reality. It follows what we called (borrowing

107

a term from the lexicon of automobiles) the structure of the *coupé*. If there is nothing behind the body, it is precisely because consciousness is out there in front of it. It is always ahead, in advance of it. "The body is perpetually that which is being left behind." The structure of the *coupé*, in fact, requires that consciousness — which is nothing, which is only the fact of not being what one is — always be out front. In this first version, the body effaces itself. It fades for the sake of the future to which it is committed, eclipsing itself before that which is not yet . . .

It happens, on the other hand, that the soul, or rather consciousness, yields to the body and allows itself to get bogged down by its presence. This second version of indivisible human reality is what Sartre calls the flesh. It is passive and immanent, bourgeois and feminine. It thus happens that existing beings remain attached to their bodies as to irreplaceable family heirlooms: this is priceless — I got it from my mother. There are also, for every individual, times when indivisible substance yields to the temptation of stretching itself out. The flesh is weak, as weak as the "body" was strong. The body was the heroic, militant, and politicized version of human reality. The flesh is its sexual, horizontal, and libidinal version. "The ultimate degree of desire," it is said in *L'Etre et le néant*, "will be a fainting away as the ultimate degree of consent to the body." Little Boris in *Les Chemins de la liberté* thus swoons conscientiously when making love with Lola. Human reality, although indivisible, oscillates between two forms of obliteration — a fading away of the body in the activist project and a loss of consciousness in the surrender to desire.

Historical urgency, after the war, diverted Sartre from all that might seem obsolete (in their metaphysical anachronism) in such academic questions. The entirety of his political writings appears, nevertheless, to be an attempt to elaborate, for the benefit of the collectivity, the equivalent of a sixth Meditation, which would propose as a third substance the indivisible unity of the working class and its class consciousness, the dialectical cohesion of the Party and the proletariat, the fusion in one and the same political body of thought and action, of intellectuals — be they party leaders, ideologues, or artists — and worker comrades. And it would pose scant difficulty to retrace, amid the copious writings of the militant, an oscillation between two conceptions of this unity which are strictly analogous with the two versions posited of the nondistinction between body and soul. The secretary-general is, in the proletariat, alternately like a formidable helmsman on his ship and like a fish in water.

The first model structures the crypto-Stalinism of the 1950s. It is now the masses who, like the body earlier, occupy the position of that which is "left behind." And the union, here too, is effected by means of a distinction. The soul is distinguished from the body by nothing other than the distinction that it confers on it: a body without soul will also be condemned to lack it. These theses are developed in "Les Communistes et la paix" and "Réponse à Claude

Lefort." "The Party," writes Sartre, "is distinguished from the masses only insofar as it is their union." And elsewhere: "The P.C. is not outside the class; it is separated from the masses only by the 'distance' created by the exercise of power: it must indeed *express* the class.'' The restrictive syntax of such propositions reinforces the effective constraint they describe. There is no distinction except to the extent, the strict extent, that it produces a union. If there is a distance, it is only internal, one belying a tension and not at all a separation. A restricted distinction that produces what might be called a unitary and distinctive re-stricture, the spasm or involuntary start which does not fail to engender the structure of an avant-gardist *coupé*, a detachment of the head producing a body behind it, as the elite heads off on its own. Consciousness is always conscious of something other than itself. The law of intentionality thus requires that class consciousness be distinguished from class: the Party must indeed express the masses. "Where did I write," Sartre asks Lefort, "that the Party was identical to the class? It is as though I were to call a 'bunch' the string binding the asparagus." A few years later, he would ponder, on the subject of that distinction binding the masses, what kind of bind it had placed them in and whether, in fact, the proletariat was in such great need of being bound.

Everything transpires as though one had to choose between two types of union: the union of the body by the soul and the union of the body with the soul. In the first, the soul imposes on the body its own distinction; in the second, the soul loses it in the body, a circumstance presupposing that the intellectual will "go into a factory and abandon his studies to become a worker among workers." It is this cultural revolution that motivated the enthusiasm with which Sartre, after May '68, became an adherent of European Maoism. The intellectual is no longer the unmoving motor whose instructions mobilize the masses; it is now he who travels in order to join up with them. We have seen flesh born of a soul consenting to the body. We now see the intellectuals, who had pretensions of guiding them, enroll in the workers' school in order to follow them. It is no longer a question of writing for the masses but of speaking with them; no longer of expressing the class but of allowing it to express itself. One is right to rebel [On a raison de se révolter], most specifically against the distinction between body and soul and the division of labor ensuing from it, against the elitist and castrating organizations that separate intellectuals from workers by infinitely reproducing the exemplary exception of the intellectual, the restriction of mind.

A topography of political speech acts is determined at just this juncture. It is delineated in most of the texts published by Sartre after 1968 (with the exception of *L'Idiot de la famille*) through a contrast between the classical intellectual, who from his spiritual haven or meditative retreat thinks of the proletariat and sometimes even for it, fervently signing the protests he receives through the mail, and the new — revolutionary and polyvalent — intellectual who goes out not only into the streets but also into the slums to live with those who toil, share the fatigue and hunger of alienated bodies, and know the burden of a body in pain. And yet what is most significant about those texts and declarations from after 1968 is perhaps that they are not from Sartre's hand but, if it can be said, from his mouth. They are found in the interviews gathered in *Situations* IX and X, in the exchanges with Gavi and Victor published under the title *On a raison de se révolter*, and in the conversations (intended for the film *Sartre par lui-même*) in front of Astruc and Contat's camera. With a single exception, Sartre speaks rather than writes in order to announce the disappearance of the classical intellectual, that is, the intellectual who writes rather than speaks. And if that announcement is made out loud, it is not because of the health problems that were to handicap the very last years of his life and prevent him from continuing to write. At the time that a series of ocular hemorrhages caused him a loss of sight, in 1973, it had already been five years since, converted to Maoism, he had ceased offering any hope of salvation to intellectuals except through "establishing" themselves in factories and dissolving into the laboring mass. Five years as well during which, despite everything, despite his stands, he continued to work on the Flaubert project that he had had on the boards since 1955 and that he would have liked to bring to completion, on the tenth story of the — by now, more or less modern — building where, ten years earlier, he had corrected the proofs of *Les Mots*.

It should not be a matter, above all, of forgetting the simultaneously courageous and pathetic acts (or gestures), the generous interventions of which we are reminded by a vast iconography, poignant at times to the point of being ludicrous. Sartre, too, went down into the streets when it was necessary and where it was necessary. His tenth story nevertheless remained the privileged locale of his existence, that is, of his writing. I remain an intellectual, he tells Gavi and Victor, who can participate in your actions only "if I have a fixed point of reference — the Flaubert I am writing."

He does not stop speaking of stopping writing, but his hand continues, the same hand evoked by Blanchot, sick and lacking in mastery, never summoning the strength to stop.

My purpose is plainly not to denounce any duplicity, the hypocrisy of a writer who would have liked to mislead us, using his work to clear his life or his life, his work. It is not a matter of calling Sartre's honesty into question. He himself dismantled the prosecution's case in any such trial by making of his innocence the principal wrong imputable to an intellectual: if he is guilty, it is above all of not being so. The Sartrean intellectual, perpetually more innocent than he would like, cannot succeed in dirtying his hands. Whatever he does, attenuating circumstances are always found for the family innocent. And if a cleric's honesty consists in betrayal, it is difficult to say precisely who — the Devil or the Good Lord — will be able to find his bearings in the process. I would like, instead, to come back to the exemplary exceptional tribunal before which the writer finds himself condemned to remove himself from what he has said. Condemned to (and not for reason of . . .). We must put an end to the social division separating intellectual workers from manual laborers, but I am not speaking of myself. For whom does one write? asked Sartre. An intellectual is someone of whom it can be said that he never speaks for himself but only for others. He cuts himself off.

There is no need to specify that when he made those declarations, Sartre himself had all the attenuating circumstances that might be needed. At more than seventy years of age, he had entered into the weakness of his years. "The future is closed." It was written that Moses would not enter into Canaan. The promised land of him who called himself Jean sans Terre, the factory endowed with lucid hands, appeared to him at an age when even the natives of the proletariat are sent off to retirement. This man in his decline and who aspires to descend is now having trouble bending over. If I were fifteen years younger, he says, if May '68 had come in 1954, if I had joined the Party at the same time as Nizan, everything would be different. I would not even have begun *L'Idiot de la famille*. But one does not choose one's time. It is equally possible, to paraphrase *Baudelaire*, that, contrary to received notions, men never have anything but the age they deserve. As for youth, Sartre, when he was part of it, agreed with Nizan in seeing it as a bourgeois sickness.

The Intellectual's Manual

Is the hand that holds the pen worth as much as the hand that holds the plow? We shall not attempt at this point to transcend the opposition between the intellectual and the manual worker but, within that opposition, to describe those twin compromising appendages dragged around by thinking beings at arm's length: the hands of the intellectual.

La Nausée is triggered by a manual collapse that overcomes Roquentin one Saturday in January 1932 and that excludes him from having any hope in the future of having a grip on things. The "Undated Sheet" with which the novel opens notes the incident: "Saturday the kids were skimming rocks, and I wanted to throw a pebble into the sea like them. At that moment I stopped, I dropped the pebble, and I went away." The only explanation for such defeatism appears a few lines farther down. It is not without interest to observe that it has something to do with the question of the cleanliness of hands. Roquentin, in fact, notes that "I held it by the edges, with my fingers very far apart, so as not to dirty myself."

Sartre will thank Husserl for having delivered him from French epistemology as represented by Meyerson, Lalande, and Brunschvieg, for whom knowing always meant effecting a kind of assimilation. For Sartre, the real is not what mind appropriates unto itself, for the real is unassimilable and indigestible; it is, rather, that with which hands get dirty. Such is the fundamental axiom of the nauseous epistemology for which to know is not to eat but to vomit. The experience of nausea, of which the episode of the pebble constitutes for Roquentin a first occurrence, will be, moreover, referred to in the rest of the novel on several occasions by the synonymous expression "the filth," [la saleté]. When he ponders it a few days later, in something of a first taking stock, Roquentin specifies the object of his disgust: "Objects," he says, "'should not *touch*, because they are not alive. One uses them, one puts them back in place, one lives in their midst: they are useful, nothing more. But in my case, they touch me. It's unbearable."

The world was previously divided into two categories of entities, those that touch and those that serve. A master and dominator of tools, Roquentin, for his part, classified himself among those that touch. He is above the useful, serves no one, and serves no end, neither God nor master. It will be recalled that it was in 1929, the year of the great crisis, that he came to live in Bouville. Existence, Heidegger more or less said, surfaces at the horizon of utensils gone off course. The sorcerer's apprentices of capitalism had a great deal of trouble during those difficult years in making sure that they were served as they wanted. And all the more, perhaps, in that they had never until then had the opportunity of differentiating between what was alive and what was not, so long as it could be used — for example, between a domestic and a tool, a worker and a machine, a miller and a mill. Exactly a year after Roquentin noted that what served should not touch, since it is not alive, two sisters, model domestics of a dull bourgeois family, also refused to serve any longer and transformed the household, which they had kept so well, into a nightmarish slaughterhouse. The most intimate recesses of the bourgeoisie felt themselves given over — by their own servants — to the anguishing experience of what the Germans call *Unheimlichkeit*. Like the ego according to Freud, the bourgeois, after the Papin sisters, was no longer master in his own house. That incident took on emblematic value for the period. Lacan, at the time of the trial, saw in the "Le Mans massacre" a confirmation of his thesis on paranoia. Genet, later on, would find in it the inspiration for his *Les Bonnes*, and the director Papatakis that for his film *Les Abysses* (for which Sartre would write an introduction at the time of its release). Simone de Beauvoir reports the details of the case in Chapter 3 of *La Force de l'âge*. There, too, what was intended to serve took it upon itself to touch, with results that were hardly gratifying. The genotext of *La Nausée* is not without homologies with its context.

But Roquentin will not be alone among Sartre's characters in deploring that reality is slipping through his fingers. All Sartre's intellectuals will, in turn, know the same failure in maintaining mastery over things. Nothing in his hands, nothing in his pockets, of course. But if the writer is to make do without a mandate, it is because he has no hands *[mains]* to receive it. *Manus dare*: to turn over one's hand(s). And then it is crucial not to be missing any, not to be one-handed. To have or not to have them is the question that anguishes the Sartrean intellectual, a question in relation to which having one or two, be they clean or dirty, remains secondary. For the hand is the male organ par excellence to the extent that it is the organ of nonsexual mastery, the instrument of the drive to domination. *Manus* in Latin indicates grip, power, strength, and, in particular, the authority of a man over a woman who has given him her own. But it is hard to see what a committed loner might do with a woman's hand, he who is already not entirely sure what to do with his own.

The central character of *L'Age de raison*, a vacationing philosophy teacher named Mathieu, suffers from a manual deficiency analogous to the one befalling Roquentin at the beginning of *La Nausée*. He mentions it to Brunet, a former friend become a salaried leader of the Communist party, who has come to pay him a visit for the sole purpose of proselytizing him. "You know, Brunet," he tells him, "I've ended up by losing a sense of reality: nothing seems quite true to me any more." *La Nausée* was originally supposed to be called *Melancholia*. Melancholia, a pathological form of mourning, develops as a sequel to the loss of what psychoanalysts call the object, that is, a love-object. Which can be sung in English, in Sophie Tucker's voice, for instance, I miss you, honey. Mallarmé's line, it will be recalled, was they've tampered with the line of verse (*on a touché au vers*). The Sartrean hero's refrain might be they've tampered with the object; I can no longer get my hands on it. Mathieu, whose own existence seems to be without object, has ended up losing his sense of reality. But he does not generalize his case. His interlocutor Brunet, in particular, gives him the opposite impression (as he lets him know) of being firmly anchored in the real. "As for you, you are quite real," he continues. "Everything you touch seems real." That statement of envy is, of course, the view only of Mathieu himself. The remainder of *Les Chemins de la liberté* will show that being a card-carrying member of the Party makes little difference; Brunet is no less alienated from the real than any other bourgeois intellectual. At the beginning of *Le Sursis*, we see him ambling across Paris, mumbling the declension of his own identity: "Intellectual. Bourgeois. Cut off forever." There really was no cause for Mathieu to be jealous. All that is left of his case is the postulate that the P.C. system would have the function of guaranteeing the reality principle against the excessively free associations of the primary processes.

An analogous situation can be found in *Les Mains sales*. Hugo, although possessing his own card, experiences in front of Comrade Hoederer the same feeling of unreality and depersonalization as did Mathieu in front of Brunet. He describes it to Jessica, his wife, who surprises him holding in his hands Hoederer's coffeepot. She asks him, "Why did you take it?" Hugo is, in fact, an intellectual, which means that he belongs to that variety of human being essentially incapable of doing anything with his hands, not even using a coffeepot. Here is his answer: "I don't know. It seems to be real when he touches it. Everything that he touches seems true. He pours the coffee into the cups, I drink, I watch him drink, and I feel that the real taste of the coffee is in his cup." The real, for Sartre, is generated through a jealous identification with the other. Its formula might be what the other touches and deprives me of, what fulfills him and depresses me, what he cuts me off from.

Gide called sight "the most depressing of our senses." A kind of optical deprivation constitutes the thing from which it separates us. The real is always what the intellectual's eye jealously observes in the other's hand. What is rational ends up being so — minimally — real. Gide continues: "Of all the joys of the senses, I envied those of touch." Mathieu and Hugo, although not apostles of pleasure, are themselves condemned to bouts of depression over a real that is given only to be seen, and that in the hands of an other. As through the blind called a *jalousie*. The memorable analyses in *L'Etre et le néant* of the emergence of Others in my surroundings evoke an analogous form of deprivation: "An object has appeared that has robbed me of the world." Hugo ends up killing Hoederer. The murderous bullet will not have, however, as Kojève would have put it, the desired anthropogenic effect. He had, in fact, just discovered Hoederer and Jessica embracing. The intellectual's jealousy takes much of the weight out of his political acts, even at their most extreme.

The real is thus no less implacable for Roquentin, a solitary man, than it is for his more or less committed successors, Mathieu and Hugo. Everything that falls into their hands falls from their hands at the same instant. At their contact there is not an object that doesn't melt, become unreal, take on a sinister air. A decisive difference nevertheless prevents any identification between Roquentin, the prewar character, and his postwar heirs. Roquentin, in effect, makes no show of impatience to dirty his hands through contact with the real. Quite to the contrary: if he let go of the pebble at the beginning of *La Nausée*, it was because he wanted to keep them clean. He preferred to let it go rather than have *les mains sales*.

A first and extremely promising gesture of a man who will choose, in the last pages of the book, to create a work of art, to bring to term what he discovers to be his fundamental project: "to cleanse himself of the sin of existing."

At the beginning of *L'Espace littéraire*, Blanchot proposes a brief psycho-pathological fable describing a disturbance in prehension apparently the opposite of the one whose symptoms are manifested by Roquentin. "It happens," he writes, "that even if a man holding a pencil should strongly desire to let go of it, his hand will nevertheless not let go. Quite to the contrary, instead of opening, it tightens up." Whereas Roquentin's hand relaxed to the point of finally relinquishing everything, the persecutory prehension evoked by Blanchot forbids any easing up of one's grip. An almost paralytic, tetanized tension prevents the hand from loosening up and relaxing. In both cases, no doubt, there is a loss of manual control, a breakdown in main-tenance. But that failure plays in opposite directions, in one case as excess, in the other as lack. I shall never have my hand, said Rimbaud at the beginning of *Une Saison en enfer*. Blanchot uses persecutory prehension allegorically to describe the incapacity to manifest that would be essential to the writing hand; an automatic and unsubmissive hand, it never writes in a masterly hand.

Another difference should be taken into account here between Roquentin's symptoms and Blanchot's persecutory prehension. One hand can't manage to take hold, the other to let go — but take hold or let go of what? Their deficiencies involve different objects that run the risk, in fact, of dismantling any appearance of symmetry between them. "It happens," writes Blanchot, "that the hand of a man holding a pencil will not let it go." It is thus a scene of writing whose solitude is not the source of any worldly mastery. Such writing is in no case a variety of action on the universe. A pencil, for Blanchot, is not a tool. In contrast, the incidents reported by Roquentin overtook him outdoors, on the beach, in town, in life. They were, moreover, induced by objects that don't write: a pebble, the doorknob. That is a first point. There is a second one. A singular and remarkable restriction will, in fact, never stop limiting the evil whose progress is recorded in Roquentin's journal. For if it is true, as he writes, that he is no longer able to take hold of the objects that come into his hands, there is all the same a remarkable exception, concerning which he does not mutter a word — the silent exception of writing. "For example, at this moment, I am writing, but I have no awareness of writing."

Blanchot's hand wrote with a pencil, Roquentin's with a pen. But that does not suffice to explain the uncontrolled handling of the one and the handicap of the other. The hand that can no longer make use of objects is, in fact, the same as the one that writes and has no trouble holding the pen with which it describes the difficulty it has in holding objects. This doesn't count for me, says writing, which counts itself out of what it is saying. I speak for the rest. Writing removes itself at the outset: as the singular exception would have it — all except for me. For it is at the precise moment that Roquentin loses control over the things he was accustomed to using that he takes up his pen to note it down. He is no longer capable of holding anything — except for his journal, where he notes it down. Writing is safe from the disaster it retraces. There is no need to worry over Roquentin's salvation: disaster never comes without a scriptural savings account. If he relinquishes everything, it is with the exception of his journal, and perhaps through the agency of that exception. The exception of the journal, the persecutory prehension tensing Roquentin's hand on the pen composing it, functions like the blind node from which are engendered the — apparently oppo-site — disturbances of prehension it describes.

In the middle of *La Nausée*, Roquentin decides to abandon the book on the Marquis de Rollebon he has been working on for the three years he has been in Bouville. In the passage of his journal relating that decision, he is seen casting a last glance at the marquis's manuscripts before allowing them to sink into what is probably definitive oblivion. That disaffection, modulated with melancholy, is the object of a passage composed in the past tense: "I took those letters in my hands," he writes. "I felt them, examined them with a kind of hopelessness: He was the one, I told myself. It was indeed he who traced these signs one by one. He leaned on the paper. He put his fingers on the sheets to prevent them from turning over." It will be noted in passing that Roquentin is not oblivious to the fact that one writes with one's (two) hands, that the corporeal technique of writing constitutes a form of gymnastics holding no secrets for him. We will soon see the interest of that remark. In the interim, the farewell to the marquis goes on for a few pages, still in the past; then the narration stops for an hour, and when it begins again, it is in the present.

Roquentin, an increasingly solitary man, now remembers the three years of shared life with M. de Rollebon to which he has just put an end. An entire period of his life, now over, comes back to him in memory — one when things still let themselves be taken in hand, life still had an object, and objects, a use. In those efficient days, he says, "I no longer saw my hand tracing the letters on the paper, nor even the sentence that I had written."

Be it duly recorded . . .

The body is what is left behind. To act is to leave behind one's body, to move beyond it. The analysis of unreflexive consciousness in the *Esquisse d'une théorie des émotions* is conducted through the example of writing. When one has something to do, when one is in the world and life has an object, one does not have time to be bothered with oneself. "It is undeniable," writes Sartre, "that we can reflect on our action. But an operation *on* the universe is most frequently performed without the subject leaving the unreflexive level. For example, in this moment I am writing, but I have no awareness of writing."

It thus happens that writing can be transitive and constitute one of the techniques through which man can act on the universe. It happens that writing can be an active form of behavior, a manner of being in the world. That is what occurs, for instance, when Sartre writes *Esquisse d'une théorie des émotions* or Roquentin a historical study of Adhémar de Rollebon: so many books written in an unreflexive script in which the hand constantly effaces itself before what it says. Morally as well as aesthetically, moreover, Sartre always condemned writing that called attention to itself, writing overly aware of itself and having its end in itself. What he calls with irritation the "celebrated problem of language" never received from him anything but an impatient refusal, and the students of May '68 were a thousand times right, he felt, to rebel against the inflation of signs of signs, discourses on other discourses, and books on other books. Zur Sache selbst, once again. Consciousness is always conscious of something other than itself: it does not call attention to itself. And if it does, it is wrong. Poor Baudelaire! The essay Sartre published in 1945 on the author of *Les Fleurs du mal* denounces all that was absurd and reactionary in the Baudelairean wish to see himself seeing, listen to himself speaking, and write (to) himself writing.

Let us return to Roquentin, whom we left at the point when he was observing that when he wrote on the marquis, he did not observe that his hand was writing. Nothing abnormal up to now. But the proprioceptive synthesis becomes undone at the very moment in which the body's present is deprived of a future binding it, the very moment in which — for lack of a future — the body no longer lets itself be left behind. This is the situation in which Roquentin finds himself now that the abandonment of his book has left him with his own — objectless — life. "What am I going to do now?" And at that precise instant, his hand becomes detached and appears to him.

The paragraph to which the event is consigned begins: "I see my hand, which is opening up on the table. It is alive," and so forth. The account of this discovery occupies more than a page, composed entirely in the present. It will be noted that Roquentin says "my hand" without specifying whether he has another one and, in that event, which of the two he considers to be his own and to whom the other would allegedly belong. And I am not mentioning the hypothesis according to which he would have more than two. My question will bear on the hand that traces the lines in which Roquentin describes the hand that appears to him at the very instant when he notices that he did not notice it when it was writing about Rollebon. In fact there is, here too, another hand that he does not notice, no longer the one that wrote on Rollebon and is the object of his description, but the one that presently, in the silent present of the indicative, conducts that description itself. This question is not of a psychological order: everything is in place on the page as soon as a distinction is made between reflexive consciousness and unreflexive consciousness, the latter being nonthetic of itself. It is rather of a physical — even acrobatic — order. The lines of *La Nausée* we are pausing over, I repeat, are composed in the present tense, which implies that their referent in the order of events is contemporaneous with their utterance. As an example, I will cite a passage that is indeed exemplary. "My saliva is sugary," Roquentin notes with his writing hand. "My body is warmish; I feel stale, washed out. My penknife is on the table. I open it. Why not? At any event, it would change things a little. I place my left hand on the pad and thrust the knife firmly into my palm."

It should be recalled here that Roquentin, who is writing this at the same time he is doing it, knows quite well, as we have seen, that in order to write one has to make use of both hands, one to hold the pen, the other to prevent the paper from moving. All of which gives him four in this case: two real — or better, plausible — ones, those that are before his eyes and that he evokes on this page (one with the knife, the other with the wound), and then their shadowy twins, which give them utterance, the phantom hands of his double. These are the ones mentioned by Sartre in *L'Imaginaire* when, after maintaining that it is impossible to touch an image, he immediately corrects himself: "I can do so, but on the condition of doing it in an unreal manner, of renouncing use of my own hands in order to resort to phantom hands acting on unreal objects." Writing, consequently, as soon as it is no longer about the Marquis de Rollebon, ceases to be the operation on the universe that the *Esquisse d'une théorie des émotions* saw it to be. That is probably why it will be so difficult to engage the hand that writes Roquentin's journal in the real. Concerning the writing hand, the victim of persecutory prehension, Blanchot wrote: "It belongs to the shadows and is itself a shadow, the shadow of a hand gliding in an unreal manner toward an object become its shadow." Roquentin does not notice it, but from the very first pages of his journal, from the moment he noted that his hands had not wanted to sully themselves with the mud of the pebble, the hand(s) with which he writes has (have) been radically cleansed of the sin of existing.

Several chronologies published in the press on the morrow of Sartre's death observed that in 1917, in order to compensate for the rigors of his exile in La Rochelle and perhaps for the jealousy linked to the remarriage of his mother as well, the thirteen-year-old *déraciné* became enamored of operetta, the musical genre he had just discovered at the local municipal theater. An active passion, no doubt, since it required him to pay for it with his pen. He thus contributed to the genre by writing two libretti: a *Horatius Coclès* and a *Mucius Scaevola*. The one-eyed and the one-handed, then, these two heroes of Roman chronicles in which Dumézil, precisely at the time that Sartre was finishing *La Nausée*, had just rediscovered the dual aspect assumed by the sovereign function throughout Indo-European ideology. I will not consider Coclès. I will merely recall that one-eyed [*borgne*] in Latin translates as *luscus*, from which the French *louche* [squint-eyed] is derived; that *borgne* itself, in the speech of the Middle Ages, meant *louche*. Associated with the Varunian and Ouranian modality of sovereignty, Coclès incarnates a power that is *louche*, the power of the *louche* as such, the magical force that fascinates as well as the panoptical gaze that paralyzes, a gaze that is *louche* precisely because one never knows whether behind it there is someone looking, because one never can tell with which eye he is looking at you, the evil or the good. "To write," according to Blanchot, "is to enter into the affirmation of solitude in which fascination looms as a threat." Fascination, in fact, as passion for the image, is linked to the confusion of sensory realms occurring when one is literally "touched" by a gaze. *L'Imaginaire*, for its part, will say that "the imaginary objects that haunt us are by their very nature *louches*." And it is insofar as they are *louches*, conversely, that we must consider unreal or imaginary the objects that melt in the hands of the fascinated and powerless Roquentin, Mathieu, or Hugo.

But we shall abandon the series of the *louche* and Coclès, its patron, to return to the other libretto, *Mucius Scaevola*, and through it to the scene of *La Nausée* in which we saw Roquentin — the solitary man who, like Pontius Pilate, would wash his hands of the sin of existing stab himself in the hand with a knife in order to be able to write a novel in peace. *Les Chemins de la liberté* are not lacking in analogous scenes in which Mathieu, literally and metaphorically, manifests a singular detachment when it comes to his hand. But I shall stop, because of its title, at the 1948 play *Les Mains sales*.

Sartre, of course, intends to show that Communists have dirty hands. But it is all to their honor; no one governs innocently. Far from condemning them for it, Sartre lashes out at the idealism which imagines that one might be involved in politics without dirtying one's hands, that one might touch the real and keep one's hands clean. And if everything that Hoederer touches seems real, it is precisely because he has dirty hands. Whereas Roquentin wanted to escape from filth [*la saleté*] and not dirty his hands, Hugo is dying of envy at the idea of one day being big enough to be able to sully them for good. Lady Macbeth is the patron saint that the Sartrean candidates for indelible staining should invoke. But goodwill is not enough for whoever would dirty his hands. Hell is not paved with good intentions alone, and Hugo's desire is contradictory. He dreams of dirtying himself but wants to do it on his own, as though it were all dependent only on himself. As though it were possible to have one's own hands dirty, to dirty them immaculately — without the slightest imperfection.

Varuna's power is interdependent with the structural dissymmetry according to which if, on the one hand, only a visible being is able to see, it is, on the other hand, always possible to be visible without, for that, being seen. If the experience of an Other's gaze is so forceful, it is above all a function of the fact that it weighs on me without my being able to see it in return.

The analysis of the Other's gaze in *L'Etre et le néant* culminates with the absence of the Other. In a definition that reopens the central Sartrean question of the boundary between imagination and perception (and Sartre himself makes the connection), the Other is posited as the object that I cannot see precisely because it is looking at me. Deictics (this very tree) is no longer possible: the Other is no longer this very Other because the demonstrative has no place there where nothing is being shown. Perceptual transcendence loses its worldly abutment, and not seeing anything, I see myself as seen. The presence-absence of the Other, in effect, induces an unwholesome thematization of the reflexive structures of consciousness. The perceiving subject finds himself brought back to himself while undergoing the experience that he is also a perceivable object. It is not enough to say that it is not necessary for an Other to be present for me to feel his gaze. Or that the Other's gaze can weigh on me even in the absence of an Other. In a certain sense, it is exactly the opposite: if only the Other could reveal himself, he would immediately stop staring at me, for I then would be in a position to perceive him; I would no longer have to introduce the enigmatic where there is, in fact, nothing. Upon facing it, I could attempt to gain the upper hand. But the Other — or at least his gaze — can never be present. He — or it — is an imperceptible object. Between Caillois' phenomenology of the mask and Foucault's technology of surveillance (which are both quite close to the Ouranian structures of sovereignty described by Dumézil), the Sartrean gaze of the Other finds the principle of its effectiveness in the fact that it is not localizable or available to domestication — a certain *nullibiété* and a certain *Unheimlichkeit*. It always takes us from behind.

This dissymmetry disappears when one shifts to the register of tactile sensibility. We are necessarily and immediately touched by everything that touches us. It is impossible for two beings in contact with each other not to touch reciprocally. Put differently: whereas it is possible to see without being seen, it is not possible to touch without at the same time being touched. One never emerges intact from any contact. And that is precisely what Hugo refuses. He would like (like Hoederer) to have a grip on reality, but without letting reality lay its hands on him. He does not want the real to dirty his hands, but wants to be able to do it himself. That, in fact, is what is at stake in the scene in which he refuses to let himself be frisked by Slick and Georges, the henchmen sent by Hoederer to meet him. He is horrified at the idea of being touched by those dirty hands — of which he, nevertheless, remains so unrelentingly jealous. "And me, they are touching me," as Roquentin already put it. "It's unbearable!"

It is then that Hoederer appears and, taking the mediator's role, proposes a compromise: "Slick!" he says, "what do you want from him? To cut off a hand? To gouge out an eye?" In other words, at what price are you ready to accept his engagement? How do you want him, one-eyed or one-handed, as Coclès or as Scaevola? It is up to the proletariat to decide what organ, what pound of flesh, the intellectual must pledge in order to be pardoned for the sin of not knowing what hunger is.

As for Hugo, he would give his right hand in order to get it dirty. "I would let my hand be cut off," he says, "in order to become a man." But Hoederer is there in order to let him know that one does not truly dirty one's hands so long as all one does is dip them in one's own blood. Self-mutilation cannot take the place of class experience. It is absolutely imperative to plunge them into what Simone de Beauvoir quite aptly calls "the blood of others."

It is known that *L'Age de raison* was originally to be called *Le Serment*: I would let my hand be cut off — or burned, like Scaevola's. But Dumézil reminds us that that votary of Mithra lied at the very moment he authenticated his oath with the loss of his hand. He gave up his hand to burn only in order to deceive Porsenna. Rather than the oath per se, the heroic figure of Roman legend is the patron of false oaths, sophistical ruse, juridical chicanery, and so-called political lies. All the power, in brief, that the cleric manages to arrogate to himself while stretching out the palm of his hand.

Chapter 8
Insinuations
(Questions of Method)

Toccata

What interests me most in the passages of *La Nausée* that have retained my attention is the fact that they have not retained anyone else's. That 1,670,800 copies of the novel (*Le Monde*, which gives that figure, does not specify whether it includes translations) were thus sold and more or less read between its first publication and the death of its author without a single reader having found anything to object to in these scenes or having felt the slightest discomfort in their presence and taken the time, for example, to count on his fingers Roquentin's hands. My knowledge of the secondary literature is rather limited, but aside from the anachronism positing 21 February as the first day of spring, I have encountered no one who has found noteworthy those lapses into irreality which, it seems to me, cannot all be considered mere local accidents without broader implications for the text in which they appear. A consensus has been reached that *La Nausée* is a novel that borrows its narrative codes from realism. But no one appears to have noticed just how frivolous and maladroit that loan is, and it is perhaps therein that what is most fascinating about the text lies.

The two preceding variations were read as lectures: like Campistron on Racine, the genre of the lecture seems to fester over the deceased Sartre. After which, I was asked what it proved. I was also accused of proceeding by insinuations. It was a reproach, but the word interests me. My approach would be neither honest nor loyal. Why, I was asked, introduce strangeness where more than a million readers have seen nothing? Some even went so far as to insinuate that I had concealed motives when speaking of the *louche*.

Perhaps it will not be sufficient to clear up any misconceptions, but I would like it to be known that I would be completely inclined (should the need arise) to deplore the complacency with which criticism in recent years has become addicted to a shameless sexualization of texts it exploits on the pretext of protecting them. The intrusions of the reader are particularly indelicate when they introduce sexuality into a text that gave no sign of desiring it. Psychoanalytic criticism is often no more than a pedantic cover for academics' most decrepit propensities to smut, hard put as they are to regain an air of youthfulness. A reading should at the very least attempt to make itself desired by the text in which it would insinuate itself. Tender [*tendre*] is the word: a question of touch, of fingering. But the margin is narrow: to what extent can these interventions be reproached for being out of place if the specific trait of sexuality is precisely to be always more or less so? What proper place should be granted to what, by definition, has none?

As for insinuation, it causes me no displeasure. Not everyone is accorded the right to penetration. Moreover, it does not commit me to anything. I don't have to dive in. I quote, and it is not by me. I arrange things so that it is always he who said it. Say I. Which does not displease me.

Concerning quotation, here is one to which no one will object. It awaited me in *Penser avec les mains* (The book was on sale; with a title like that, I was not about to deprive myself), a 1936 work by one of the pioneers of commitment, Denis de Rougemont. "He who touches an object without profoundly marking it with his imprint and making it his own can never," writes the author, "touch the property of others. What he has taken can never belong to him: it is not in his power to appropriate it. The scholar and the person inclined to quotation profit from greatness that they are unable to mark." Loan or imprint: I have nothing to add. The quotation is sufficient to my needs and to its own. It is, by itself, without my having to add anything of my own, perfectly suited to my purpose: ready-to-be-quoted, let it then be, there where I insinuated it, the living proof of what it says.

The adulterous practitioner of quotation: he touches what he cannot appropriate. Was Roquentin, who could not succeed in leaving his imprint, also an adulterer? But in his case, there is something else that Rougemont does not mention: it was he who was marked by the objects on which he could not manage to leave his mark. Marking nothing, marked by all. So goes it as well for the practitioner of quotation whose borrowing is but the belated remarking of a prior imprint. He has allowed himself to be too precociously affected by what belongs to an Other, victim of a seduction for which he was not yet sufficiently mature. Quotation is but the belated effect of the premature advances that an Other has made toward me, the deferred effect of the insinuations through which he wedged his way into my desire: I have in myself an idea of him before even of myself.

Guilty Hands

It is not the hand absolutely speaking, that is a part of man, but only the hand capable of accomplishing work, that is, the living hand. Inanimate, the hand is not part of man.

Aristotle, Metaphysics.

On the screen, there is no one: a landscape, an empty room, or, placed on a table, a letter yellow with age. A voice is nevertheless heard, but one does not know from where it comes. Sartre, who wanted to make the novel profit from the innovations of motion pictures, inaugurates with *La Nausée* the novelistic equivalent of the technique of the offscreen voice, the procedure of the offscreen hand.

Most of the bodies appearing in *La Nausée* are reduced to their upper (or rather anterior) extremity. Their description encounters in fascination that singular organ almost always designated by Roquentin as "the hand" (should the singular be used, where there are two?). At the approach of his gaze, bodies delegate to their hand the business of representing them. Placed in a position of detachment in relation to the body where they originate, they are the ambassadors of the body proper, its diplomatic corps. Or perhaps its refugees. Its renegades.

On 2 February ("Friday," "5:30 P.M."), as Roquentin sits on a bench at the Rendez-vous des cheminots, a waltz of hands whirls above a neighboring table. The gentlemen are playing cards. One recalls the rules of the card game called *manille*. A hand is passed. I pick it up. "A reddish flash covered with white body hair: it's a hand. . . . Hands with ringed fingers come to pick them up. . . . The hands are so many white stains on the table surface. . . . The hands move back and forth. . . . That gesture, for instance of the red hand picking up the cards . . . " As the bodies nap, the hands become the grammatical subject of the game. It is not the young man but his hand that cuts the deck. And even then the fact that reference is made to its bearer is an exception. Most often, the text restricts itself to mentioning (the) hand(s) — it not being easy to keep count — without indicating their owner. Hands pass, but one doesn't know to whom they belong. Attributions require judgment. A player smiles. Roquentin corrects himself: "The red hand doesn't belong to him, but to his neighbor." They were almost about to argue over it.

Two weeks later, on the 16th ("Friday" the day on which Bouville is invaded by fog), Roquentin has his breakfast at the Café Mably. Facing him this time (the *manille* players were at his right) are a couple of artists about to leave. In order not to instill a sense of strangeness where there is nothing, Roquentin is discreet, acts as though nothing is happening and looks at them from the corner of his eye ("I had lowered my eyes in order not to seem to be staring at them.") And that is enough for the hands to take off forthwith. Concerning those of the woman: "Her hands were in constant motion. . . . Her hands ran along her blouse and on her neck like huge spiders. . . . one hand began to descend." They shift into action automatically as soon as Roquentin's oblique gaze absorbs them into his conscientious distraction. They allow themselves to be seduced, led astray, detached in turn by his pseudodetachment.

There are above all, on the 29th (Monsieur Antoine's last day at Bouville), the hands of the Self-Taught Man. Roquentin goes for the last time to the library. From his seat he can see the Self-Taught Man. But he prefers not to be seen seeing. To that end he places a newspaper as a screen before him, pretending to read it and installing himself behind it in a position of peripheral perception:

> I lowered my head to my newspaper and made believe I was reading; but I wasn't. I raised my eyebrows and lifted my eyes as high as I could, trying to see by surprise what was going on amid the silence in front of me. . . . turning my head slightly, I managed to catch something with the corner of my eye. It was a hand. . . . At present it was resting on its back, relaxed, nice and sensual. It had the indolent nakedness of a bathing beauty basking in the sun. . . . A brown, hirsute object approached it, hesitantly. . . . It was a fat finger yellow with tobacco; it had, beside that hand, all the uncomeliness of a male organ.

These three scenes have in common, beyond the fact that hands forget the bodies they are attached to, the position adopted by Roquentin to make his observations. For Sartre, as is known, perception is an active mode of behavior, a motor and motivating act entailing that its subject virilely confront what he has before him. In the hodological space of existential commitment, to perceive is to go forward, to advance. For which reason there is no reason to overestimate the difference between the retrograde position (that of Faulkner or Baudelaire) and immobility (Roquentin's). One must never stop perceiving: the real collapses at the precise instant that the perceiver stands still. Movement, in Sartre, is the most trustworthy of the binding processes. The perceptual stasis into which Roquentin congeals in the course of these three scenes thus enters, more than he seems to say, into the staging of the movements which he claims to be merely witnessing. "I never perceive," writes Sartre in *L'Etre et le néant*, "an arm rising alongside an immobile body. I perceive Pierre-who-is-raising-his-hand." That is the whole difference between "I" and Roquentin, before whose eyes bodies are detotalized. He is seated. Doesn't move his head. Pretends to be looking straight in front of himself, but — given his lack of sympathy for his fellow members of the species — thinks nonetheless and looks askance at everything going on around him. In the first scene, at the Rendez-vous des cheminots, he is depressed. ("I don't have the courage to look at them," he says of the card players. "I must have a broken spring somewhere. I can move my eyes, but not my head.") In the second, which is more perverse, if he plays dead, that is part of his predatory strategy: he wants to reserve for himself a monopoly on the Other's gaze and arranges not to be seen seeing. Like the little girl who came back on tiptoe to the garden she had just left because she wanted to see what it was like when she wasn't there to look at it.

In renouncing frontality, Roquentin settles little by little into an immobile, inactive mode of perception, an uncommitted and almost dreamlike perception which, instead of focusing attention, diffuses it distractedly, in a kind of centrifugal disintegration, on the margins of its field and allows the last glimmers of an almost crepuscular consciousness to haunt its fringes. It is then that hands arise and detach themselves and that instead of perceiving — as you and I would, without any affectation — Pierre-who-raises-his-hand, he perceives a hand that starts trotting over an immobile body like a spider. Without hyphens.

At the time he was working simultaneously on *La Nausée* and on his inquiries into the phenomenology of the imagination (in 1935), Sartre had himself given an injection of mescaline under the supervision of his friend Lagache, a physician. Just to see . . . Or to imagine. To see what it was to imagine. One of the results of the experience was to be a severe depression, lasting six months. As for the injection itself, *L'Imaginaire* describes its immediate effects in pages devoted to the pathology of the imagination and, specifically, to hallucinations. They present significant similarities to phenomena described by Roquentin in the pages of his journal where, at the limits of his perceptual field, hands become autonomous and take to acting in the most headstrong manner. "I" and Roquentin, here, are no longer entirely distinct. "I was able to observe," writes Sartre, "at the time of a shot of mescaline that I had administered to me, a brief hallucinatory phenomenon." There follows a description that emphasizes, as the crucial element triggering the phenomenon, a lateral and peripheral cathexis of consciousness. I had stopped, he says in effect, "looking in front of myself."

Not that he was looking elsewhere. With his eyes wide open but vacant, he was no longer looking but straining his ear to seize the noises coming from the next room. And it was at that moment that there suddenly surfaced three little parallel clouds that Sartre calls "spontaneities freed *at the edges* of my consciousness." Those images that the hallucinating subject imagines he is perceiving are defined, first of all, by their place of origin: they belong to a perceptual limbo. At the fringes of his perceptual field, Roquentin also stages for himself (by confiscating other people's hands) the emergence of similarly liberated spontaneities. In secret. Furtively. As he reports in his voyeur's journal.

The integrity of the bodily schema of the Other is thus placed under the responsibility of my own perceptual commitment. In a way it depends on me whether he undergoes detotalization, becomes fragmented, disintegrates. It is enough, we shall see, that I desire him (that is, that my body consents to its own flesh and that instead of being transcended, it gets sexualized). Love traffics only in details. My desire destines the bodies it covets to being partitioned, a promise of sharing.

In the analysis of the category of the obscene proposed in *L'Etre et le néant*, it is not a question of hands but of the rump. The descriptions found there nevertheless offer a sufficient number of analogies with the pages of *La Nausée* that have retained us for us to classify as "obscene" the hands Roquentin sees freeing themselves from the bodies on which he spies, or rather the hands which his sadistic gaze removes from the bodies bearing them. Obscenity is, in effect, the specific characteristic of a corporeal zone that detaches itself from and stands out against the body serving as its support. An organ juts out, applied to its surface like a prosthesis or tattoo, without being integrated into it. The obscene is characterized by its quotationlike aspect, an air of being borrowed that is evocative of an insertion or the incision of a graft. Inset, almost superimposed, at skin level, it does not seem to be in its place. Sartre's terms are "superfluous" [*en trop*] and "contingent." It is a borrowed part. It does not bear a family likeness to its surroundings, is not related to the context in which it stands out with an incongruous, inappropriate strangeness. It has with them only a relationship of contiguity — that is, no relationship at all. A foreign body amid the body proper, a fragment detaches itself in the first fissure of an analysis. It is enough for it to be sexualized for substance to become divisible.

Roquentin, before recounting the events in the library, himself notes that the Self-Taught Man's misdeeds were, in the last analysis, rather innocent. And it is clear that the sexual tenor of the manipulations for which he is reproached boil down to rather little if one eliminates the insinuations to which Roquentin has recourse in describing them. He took an adolescent's hand. But why was it necessary to make of it a sensual, nude, bathing beauty? Why describe the guilty finger as an uncomely male organ? Before subscribing to the thesis of flagrant homosexual abuse, we should examine with due suspicion (in the manner of Robbe-Grillet) the intentions of Roquentin, who, for his part, is caught here in flagrant metaphorical abuse. *Esse est percipi*: he commits Berkeley's error by imagining that he is perceiving while taking his fantasies for reality. In choosing to see not the-Self-Taught Man-who-moves-his-hand but the hand that moves (like a spider or male organ), it is he who stages the ill-famed scenario of the obscene. He casts a spell on it. Perhaps it would not have been sexualized had he not detached it.

(In "L'enfance d'un chef," Lucien follows with his eyes M. Bergère's hand as it fondles his body. The young uninformed homosexual scotomizes and decides that he is dealing with two different things: "Bergère was frightening," we read, "but Bergère's hand, on the contrary, vital and deft, seemed a person.")

Clean Hands

In these three scenes, we find the hands of Others detaching themselves from their bodies. But I should like to return once again to the subject's own (clean) hands — *ses mains propres*.

In the pages of *L'Etre et le néant* describing the sexual experience of one's body (consenting to the flesh, the sinking of consciousness into desire), Sartre develops an opposition between the hand and the sexual organ, the organ of technical activism, through which the body is affirmed through self-transcendence, and that of libidinal liquefaction, delivering him over to wallow in the immediate. The antithesis is so marked that one is inclined to say that, just as the genital organ is what will never be in its place in a body, in exactly the same manner the hand is excluded from a flesh with which it has nothing to do. "There is no supple, prehensile organ, bound to striated muscle tissue, that could be a sexual organ, a *sex*; a sex, were it to appear as an organ, could be only a manifestation of vegetative life." The sexual organ is effectively defined strictly and exclusively by its insubordination: it is a fragment of one's body escaping the technical or gymnastic controls of the centers of volition. It is absolutely necessary, Sartre continues, that erection "not occur *voluntarily*." "Autonomous and involuntary, it signifies the sinking of consciousness into the body." It is that inertia, that sort of essential passivity, which engages desire in the paradoxical maneuvers described, for example, in *Saint Genet*.

In 1929, between the written and oral sections of the *agrégation* examination, Sartre made a declaration of love (or almost so) to Simone de Beauvoir: "From now on, I am taking you in hand," he announced to her. Is she alluding to that prehensile organ in her memoirs when she acknowledges: "I reproached Sartre for regarding his body as a pack of striated muscles"?

In contrast to the hand, which is the organ of mastery, the sexual organ is the place in his body where the subject escapes and which escapes from the subject. A failure of possession (it is no longer in possesion of itself); an unenslaved enclave undoing its mastery. Topographically, the genitals are defined as the part of a body that does not belong to it. A heterogeneous insinuation, the foreign had always already been introduced. There is where I encounter the Other who had forever been lying in wait. There do I make myself desired by one who sates himself with my expropriation. The sexual enclave entrenches itself in a position of fundamental irredentism: within it, the sin of existing cannot be redeemed. The experience of sexualization begins with a hesitation concerning the limits of what is one's own. Where does my body begin? And where does it finish? A part generally considered integral, the hand, for instance, can suddenly effect its own exclusion. A supplementary item such as a piece of clothing, on the other hand, can lose its exteriority and be integrated. It will be observed that these descriptions (as is implied by the indistinguishability of what is yours and what mine) merely apply, to one's own body, remarks that, concerning the category of the obscene, had had the body of the Other as their object. What is obscene, in fact, is an organ of the body of the Other which seems not to belong to him.

A few pages later, the incompatibility between hand and genitals (the fact that they cannot coexist within the same set) is further emphasized in the context of the failure besetting desire when the subject moves from caressing to conquest and possession. In order to reach consummation, one is obliged to resort to hands, whence a return of the body which the flesh will not survive. The schema is no different from that drawn up by psychoanalysis in order to elaborate the concept of sublimation. The hand is the antisexual organ because of its absolute subordination to the subject's wishes, a subordination making of it the organ of technological achievements. First Freud, then Eissler have compared Leonardo da Vinci's fascination with machines in general and flying machines in particular to remarks concerning the mechanism of erection found in the fragment of his notebooks entitled "Della Verga." There, Leonardo insists on, and deplores, its involuntary, uncontrollable character. The organ that does not rise when asked to but occasionally takes off when it shouldn't eludes its owner's will. And the dreamed-of airplane would be precisely a penis over which its pilot would have absolute control, a penis with neither autonomy nor spontaneity.

And yet hands, and even clean ones, are but rarely in Sartre the organ of technical sublimation described in *L'Etre et le néant*. Is Roquentin's hand truly a "prehensile organ," the one that opens *La Nausée* by not managing to hold a pebble that might dirty it? There is not much eating in Sartre's novels. But at the end of his lunch with the Self-Taught Man ("Wednesday," 21 February), during the cheese course, Roquentin is stricken with another attack of nausea. He takes in his hand a cutting object and notes (I won't comment on the present): "My hand is tensed around the handle of the dessert knife. I *feel* the black wooden handle. It's my hand that is holding it. My hand. Personally, I would be rather inclined to let the knife be." What is left of the opposition between hand and sex organ when the former lets itself be won over by the involuntary movements defining the latter? And if the insinuation of sexuality is deemed precipitous (the cheese having only just been served), we have only to refer to the description in *L'Etre et le néant* of a yearning caress. It depicts in rigorously identical terms the obscene strangeness of a dissident hand. When I caress her flesh, we read, I do not take a part of the Other's body, but "I *carry* my own arm and *place* it alongside the desired woman; my fingers, which I *promenade* on her arm, are inert at the extremity of my hand," and so on. To caress, to desire is not to take. The hand itself is sexualized as soon as it ceases to be a prehensile organ. That is the source of Roquentin's nausea as he traces in his journal the gradual sexualization of his organ of antisexual defense.

Perhaps an interpretation might be attempted in this context of the numerous scenes in which a Sartrean character cuts his hand (lets his hand be cut) or tries to. If your eye be for you an opportunity for downfall, we are told in the Gospel, tear it out. It might be thought at first sight that it is because his hand is guilty that he feels obliged to have it cut off. A hand is not made for caressing but for seizing. If it has allowed itself to be perverted, one must separate from it. Mathieu, for example, in *L'Age de raison*, has allowed himself a second time to lay a hand on the beautiful and ungraspable Ivich. She puts him in his place: "You still take the liberty of touching me?" And he takes a knife, which he plunges into the palm of his hand — radical punishment that should cleanse him forever of the sin of touching. The same Mathieu, at the end of *Le Sursis*, will free himself once again, while crossing the Pont Neuf, of his tenacious appendages, this time by resorting to philosophy and disregarding them. He places them on the railing of the bridge and gives them absolution: "Precisely because he could see them, they were no longer his. They were the hands of an Other, outside, like the trees, like the reflections trembling in the Seine, hands cut off." I do not recognize as my own an organ that does not obey me. One frees oneself of one's criminal hands: they have sinned and must be disposed of. Their expulsion is at once punishment and remedy.

And yet if, as we have seen, what defines and produces the sexualization of an organ is precisely the fact that it is not integrated into the bodily schema, that is, that it does not succeed in being part of one's own body, if an organ is sexualized whenever it allows itself to swell with a coefficient of strangeness, then one should, rather, maintain the opposite: not that hands should be cut off to punish their guilt but, on the contrary, that this guilt itself is the result of the fact that they have become detached from their tutelary organism, cut off from their mainland. Their secession is the cause and not the effect of their sexualization. I would not cut you if you had not already cut yourself.

At the end of *L'Age de raison*, Daniel, the homosexual, who has just dirtied himself, takes a shower and then decides to return to the fount: If your eye is for you an opportunity for downfall, tear it out, said the Gospel, and Nietzsche commented: "It is not quite the eye that is in question." It is not quite his hand that Daniel will cut off, but the organ that has just made him do again what he still can't succeed in doing voluntarily. He thus takes his razor in his prehensile organ, to which — unforgivable sin — he delegates the task of carrying out his most extreme intentions. "My hand will do everything," he says. . . . "It is my hand, my hand that is to do it all." That which forthwith plunges into guilt without thinking twice about it by cutting itself off from the decisions of its head. He has not found the technique allowing him to cut himself without touching himself: "One is first forced to resort to that obscene gesture." For sexuality being always within hand's reach (and the hand, reciprocally, always within sexuality's reach), it is not with one's bare fists that one is about to bring about one's deliverance from the sin of existing. In the absence of castration, Daniel will offer to marry Marcelle, which is, after all, as much a defense as any other. He gives her the hand that had not wanted to cut it off for her. Without hyphens.

The hand, the sexual organ: neither one nor the other, in the last analysis, does what one asks it to.

Insinuations

By male we understand the being that engenders in another, and by female, the being that engenders in itself.

Aristotle, *On the generation of animals*,

In 1963, Sartre published an essay on Wols, "Doigts et non-doigts," which he incorporated a year later in *Situations* IV. I shall point out an effect of tangency — or rather, of self-tangency — through which the author puts his finger on a particularly sensitive zone of his own text. In it, he touches on or grazes himself across a thin membrane of quotations marks. At one of the turning points of the text that he devotes to the painter of mucous membranes, Sartre, in fact, quotes Wols, who has quoted him on the subject of touch. He allows himself to be surprised at encountering himself in the painter's writings, at a tangent to himself, but in the Other; simultaneously within and without; with Wols and nothing other than between himself and himself: to one side and the other of the Other, the Other on whom he touches and caresses himself.

Sartre, then, writes of Wols:

"He once quoted me: 'Objects touch me, it's unbearable. I'm afraid to enter into contact with them.' It matters little what those words mean for me. What *he* means is that objects touch him because he touches himself on them."

Carried away by the pleasure of touching himself on Wols, Sartre does not confess, he accuses. But there is no reason to think that he meant anything other than what he says Wols meant.

To be sure, *La Nausée* provoked a scandal in its day. It was not, however, for having transgressed any sexual taboos. Roquentin's journal contains no description of the sort qualified as explicit. As for Sartre's language, it is too aggressive to let itself be affected by a libidinal vibrato. A somewhat nervous censor might find objections to two or three passages (the exhibitionist episode, the rape fantasy focusing on little Lucienne, the Self-Taught Man's pederastic gesture), but the protagonist, Roquentin, is essentially beyond attack. He rarely resists the pleasure of using crude language, to be sure. But in no way does he offend standards of behavior (if not of diction): his deeds and gestures are not those of a libertine. In the quasi-monastic life he leads in Bouville, sexuality, if we can trust his journal, is the least of his temptations. During the whole of the month of February 1932 (particularly long that leap year), his journal mentions only one instance of intercourse. And even then, it is performed without enthusiasm. On the evening preceding Mardi Gras, he goes to dine at the Rendez-vous des Cheminots and, he notes, "the proprietress being there, I had to screw her, but it was out of politeness." He and his body are separate and distinct. But he nonetheless has a sense of manners. This specialist of the eighteenth century maintains the traditions of gallantry.

Once a month, all the same, for a man of thirty, is not very prolific. But Roquentin does not seem to be torn apart by the circumstance. It is possible, of course, that his journal is not telling us everything: his journal already neglects to include so much. It is also possible that his peculiar publishers, without warning the reader, took it upon themselves to censor his journal. It is even possible that it was Sartre's publishers (rather than Roquentin's, who were fictive) who, in reality, would have performed (or requested) the cuts. All the same (and with no wish to introduce strangeness where there is nothing), it is curious that despite all his manual problems, masturbation remains a subject on which the solitary man's journal does not touch a single time in the course of the month. But it was Wols, he said, not I, who was afraid of touching (himself to) things.

In fact, on one occasion it did befall Roquentin, who no longer wanted to touch things once they had begun to touch him, to be on the verge of touching himself. There are three modes of the verb: active (I touch), passive (I am touched), and reflexive (I touch myself). Sartre, who has no fondness for third paths, will not carry that third form in his heart. He will accuse it, in particular, of being fatal simultaneously to the categories of the object and the subject. On 2 February ("Friday," "5:30 P.M."), Roquentin arrives at the Rendez-vous des cheminots — "to screw," he says (for he likes crude language). That is not a reflexive verb. But it is perhaps already an activity without object to the extent that the verb does not go so far as to realize its full transitive potential. For lack of a (direct) object, it will be obliged to resort to an (indirect) supplement. In any event, the object that would have been able to bring about the transition is not there. Madeleine, the waitress, lets Monsieur Antoine know that the proprietress has gone out to run errands. You just missed her. Which makes him shift from one absence to the other, from the absence in whose core he had just been desiring to that in whose core he now experiences that desire's disappointment. Roquentin notes that at that precise moment, he "felt a stab of disappointment in my groin. . . . At the same time, I felt my shirt rubbing against the nipples of my breasts." Two simultaneous sensations — on the one hand, in the form of a disappointment, that of the loss or absence of the object of sexual desire; on the other hand, but at the same time, a contact with oneself through the intermediary of the cloth of a garment wrapped around oneself. The autoerotic character of the shirt's tactile appearance is beyond doubt. Among numerous occurrences of the same fantasy in Sartre's text, one has but to recall that in which Roquentin — on 21 February, in the course of a meditation in the Public Garden — is seized by the vision (bordering on hallucination) of a young woman whose "lovely bosom ceaselessly caresses itself against cool fabrics" and who "smiles mysteriously, attentive to the swelling of her breasts that titillates her." For a caress — that is, the fundamental gesture of flesh, which, in contrast to a body does not grasp but extends itself — is an intransitive movement, a gesture without direct object, a gesture through whose magic the object loses its transcendence.

"To perceive an object, in a desiring attitude, is to caress oneself on it," we read in *L'Etre et le néant*. If a caress wants an object, it is thus not in order to touch it, but to touch itself on it. What object? It is identified two sentences later. "My shirt rubs against my skin, and I feel it."

That was not Roquentin speaking, but his author. Wols did not want to touch (himself to) things. And neither did Sartre (nor Roquentin) touching himself in Wols. Autoerotism ("I felt my shirt rubbing against the nipples of my breasts") appears at the very moment of the loss of the object (the proprietress is not there), at the precise moment that the absence of the direct object of the verb "to screw" [*baiser*] surfaces.

But what else exactly did he want? Is there a fundamental difference for him between touching himself on the proprietress and caressing himself with his own shirt?

At the Rendez-vous des Cheminots

The Rendez-vous des Cheminots, where the scene of 2 February takes place, is a hotel which simultaneously serves as a bar and restaurant. As its name indicates, it is located near the train station. Roquentin doesn't live there. He has his room elsewhere, at the Hôtel Printania, on rue des Mutilés. Similarly, the Café Mably is where he goes most often to order a beer — sometimes in order to drink it, sometimes to think about it (and make sure it's philosophy). As for restaurants (there is not much eating in Sartre's novels), if Roquentin dines once at the Rendez-vous (and it is the only time) the day before Mardi Gras (the evening of the 12th), on the 11th ("Sunday") he had lunched at the Brasserie Vézélize, on the 13th ("Mardi Gras") he was to lunch at Chez Camille (a cassoulet) and on the 21st ("Wednesday"), invited by the Self-Taught Man, at Maison Bottanet (oysters, chicken, cheese). As a rule, when he goes to the Rendez-vous, it is neither to drink nor to eat. It is not to accomplish the motions necessary for his self-preservation. The place, in fact, procures him two very specific kinds of service:

1. The first that he mentions are sexual services. This is where, as he lets us know in the first pages of his journal, he makes love with the proprietress (named Françoise); the affair is transacted on mutual terms. She derives pleasure from it ("she never says no"), and as for him, it brings him relief, like a visit to the doctor or a hygienic exercise through which he purges himself "of certain melancholies whose cause," he specifies, "he knows only too well."

Roquentin mentions his desexualizing gymnastics among several examples intended to establish once and for all that he, the loner, has exchanges with no one, that he lives without exchanging a word with anyone at all, without speaking to a soul. Even when he relieves himself of his melancholies, he does not communicate. The tight association that this page forges between silence and sexuality, a sexuality exempt from desire and dispensing with seduction, calls to mind quite markedly the taciturn loves from which Poulou is spawned as the opening credits of *Les Mots* are listed — with his grandfathers, one of whom impregnates his wife "without a word" while the other is not even able to distinguish between health and beauty. Might it not be a family tradition that (in contrast to cocktails) when one speaks of sex, it is not philosophy?

In any event, without our being able to decide for sure whether it is merely in his journal or also in his life, whether he has nothing to say (because nothing happened) or nothing to say about it (precisely because it happened, and health is but a silence of the organs), Roquentin does not tarry over the facilities of the place, except, curiously, to note that they are not very suitable. For if, on the 12th, he screws, as he puts it, the proprietress, it is strictly out of politeness, and he does not hide the fact that he could very well have done without it. On the 2nd, on the other hand, he arrived to do it, but she wasn't there, and he was obliged to make do without. Solely on the basis of what is given in the journal, then, she is there when one could do without her and not there when one needs her. Despite the arangements "on mutual terms," desire and its object are not on the same wavelength.

2. Along with such sexual services, the Rendez-vous des Cheminots is also for Roquentin a place for the procurement of aesthetic services. It is there that he manages to arrange regular encounters for himself with Beauty, represented locally by "Some of These Days," the ragtime that he has played for him on the phonograph.

On 2 February, for instance, the day he goes there to screw and realizes to his disappointment that the proprietress is not there, he asks Madeleine to play it for him. That is the first occasion on which it is heard. Roquentin will think of it a number of times but will have it played for him again only once, on 29 February, the day of his departure for Paris. On the 12th, for example, when he yields under duress to Françoise's requests, it does not appear that he was thinking of listening to it.

We don't know whether Roquentin understands English and even less (in the event that he does) since when. (We don't know, for example, if he would have been able to understand the song's lyrics in the event that his first hearing of it, in the streets of La Rochelle in 1917, had been that of American soldiers, not whistling, but singing it.) We know nothing, more generally, of his attitudes regarding the Anglo-Saxon world. (What does he think of Hume, Berkeley, Newton, Bentham, John Stuart Mill, the American neo-realists, Virginia Woolf, Faulkner, Dos Passos?) All we know is that in the spring of 1927 he was in England with Anny, the woman he loves, on vacation. We also know that she remained there to pursue an acting career. Finally we know that it is there in London that the same Anny, the woman he loves, the sole object to which our loner is still attached, will be taken from him. For it is there that a man, an Egyptian, will let her know a pleasure that will detach her from him forever, a pleasure in which she will lose herself for him, and he will lose her.

"Some of these days," goes the song, "you'll miss me, honey." A third line is also quoted: "and when you leave me." A black woman does the singing, but the words are by a Jew. Who left? Whom are we to listen to? The woman's voice? The man's words? For whom does one write "You'll miss me, honey"? To whom does one sing it? And for whom does one listen to it in the streets of La Rochelle in 1917? Who is missing whom in the refrain? And moreover, why say "You'll miss me" instead of "I miss you"?

Roquentin enters the bar. The proprietress is not there. It's the waitress who tells him. "You just missed her, Monsieur Antoine." As in the song he is about to have played in order to overcome his disappointment, think of something else, and desexualize his preoccupations a bit. It might be imagined, in fact, that for lack of what he was after, Roquentin falls back on a musical moment and, all by himself in a corner, sublimates himself up a small aesthetic experience. And yet that is far from the case. He expressly excludes that charitable interpretation on the 29th, during the second and final hearing of "Some of These Days." "To think that there are imbeciles who draw consolation from the fine arts," he notes while listening to it. "They think that beauty has compassion for them. The schmucks." Beauty — and more specifically, melody — partakes of an inflexible and pitiless rigor. It does not let itself be moved to pity. Far from being a consolation prize for losers, a substitute pleasure to compensate libidinal rejects, there is something in it as wrenching as a departure. The leitmotif of the loner's reflections is pain: "A glorious bit of suffering has just been born: an exemplary suffering. Four notes on the saxophone." Beauty does not console one for the pain caused by absence, but rather measures it. "One has to suffer in rhythm [en mesure]," as Roquentin says. And Mathieu, in another bar scene, this time with live music (Lola singing): one has to "suffer in beauty." It is thus not true that Roquentin has "Some of These Days" played for himself because he is unable to screw the proprietress. "Some of These Days" does not make one forget anything but, rather, recalls the absence that it sings of. Which is in the song. The lyrics are, in effect, circumstantial: they sing their context. They sing the place from which they sing.

Sartrean existentialism does not subscribe to the structuralist slogan according to which woman does not exist. It implies, on the contrary, that a woman exists all too much, which is why the resultant spectacle is not very pretty to behold. Thus it is that the end of *L'Imaginaire* will contrast, term for term, aesthetic experience and sexual experience. A beautiful woman, we read, does not exist. Which does not, moreover, prevent one from dreaming of one. Either one desires her, and the poor dear is real. Or one imagines her, and she is beautiful. For the real can cause pleasure, but one suffers in beauty: whence the "pained disinterest" with which man embellishes the woman he no longer desires.

That opposition, however, seems a bit sketchy in light of the events of 2 February, which suggest, on the contrary, a rather strict proximity between aesthetic and sexual experience. Roquentin, in Bouville, does not go to concerts, the theater, or the movies. When he goes to the museum, it is in order to procure for himself the pleasures of social satire. It does not occur to him that the paintings might also be works of art. As for the library, it does not appear to afford him any literary emotions: he restricts himself to consulting the Rollebon archives. It is thus precisely and exclusively at the place where he has managed to find sexual accommodations that he arranges to find, on the same occasion, a correlative to his aesthetic tastes (if indeed things transpired in that chronological order and at the origin of his frequentation of the spot sexual motivation preceded musical devotion). Far from excluding each other, as the conclusion of *L'Imaginaire* would have it, beauty and sexuality are thus literally placed under the same sign by *La Nausée* sheltered in the same enclosure, at the same address, officiating each in place of the other, at the Rendez-vous des cheminots.

Moreover, that is not exceptional: on two occasions in *L'Age de raison*, Mathieu, driven wild by the unattainable beauty of Ivich, allows himself to lay his hand on her, and each time, it happens in the proximity of works of art, in the context of an aesthetic experience. It is of little use for Ivich to be present (unlike Françoise); she is no less beautiful. The first time is in the taxi taking them to the Gauguin exhibition. The second in the Sumatra, the cabaret where Lola sings and suffers in beauty.

Sexuality, we might say in summarizing what is at stake in these scenes, is thus what is refused in beauty. Beauty occurs where sexuality is lacking, but it is because sexuality itself is produced through a lack. Beauty thus has as its ground and point of origin the constitutive absence of the sexual object, an absence which it restricts itself to singing, without adding anything to it or substituting anything for it. "Some of These Days" is Perdita's song, the refrain of lost women. As though the *Tristes* had been Ovid's true *Ars amatoria*.

Proustiana

Sartre's line in 1938: "Proust's psychology? It's not even Bergson's; it's Ribot's."
.Lévinas, "L'Autre dans Proust," *Deucalion*, 2, 1947

The real is the correlate of perception, but to desire is not to perceive because instead of touching, one caresses oneself on what one touches. For failure to speak the language of our desires, the real is incapable of answering them.

On several occasions and in various contexts (the Collaboration, the crisis of language, hallucinations, poetry), we have seen Sartre refer to a concept much appreciated by the psychiatry (and the nascent psychoanalysis) of his day, that of depersonalization. The syndrome of depersonalization, which is also called the feeling of a loss of reality (Sartre, using Janet's vocabulary, occasionally speaks of neurasthenia), would, according to the mental hygiene of the *années folles*, be prone to pounce on those subjects — naturally inclined to analyze their feelings — who allow themselves to follow that inclination beyond what is reasonable and begin imagining (or even masturbating) themselves. Hesnard, for example, relates the impression of unreality to the practice of what he calls in English "self-feeling," that is, the practice of self-affection in all its forms, be they psychological or manual. "The imagination," he declares, "is an essentially autistic, self-sexual function." The phenomenologies of perception were never to say anything different. The difference between perceiving and imagining is no longer a function so much of the position of the object (present if it is real, absent if imagined) as of the structure of consciousness (intentional if it is perceiving, reflexive if imagining) or, what amounts to the same thing, of the opposition between the interior, the intimate folding back upon the self that is generative of the unreal, and the existential (ek-sistential) exteriorization in which reality is founded. Imaginary illnesses begin with analytic introspection, an art that finds its most accomplished and unpardonable representative in Proust. "He takes pleasure in analysis," says Sartre, "and I tend strictly toward synthesis." Tending — *tendre* — is the word, but it's a verb with an asymptotic object.

Among the ironclad distinctions around which Sartre's text is elaborated, the most important is that separating consciousness from its objects. "The first initiative of a philosophy," we read at the beginning of *L'Etre et le néant*, "should be to expel things outside of consciousness." Consciousness is, in effect, always conscious of something other than itself. But the transcendence of objects, the counterpart of the intentionality of consciousness, is more than a law of essence, for it also has a normative value. It constitutes the hygienic-cum-ethical imperative on the basis of which virile (allo-erotic and heterosexual) commitment will wage its campaign against the temptations of depersonalizing self-affection. It is in the affirmation of the transcendence of the object that one finds the inspiration of that antireflexive ethic that Sartre had no need of spelling out, since it already implicitly traverses the entirety of his writing.

Sartre argues in *L'Imaginaire*, against Proust, that "love is not above all consciousness of itself: it is a consciousness of the charms of the beloved." The normal use of the verb *to love* [*aimer*] is transitive; the reflexive form is but its perversion. *Amabam amatam*: to love is not to love oneself; autoerotism, far from being the essence of sexuality, is only its accidental form, an impoverishment. Along with Proust, Sartre lashes out at psychoanalysis, which also thinks that one can account for affective life through the chemistry of "transferences, condensations, sublimations, and derivations," as though feelings and emotions were entirely independent of the objects that give rise to them and even, in limited cases, as though they had no objects.

And yet it will be recalled that in describing desirous flesh and caresses, Sartre pursued a quite different line of discourse. The crucial moment in Freud's description of the genesis of the sexual drive involves a form of object-loss occurring after nursing when the infant gives himself over to a sensual sucking without object, caressing his lips against each other or having them caress his mother's breast. This constitutive brushing back upon itself of the sexual drive is exactly identical to the gesture of the caress as described by Sartre, a movement in which the object vanishes because the subject, instead of taking it, caresses himself with it. From which it follows that even in Sartre, sexuality runs a considerable risk of never encountering that object which would finally deliver us from Proust and Freud. But from which it also follows that Sartre's insistence on the transcendence of the object should be considered one of the crucial elements in an antisexual campaign of repression, a program for desexualizing the object: the intentionality of perceptual consciousness figures in the first ranks of the resistance to sexual reflexivity.

"If we love a woman, it is because she is lovable," said the article on intentionality, which continued: "And there we are, delivered from Proust. Delivered at the same time from 'inner life'; we would search in vain, like Amiel, like a young child kissing her own shoulder, for the caresses and fondling of our most intimate selves." It will be recalled that on two occasions Roquentin expressed concern about what kind of a person keeping an intimate diary was making him look like. In this case, things occur in three stages. First, the magisterial plural of a man ("we") who loves a woman. Then Proust. And to finish off, a child coiled around herself. Her- and not himself, according to Sartre: it is the fold that feminizes. The intentionality of consciousness, at the same time that it desexualizes the object, effectively guarantees the virility of the subject. The woman's object is a mirror, but the male body knows no creases; it affirms itself by moving beyond itself and does not caress itself with the objects it encounters. Simone de Beauvoir herself would describe the second sex as condemned to the folds of immanence, failing to emerge from its flesh. Intentionality, in fact, does not play identically on both sides of the divide. A woman has great difficulty in being conscious of something other than herself, which is the whole — anatomical, if one likes — difference between the sexes. And the folding back upon the intimacy of the self infallibly denounces in Sartre, if not femininity properly speaking, at least a flagging of virile power: Lulu, in "Intimité," likes to "caress herself with her sheets"; Lucien, in "L'Enfance d'un chef," "to kiss himself at the bend of his arm." In *La Mort dans l'âme*, Philippe offers Daniel, who is swooning, the spectacle of the delectable nape of his neck, which was caressing itself "with its jacket collar and deriving pleasure from itself"; later on, beneath Brunet's more severe eyes, the mass of prisoners indulge in "caressing themselves with their fatigue." But pride of place in the series goes to Baudelaire, the man given to bending over himself.

SARTORIAL PATCH. I stop where I like, and a text interests me only to the extent that I interest myself in it, that I accord myself the pleasure of weaving my way among the quotations I insinuate. I have to be able to feel myself comfortable there. For I in turn derive pleasure amid the sinuosities of this text that is less his own than he imagined, with its recurrent pleats in which I coil up [*je me love*], as the critic says, every time he irons them out.

("*Je me love*," she told herself, her cheek on her shoulder, almost in the hollow of her ear, so that there might be an echo.)

My insinuations, at bottom, are not so nasty. It will be seen that I have a great deal (and more and more, for the pleats are accumulating) of self-affection for Sartre's text. Perhaps that would have annoyed him, that I accord myself such pleasure that way, he who thought, without reflecting, without any affectation, that language ought not to make a wrinkle. But in those creases, after all, what interests me is the object, the thing that insinuates itself, the lost object, the breast. For the breast, it goes without saying, is but what is implicit in the pleats, the inexplicable breast, the cryptic content that a pleat — or crease — at once engenders and snatches away. The metonymic effect of a fabric coming back upon itself, of a text whose tread amounts to touching itself, border against border, applied [*appliqué*] to itself.

It is here that politics intervenes. For it happens that the transcendence of the object, as well as being virile, is simultaneously progressive in orientation. Members of the bourgeoisie, whose lives are without object, are also inclined to depersonalizing analysis. Instead of living outside, "a man among men," they effeminize themselves in their threatened interiors. A long note in *Saint Genet* kills two birds with one stone: at the same time as it attacks erotic literature, it lashes out at bourgeois reflexivity. The starting point is the episode in *Ulysses* in which Bloom "breathes in with pleasure the intimate odor rising from beneath him." *L'Etre et le néant* had already indicated the "profound tolerance of facticity" betrayed by that scene. Sartre comes back to it in *Saint Genet*: "The bourgeois's affection for his own excrement, M. Bloom's for 'his own odor,' presses our civilization of solitude and individualism to its final consequences. Lost and abandoned amid a hostile and indifferent society, the individual wraps himself up in himself and attempts to find recourse in immanence against an impossible transcendence." A few lines farther down, it is the couple itself that is absorbed in bourgeois autoerotism. Sartre shows it trying to be no more than a single beast which "feels itself, chews on itself, sniffs itself, and touches itself with its eight groping paws and pursues in the moistness of its bed the sad dream of absolute immanence."

Moreover, the bourgeois, more generally, has a hard time perceiving. He has no grasp of reality because he wants to possess the world instead of transforming it. He is man intent on having, as the proletarian is man intent on doing. But possessing, precisely, is once again touching oneself with: "It is myself whom I am touching with this cup, or this trinket," says the collector. Similarly, the heir "touches himself with *his* gravel, with the diamond-shaped panes of *his* veranda." The Sartrean taboo on private property is a direct consequence of the phobia of touching oneself whose prey Roquentin becomes from the day he opens his diary: both are the effect of an impatient repression of autoerotism.

Contiguities

1. In the campaign launched by Sartre to promote Husserlian phenomenology on the French market, there are several things at stake. The most obvious is the valorization of the exterior at the expense of the intimate, a valorization that does no more than translate in terms of topography a restoration of sexual hierarchy. The exterior is masculine space, the place where a man feels at home ("a man among men"); the interior is feminine space, that in which a man feels superfluous, threatened with a feeling of strangeness. (One recalls Boris's joke in *La Mort dans l'âme*: "Women, when they are by themselves, speak of their interior or their interiors.")

2. But that valorization presupposes a more fundamental move of ejection, a move tracing the line of demarcation between the interior and the exterior: the object is what is rejected by the subject.

"The first initiative of a philosophy should be to expel things outside of consciousness." And Sartre does indeed begin his philosophical career with *La Transcendance de l'ego*, in which he evicts from consciousness its long-standing tenant, the ego, which, he shows, "is neither formally nor materially *within* consciousness." That, of course, is but the first of a long series of expulsions whose most frequent victims will belong to the empiricist and analytical tradition of Anglo-Saxon philosophy (Hume, Berkeley, Locke, Bentham, the neo-realists). They are the target of both *L'Imagination* and whole sections of *L'Idiot de la famille*. Sartre takes up on his own and relaunches the polemic intrinsic to Husserl's project against what he calls "the errors of a certain immanentism that would constitute the world with the contents of consciousness." He then mentions "Berkeley's idealism." Berkeley's philosophy (or "error," as he elsewhere calls it) does indeed ask to conceive external reality in a way such that things would be neither things-in-themselves nor appearances but, in Gueroult's phrase, "things in us." *Esse est percipi*: the *perceptum* is contained in the *percipiens*. And for Berkeley, to imagine is not, as Sartre would have it, to posit outside of myself a certain object as absent, but to have within myself an image of that object. Here, too, the opposition might be formulated in terms of doing and having. With the most imperturbable intolerance, Sartre will relentlessly clean out all pockets of exteriority, those immigrant parasites that an insufficiently vigilant philosophy has allowed to infiltrate. But any resident of consciousness, whatever it be, would find itself with immigrant status. Consciousness, in fact, has no contents, only correlates. There can be no question, consequently, of impregnating it: to be conscious is to empty oneself. And there we are freed from the "illusion of immanence," from "internal objects," and from that "exteriority within" to which a number of English ideologies wanted to reduce consciousness.

Behind such attacks, which are directed against Hume and Berkeley, what is being augured is a rejection of psychoanalysis. "The whole theory," Sartre notes, "presupposes a notion that is nevertheless never named, that of the unconscious." Psychoanalysis, being but a form of analysis, after all, Sartre's Freud need not await the entry of the Nazis into Vienna to become English. And the repression [*refoulement*] — in the sense of the term understood by the Ministry of the Interior — the expulsion of things beyond the borders of consciousness, goes together in his case with the repression of the unconscious beyond the borders of the psychical, that is, with the repression of repression. It is a fact, moreover, that psychoanalysis also proposes to proceed with an irredentism comparable to the one from whose elimination Sartre's philosophy draws its inspiration. But it does so in a less militant, more diplomatic manner. For the sexual drive, after all, like an irredeemable debt, is but the trace of the Other in me, what in me separates me from myself, the intromission within the infant of the mother's desire. Laplanche, in describing it, uses the phrase "alien internal entity," which is precisely the name Sartre gives to the object of his most persistent allergies. One might also evoke (since, were it up to him, *La Nausée* would have been called *Melancholia*) the problematic of melancholic *Erinnerung*, which Lagache, his buddy the doctor, invited by Janet and Bataille, developed in 1937 before the Société de Psychologie Collective, with references to Abraham and the concept of introjection. The tenacity with which Sartre, to the point of nausea, opposes any form of introjection and incorporation, the violence with which he would vomit up heterogeneous insinuations, calls to mind the fundamentally "bad" character attributed by Melanie Klein to internal objects. The object becomes a threat for me from the moment that its disappearance from the external world (or perceptual field) forces me to introject it and makes me fear, as a result, the worst reprisals against the integrity of my body.

For to sing "Some of these days, you'll miss me, honey" to someone who is leaving or (even more) to someone who has already left you is, in the last analysis, a threat whose absurdity might well suffice to characterize melancholic aggressivity. I'll punish you for dying: at that point, one has moved beyond sulking and even blackmail.

3. Husserlian intentionality answers a third exigency in Sartre's textual system: it allows for an escape from the perils of contiguity.

Man is not in the world, says the existentialist, he is (present) to the world. He is not simply an object of the world alongside other objects of the world (in the sense that the world includes minerals, vegetables, and animals, among whom is man). He is an object of the world for which there is a world: he understands the world without allowing himself to be explained in terms of it. For unity comes to the world through a consciousness which — because it is not part of it — makes of it a whole. As the divided structure of the *coupé* would have it. I do not call the string holding the asparagus together a bunch. "Matérialisme et révolution" says the same thing: it is in the whole "which does not exist" that the parts find their unity. The whole thus never allows itself to be reduced to the sum of its parts: it is not enough to be together [*ensemble*] to form an ensemble. Consciousness, in this syntax, is never in the position of a noun: it partakes, rather, of hyphenization. Sartre's work swarms with pages denouncing nonsynthetic sums, heteroclite collections: unity will never emerge from such bric-a-brac. Analysis, the triumph of the part over the whole, sounds the defeat of totalities, *partes extra partes*. Sartre's anthropological totalitarianism is first of all a resistance against the threats of atomistic detotalization induced by the effects of contiguity. For *he* takes no pleasure in analysis; he tends toward synthesis.

One remembers love à la Proust: "I am in love, and beside me there is this woman" becomes, in short,: "I love her." It was to contiguity that the various eighteenth-century thinkers competing for the title of Newton-of-the-human-mind were to entrust the task of explaining the totality of psychical phenomena. "It allowed one," we read in L'Idiot de la famille, "to link up through subtle gravitations objects whose sole point in common lay in not having any relations with one another." But without attaching undue importance to the love of what is most distant, it is not enough for two beings to be side by side for an attachment to be born. Contiguity explains nothing. Contingency and contiguity, moreover, are etymologically close to each other: they come from the Latin *contingo*, to touch, that is, from the verbal root that causes so many problems for Roquentin. And it happens, precisely, that Roquentin discovers his contingency by discovering that things are merely contiguous and nothing more, that they touch one another but do nothing but touch one another. "Everything in existence is born without reason." It is not, then, because things do no more than touch one another that they have relations. Or better still: "Where do children come from?" Answer: there is no sexual relation between beings who do nothing but touch themselves.

The note from *Saint Genet* described the couple as a false totality into which each partner enters only to touch him(her)self. If, consequently, in order to be together it is necessary to no longer touch oneself, to no longer do nothing but touch oneself, it is excluded that one can be together as two. But the argument can be turned around: if, as long as one is contiguous, one does not yet form a unity, from the moment one begins to touch oneself, one effects a detotalization. That is the reason why Sartre insists at such length on the fact that there are no double sensations: I can no more touch myself touching than see myself seeing. If it may no doubt happen that I touch my leg with my hand (while slipping on a pair of pants — Sartre's example), my hand touches, my leg is touched, but my hand that touches is not touched. And my leg is touched by my hand exactly as it would be by any other hand. From that impossibility for the subject to catch up with himself comes his necessity to double up every time he approaches himself. It is thus precisely because there are no double sensations that I duplicate myself every time that I self-affect myself. So that a subject who touches himself, divides himself by touching himself, becomes contiguous to himself, finds (and loses) himself alongside himself, being his own neighbor, having taken his own place: himself in place of himself.

Lucien, in "L'Enfance d'un chef," recalls in front of a mirror his still fresh homosexual adventure with Bergère. "He touched his loins," we read, "and regretted not being an other to be able to caress himself with his own flesh as with a silken fabric." It is obvious — and that is what allows the fantasy to give the wish all the present force it has — that were he an other, it would not be with his own flesh that Lucien would be caressing himself. But the autoaffective circuit is not a short circuit; it entails a detour through heteroaffection that the subject is obliged to take in order to join up with himself anew, but to join up with himself while alienating himself, disjoining himself, inserting between himself and himself that stranger who reduces his relation to self — all intimacy lost — to a pure relation of contiguity. The autoaffective junction is not without danger for the self proper: it is sundered from itself, just as the futureless present in Faulkner cut itself off from itself. An odd couple: the self proper takes off, splits.

Define sexual as any organ of my body that does not belong to me. *L'Idiot de la famille* lingers at length, in some astonishing pages, over the manual gestures a subject accompanies himself with for the pleasure of it. There are, in particular, scenes of Flaubert before a mirror in which the author of *Novembre*, like Lucien, tricks himself into imagining that the hands he lays on his body are those of an Other. There is, above all, the passage in which Léon is described as caressing himself after slipping on the glove he has just pilfered from Emma. His hand, inside the glove, touching his body outside the glove. And he himself, through the glove, double: at once within and without, internal and external, on one side and the other of the Other, following the silky crease of self-affection. Contiguous to himself.

Like Sartre citing Wols who cites him, separated from himself, like a glove, by the silent space of quotation marks.

Far from Berkeley

And there we are, quite far from Berkeley and Hume.
Sartre, *L'Imaginaire*

Sartre published his first book in 1936: *L'Imagination*. On the title page, the author is identified as a "teacher at the Lycée du Havre." The same collection — Nouvelle Encyclopédie Philosophique, published by Alcan — had brought out a year before the slim volume that Raymond Aron had brought back from a year at the French Institute of Berlin, *La Sociologie allemande contemporaine*.

We are already familiar with the anecdote of the Bec de Gaz, the Montparnasse bar in which Aron, passing through Paris on vacation, no doubt at Christmas, during that year of 1932–33 which he was spending in Berlin as a fellowship holder at the French Institute, initiates Jean-Paul Sartre, age 27, a philosophy teacher at the Le Havre lycée (also on vacation), to the humble mysteries of Husserlianism: "You see, my little friend [*petit camarade*]," he tells him, "if you are a phenomenologist, you can talk about this cocktail and it's philosophy!" The story, told by Simone de Beauvoir, specifies that the cocktail in question — "this cocktail" — was apricot flavored, the house specialty. Rather sweet, then, sugary even, and probably lacking in tang. It must have had a taste close to that of existence. Sartre's emotion, in any event, was immediate and unbounded at the thought of such a technique, which just beyond the Rhine would allow philosophers to have as the object of their discourse neither ideas nor any other form of abstraction but things themselves, to have as philosophers full access to the real world, the one found in bars. Simone de Beauvoir comments: "That was exactly what he had been wishing for for years: to speak of things the way he touched them, and for it to be philosophy."

Without any wish to insist unduly on the relations between a philosopher and his passport, it is not completely irrelevant to observe that within the economy of this scene, it is German philosophers who, to the stupefaction of their young colleague from Le Havre, would allow themselves to speak of what their hands touched. Between Sartre and the reality of his desires, there is always a border to be crossed. The revelation whose messenger Aron will have been does not fail to conform to the jealous structure governing the engendering of the real. A whole diplomacy of philosophy is put in place, which will emerge fully developed a number of years later when Sartrean existentialism has become committed and acquired, in the process, an international status. And since, like bananas, works of the mind, including phenomenology, should be consumed on the spot, Sartre will not hesitate to file his candidacy to be his initiator's successor. The following year, like an anthropologist, he takes off for the field, taking the train toward the concrete, *Zur Sache selbst*, to the French Institute of Berlin. He had already crossed a few borders and would subsequently cross others (of every stripe). But this stay in Germany (September 1933–Summer 1934) will be his longest and, in a sense, his only true stay in a foreign country. With the exception, to be sure, of the seven months he was to spend in the same country as a war prisoner seven years later, on which occasion a second lesson in the real was to allow him, in turn, to go beyond the lesson of phenomenology.

He had already crossed the Franco-German border several times as a small child. But that was before the war (of 1914), and at the time, one reached it long before coming to the Rhine. In the company of his grandfather — whom it crossed (Charles on one side, Karl on the other) — he was accustomed to crossing it during vacation time. The old man was returning to the land of his birth, become *unheimlich*, since Alsace was now foreign territory.

Sartre would always remain quite sensitive to the events of the year 1870. In *L'Imagination*, the entire history of French philosophy under the Third Republic is interpreted as a reactionary reaction to the defeat, the fall of the Empire, and the Commune that ensued. In *La Nausée*, the Bouville Museum glorifies the repression and the triumph of the moral order that permitted, after the "terrible year," as it was called, national recovery and the restoration of bourgeois power. Finally, it is also acknowledged that one of the points of fixation of Sartre's myth of Flaubert is the inexpiable relief expressed by the family idiot when he learns that the Commune has breathed its last breath. It is significant from this point of view that it was in the context of another French defeat, that of 1940, when he would be a prisoner in Germany, that Sartre read Flaubert's correspondence.

But the importance of that date should not be underestimated, not only as an objective point of reference for his historical discourse but also as a starting point for his family romance, since it was the defeat of the Empire in 1870 which forced Karl Schweitzer to leave Alsace for Paris. He preferred to remain French rather than become German but, at the same time, condemned himself to being a kind of Germanic enclave within

French territory. As a teacher of French to Germans passing through the capital, he was, as the author of *Les Mots* remarks, being supported by the enemy. At home abroad but a foreigner at home, it is he, the grandfather, long before Genet and Nizan, who will be the prototype of Sartre's traitors. Just as Alsace, in its internality-externality, will be the prototype of those double-edged phenomena against which the integrity of the body proper will request the protection of the P.C. System.

In the meantime, under the spell of the emotion aroused by Aron's words, perhaps without even having touched the apricot cocktail, Sartre rushes off to a bookstore in the Latin Quarter and buys Lévinas's book on Husserl, which he begins to read, feverishly, while walking on the sidewalk, prey to one jealous concern: might somebody already have touched on his subject, already have laid hands on it? A few minutes will be enough for him to emerge reassured from his reading: contingency is still a virgin. "I came to phenomenology through Lévinas," he would later say, "and left for Berlin where I stayed nearly a year." In the account she gives of this episode, Simone de Beauvoir observes that, caught up in his impatience, Sartre did not even take the time to cut the book's pages.

> London offers a remarkable point of view for anyone interested in observing bourgeois society.
>
> Marx, Preface to *The Critique of Political Economy*

It was probably during the vacation of Christmas 1932 that Aron brought from Berlin the phenomenological revelation that was to constitute the point of departure of Sartre's work.

But it was not until the beginning of school the following year, in the autumn of 1933, that the latter, freed from his obligations in Le Havre (having taken a temporary leave), would be able to succeed his *"petit camarade"* in Berlin.

In the interim, Simone de Beauvoir took advantage of the next vacation, at Easter, to have him visit London. It is she who recounts the episode in Chapter 3 of *La Force de l'âge*.

She was enchanted, it is clear. And Sartre followed.

"We had decided to see everything," she says. The common front of that first-person plural, however, quickly breaks down, in the course of the events recounted, into two propositions which might occasionally have a hard time remaining compatible: (1) he accompanied me to museums and other places where the mind's achievements could be found; (2) he dragged me to the "crowded suburbs," eager to discover the hunger of others in joyless streets haunted by the unemployed.

There is, in fact, a specifically Sartrean mode of tourism that would be defined and illustrated, twenty years after that British vacation, by the "antiguide" that

La Reine Albemarle et le dernier touriste would have been. In the absence of that abandoned work, a brief ABC summarizes its essence in a preface to the Nagel Guide to the Nordic countries. "I believe," Sartre says there, "that the following sentence by Camus summarizes rather well the state of our present curiosities: 'A convenient way of coming to know a city is to find out how people work, love, and die in it.'" Beauty is not worth the trip. That is not what one goes abroad for, but for the real. The secret of a city is not in its museums or its monuments but in its present. The existentialist tourist travels only in order to discover what is not very nice to behold.

During the summer preceding that Easter in London, Sartre, in Spain, had given a sample of the conflicts to which such principles might lead. For a few weeks, he crossed the Iberian peninsula with Simone de Beauvoir in a car that their friend Pagniez was nice enough to drive. Does one necessarily share the perception of the class in which one travels? Apparently not: Sartre, even as he was transported about on the backseat of a car he did not know how to drive, looked straight ahead and began training himself for proletarian perception. A class conflict resulted between the passenger and his all too bourgeois chauffeur, who was not long in interfering with the program of visits. Sartre did not want to "waste his time seeing Murillos" and refused to accompany Pagniez to the churches of Cádiz. But this refusal to stop at what is beautiful to behold was not limited to artistic institutions. It can indeed be the case that the real itself is not sufficiently proletarian to merit a glance. The next stop, Ronda, relaunched a quarrel that was no longer in any need of museums or cathedrals: "All that," says Sartre, "is nothing but aristocrats' houses." Seen already.

In London, it was Simone de Beauvoir who strolled through the past. She sought out, in the heart of the city, "the memory of Shakespeare, of Dickens." The older neighborhoods bore her aloft to a pinnacle of cultural euphoria. But Sartre was thinking of the future: "He told me," his companion recalls, "that when we returned to England, we would visit Manchester and Birmingham, the great industrial cities." He always needed the synthetic class in order to be comfortable in his perceptions.

That divergence in their respective interests culminated in a scene that erupted in front of a dish of cold meats of the type the French call an *assiette anglaise*. It is not known whether he touched it, but he did speak about it, and it was philosophy. In the land of tolerance, she listened. "I could accept," she says with amusement, "his comparisons between English cooking and Lockean empiricism, each based on the analytic principle of juxtaposition." Such gustatory mosaics do indeed lack the unifying hyphenization of meats prepared in sauce. Up till now, however, nothing serious. Things get worse, however, when Sartre, not satisfied with criticizing the "insipid analytic platters" of English tables, launches into the domain of synthesis. For there he was, in fact, "enamored as always of synthesis, trying to define London as a whole." The result is not exactly distinguished. She was of the opinion that he hadn't seen a thing, that his perception was totally amiss. *You missed it, honey.*

From which it follows (1) that femininity, even when it is that of an existentialist, is as spontaneously refractory to synthesis as virility is to analysis.

From which it also follows (2) that the Anglophile tends to be feminine and the Germanophile masculine.

I do not know if there are any gastronomic anecdotes concerning Sartre's stay in Berlin. But it was in Berlin that he wrote the article on intentionality, which begins with a formal attack against the Brillat-Savarins of the brain, the French-speaking advocates of an "alimentary philosophy" maintaining that to know something is to assimilate it. The reading of *Ideen* had revealed to him the transcendence of cocktails: they are there not to be sipped but to be talked about — and for the result to be philosophy.

From Easter 1933 to the beginning of school in October, Sartre would thus pass from analytical dishes to transcendental dishes, from London to Berlin. That is also the itinerary, from Hume to Husserl, traversed by *L'Imagination*, the 1936 text much of which was brought back from Berlin by its author. It might also be said that he went from the eighteenth to the twentieth century. In between, a few French names: Taine (a friend of Flaubert and one of the ideologues responsible for the events of 1870, the year in which he published the book Sartre attacks: *L'Intelligence*) and Ribot and Bergson, who both ignored that their era was philosophizing in German and even believed that it was still possible to think in English. For if Sartre's eighteenth century, because it did not see very far ahead, could think English, the nineteenth, which invented the future, spoke German. And the twentieth, as was appropriate, would speak French (that is, would give German lessons to the Anglos). That, moreover, is what Sartre graciously does at the end of the article on *The Sound and The Fury*, in which, without any fuss, he initiates Faulkner to a number of Heideggerian questions that he advises him to consider.

One last tourist's anecdote:

Did Sartre and Simone de Beauvoir return to England to visit, as he had hoped, the industrial cities whose absence had spoiled his perception in 1933? It appears not. Apparently, Sartre's next expedition to Anglo-Saxon territory was to be the journalistic assignment that brought him in 1945 to the United States (without Simone de Beauvoir) and from which he would bring back the articles on America included in *Situations* III.

An episode from that trip is evoked in "Des rats et des hommes," a preface written for Gorz's book *Le Traître*. Sartre relates a kind of pedestrian stroll he had the unfortunate idea of taking in Brooklyn and the dizziness that gradually overcame him as he attempted to advance in those similar and successive streets. The serialized sprawl of the identical, the same alongside the same, induced in him a nausea that leads us to compare that recollection to the episode of Roquentin in the Public Garden. In both cases, in fact, the revelation of contingency springs automatically from the spectacle of contiguity. "My presence within the mechanical universe of repetition became a sheer accident, as stupid as my birth," writes Sartre concerning that depersonalizing experience of American space. And like Roquentin, he abandoned the puzzle, which had no appeal for him, and took refuge in his Manhattan hotel, from which he drew the lesson of his depressing experience. It was my fault, he says. "I was taking a walk; one does not take a walk in the United States." The asyndeton is worth noting: this is not a country for hyphenization.

A good metaphor is worth the trip. How far would one not go for the sake of a quotation? But the law of insinuation implies that one finds them only where one happens to find oneself (if one must speak of where one is speaking from).

Chapter 9
A Winter's Tale

PERDITA: these are flow'rs
Of middle summer, and I think they are given
To men of middle age.

Shakespeare, *The Winter's Tale*

Having or Doing

At the end of the credits introducing *Les Mots*, Sartre pays homage to his father for his discretion. A good father does not exist. Jean-Baptiste accepted as much as a matter of course and did not insist. "Making [*faire*] children," the son concludes, "nothing better; *having* them, what an iniquity."

The verb *to have* [*avoir*], in Sartre's idiom, is in no way active and does not lend itself to the establishment of a properly transitive relation with objects. An object, in fact, preserves its transcendence only if it does not allow itself to be appropriated by a subject who would make of it his property and attribute it to himself. Such is the source of the frustrations generated by the possessive: an object which has been subjected is no longer in any condition to object. From which it follows, in particular, that the proletariat alone, insofar as it is the nonpossessing class, is up to experiencing the real. Its life is not without object, since no object belongs to it. A man without qualities, attributes, properties: *ohne Eigenschaften*. Existentialism defines man by what he does: he is only his deeds, without reservation and without either virtuality or hidden quality. The

149

opposition between doing and having already schematized (for existential psychoanalysis) the alternative facing being-for-itself in seeking to surmount its lack-in-being [*manque-à-être*]. A whole section is devoted to it in *L'Etre et le néant*. And *Qu'est-ce que la littérature?* campaigned for a literature of *praxis* and not *exis*: "it is *doing* that is revelatory of *being*."

Sartre — self-proclaimed self-made man — was proud of never having had anything, beginning with a father. It consequently befitted him to denounce as inauthentic any flight toward the imaginary solidity of the goods of this world or any other. Consciousness is conscious of something other than itself, but on the condition that it does not appropriate it. The owner's solipsism stems from the fact that he necessarily identifies with what he has. Politically, Sartre will have been opposed to private property: what an iniquity, indeed! But such reprobation is far from restricted to the realm of the means of production. Without ever having had to take a vow of poverty, he will have received quite early on the gift of not having anything; his lot will have been the unencumbered revenue of dispossession. Man does not inhabit as an owner. "We have never been at home." The habit does not make the cleric.

To Madeleine Gobeil, who questioned him for *Playboy*, Sartre confided: "I detest possessing. When I like an object, I want to give it to someone. That's not generosity; it's simply that I want the *others* to be enslaved to objects." But why would that not be generosity, since *L'Etre et le néant* had shown precisely in that emotion the surest means of subjugating and subjecting others. "To give," we read there, "is to enslave." And *Critique de la raison dialectique* returns to the analysis of potlatch, which those words concluded, to recall all that is constitutionally aggressive in every gesture pretending to generosity.

But the Sartrean analysis of potlatch does not stop there. Generosity not only constitutes an irreproachable method for enslaving the recipient of our gifts but is also the best means for ensuring one's own appropriation of what one is giving. I give only what belongs to me: a gift is the supreme form of possession. You would not give to me if I were not already yours. Translation: I am yours because you are giving to me. Goetz in *Le Diable et le bon dieu* is pitiless in the acts of charity he performs; his generosity strikes blindly through the distribution of lands he has taken from his brother. "I will give them away, those lands; how I will give them away," he threatens. But the ruses of Jean sans Terre should not catch us off guard. For him, it was merely a way of possessing those who received them. "They are mine at last," he concludes at the end of the second act, while contemplating the mass of those who are now his men. Just as destruction appears to be the *nec plus ultra* of appropriation, the gift can be defined as the most profitable form of generosity: what I give comes back to me; what I give is guaranteed only to accrue to myself.

The Possessive

He never married; he never acquired any property; he does not even possess a bed, a table, a painting, a memento, or a book. . . . He has passed his adult life in a series of hotel rooms in which there is never anything belonging to him, not even a copy of his last book, and which surprise by their bareness.

Simone de Beauvoir, "Jean-Paul Sartre: Strictly Personal," *Harper's Bazaar*

Sartre would later confess to Contat that in all circumstances he insisted on having within his reach, as one might a piece of clothing, the totality of everything he might need: his cigarettes, his lighter, and "a lot of money." ("I often had more than a million [old] francs in my pocket.") He explained: in this situation he was well disposed, he did not depend on anyone, and also, he added, "it represents a kind of way of feeling myself superior to other people." The conversation then turned to the more than generous tips Sartre gave to café waiters. And he insisted that there was nothing aggressive about it.

All that is in perfect agreement with the position developed on the subject of the object in the *N.R.F.* article on Husserlian intentionality. That early text did indeed lash out at a philosophy of assimilation that would have it that knowing an object consisted of appropriating it and would end up making of it a simple property of a mind that would lose itself in it while appropriating it. Contrary to the postulates of such idealists, the object persists only in adversity and is affirmed only in a rejection (by opposing an objection) or a project (by becoming an objective). For in wanting to possess objects, in wanting to appropriate them, one becomes their thing oneself and becomes possessed by them. It is enough to attribute them to oneself to become alienated in them. The hardened orphan of *Les Mots* waxed ironic, as well, on the fate of the young heir who, in his words, "touches himself with *his* gravel, with the diamond-shaped panes of *his* veranda." The emphasis is not mine. As soon as the object reverts to me, it becomes reflexive and loses its transcendence. And since a mirror is a woman's object, one need not be surprised that virility is proletarian. A man would not allow himself to pretend that an object reverts to him. (Roquentin also did all that was possible to differentiate himself from the race of owners. Despite the two trunks following him to Paris, that traveler without baggage did not lack conviction when he declared, "I possess only my body." Recalcitrant as to the possession of things, he is obsessed with touching himself with them.) For the true object, according to phenomenology, is always the corrrelative of a deictic: the demonstrative supplies it ("this cocktail," Aron had said, and the article on Husserl: "this precise tree"), the possessive takes it back.

These remarks are a plot summary of *Les Mouches*, which might, in effect, be reduced to the grammatical exercises of Orestes, as he attempts, suspiciously, to decline the possessive. Note the insistence with which the possessive adjectives, throughout the play, are weighed down with italics: "*your* heart," "*my* palace," "*his* master," "*their* good." Orestes has had enough of cosmopolitanism, of the freedom of indifference, and of continuous creation. He wants to break with the Stoicism that prevents him from suffering. To step out of the abstract universal. To no longer play the role of the traveler without luggage — or with an "empty valise." As a result of being everywhere at home, the man without a country is at home nowhere. *Qual piuma al vento*. Orestes wants to commit himself to a location, to belong to a space, making a place for himself, rooting his habits, choosing a habitation, a fixed point or home port. The intellectual in his flight dreams of escaping from the weightlessness of the fixed stars, knows the nostalgia of bodies gravitating earthward. He would like to be able to no longer speak lightly, to give some weight to his signature in order to implicate his spirit in the movement of bodies falling. Weigh my words. What I am saying is grave. Orestes thus commits himself to an irreversible space, where the difference between high and low, left and right, motion and rest are reevaluated. Or rather, through that very act of commitment, he restores those differences and reorientates qualitative space. The world is hodological: one appropriates it by making one's path in it. "God knows where it leads," says Orestes, "but it is *my* path."

Les Mouches dates from 1943. That same year, Sartre publishes in (the clandestine) *Les Lettres françaises* an article in which he attacks the myth of the "empty valise" in Drieu la Rochelle. The same attack would appear a few years later in "Qu'est-ce qu'un collaborateur?" and *Qu'est-ce que la littérature?* It is in 1943 as well that he publishes his "Explication de *L'Etranger*," an article in which he denounces the novelistic sleight of hand through which Camus produces the absurd: the pane of glass which he inserts between Meursault and the world in order to exempt him from using the possessive and from behind which he can play the "idiot" in all innocence. But an intellectual plays the idiot in vain, which is precisely the major accusation retained by Sartre in the prosecution of his case. Before the tribunal of history, his "lightness [*légèreté*]" is more grave than all the crimes he might have committed.

Orestes no longer wants to "live in the clouds," to float "ten feet from the ground." He aspires to descend. No sooner has his preceptor revealed his origins to him (Argos, the adulterous affair of Aegisthus and Clytemnestra, Agamemnon's murder, his own expulsion) than he rushes to where he comes from. A return to his own sources: to rejoin them, destroy them, ground himself in them. Such is the first gesture, one of landing. It consists of responding to the attraction of the soil, of making of the earth my earth, and of possessing those for whom I speak: "Tomorrow, I shall speak to my people." The world, in this shifting from *Welt* to *Umwelt*, becomes the theater of my performances. It is not enough to gaze at it; one must also "make" it. Orestes approaches what belongs to him, appropriates what he approaches. "I want my memories, my land, my place amid the men of Argos," he says to her whom he has just recognized as his sister, and a few lines later he repeats the conclusion of the article on intentionality: "I want to be a man from somewhere, a man among men." The strangeness of the singular condemns the loner never to be home. To be in one's home is not to be single; it is to be with one's own.

But a second movement is sketched in a direction opposite to that of the first. In accomplishing *"his"* deed, Orestes realizes what is his, actualizes his properties; he takes possession of what belongs to him, of what he belongs to, appropriating for himself a place and leaving his mark. And yet that very deed separates him from those whom it allowed him to rejoin, detaches him from the people from whom he did not want to be cut off. Sartre would speak of Orestes' deed as "exceptional." The word should be taken quite literally, since it excepts its author from those it allows him to appropriate. The divided structure of the coupé: exile and the kingdom. Thus, at the end of the play, no less exiled (no less foreign) than he was when the curtain went up, he must depart from the city he had wanted to approach. He wanted to find his place amid the men of Argos. Now he leaves them. "I want to be a king without a land and without subjects."

He will have done no more than pass through the city. Just long enough to possess it. That is: to reject it. To make it [*se la faire*].

The Eternal said to Aaron: "They shall have no possessions among the children of Israel." He was speaking of the Levites. And there came an intellectual who begat a cleric whose apartment was not of this world.

Immobilities

Among the examples invoked by Braudel to illustrate what he means by "long duration," the two most important come from almost contradictory domains. The first is borrowed from the most material infrastructure of civilizations and is a function of the soil on which they are established and the geographical configurations they must assume in order to survive. Many things have moved around in Paris over two thousand years, but Paris itself has not moved, and if it is not always the same boats that follow the Seine, it is still the same Seine that they follow. The second example of historical immobility referred to by Braudel belongs, in contrast, to the level of what a Marxist would call the ideological superstructures of a civilization: its mental schemata, intellectual and emotional traditions, and representational frameworks. Thus it is, he notes, that Aristotelian patterns of thought were able to traverse without being crucially modified the quarrels and disorders they engendered throughout the Middle Ages. During that entire period, for instance, immobility was always regarded as more natural than movement, and movement itself, as always passing and tending toward repose. It was the scientific revolution of modern times (from Copernicus to Galileo) which (as Koyré has demonstrated) finally overturned that hierarchy and dismantled the opposition that had governed the relations between immobility and movement for fifteen centuries.

It would not be lacking in interest to read in the light of this evolution of the concept of movement Braudel's account of a slow history, a history centered on the immobilities around which gravitate various historicities in flux, tiered like so many variations or modulations around an unchanged theme. I shall attempt, instead, to describe — with reference to what I shall call Sartre's "revolution" — the persistence of one of those immobilities: the topography of clerical utterances. Ideological speech acts are, in fact, subject to constraints which are infinitely more powerful than the messages they emit. The cleric can change his mind. He can even express the most severe opinions concerning the clerisy. It does not affect his position: he nonetheless does not move. *Eppur non si muove.* Which does not mean, moreover, that a certain immobility cannot be revolutionary, more overwhelming than a movement in whose favor it is, all the same, a bit too conventional (modern) to participate. It will consequently be a question, at this point, of asking a text where it comes from. "From where are you speaking?" as one used to ask, is a question no less decisive for the interpretation of a message than one bearing on its meaning. A critical reading owes it to itself to reactivate what has been uttered at the site of its utterance. What a text owes to its place and date of birth, if it is a text of any weight, is by no means of mere anecdotal or regionalistic interest.

Bariona

Bariona ou le fils de la terre was Sartre's first play. He wrote it for Christmas 1940, while a prisoner of war in Stalag XII D, near Trèves, to celebrate with his companions in captivity that holiday of the Christian calendar. He wrote it but did not for all that quite acknowledge being its author since, for example, he did not include it in 1947 in the first volume of his *Théâtre*, which opens with his second play, *Les Mouches*, written after his return from captivity. In 1962, he consented to a publication of *Bariona* only because it was in an extremely limited edition not for sale. It was only in 1970, thirty years after it was written, that the play was to be commercially available, when it was inserted by Contat and Rybalka in *Les Ecrits de Sartre*, a volume of texts by Sartre whose author is not Sartre: a volume (by Contat and Rybalka) of texts (by Sartre). *Bariona* thus figures among the numerous texts that Sartre wrote but over which he refused, for a variety of reasons, to exercise his rights as an author, his authority, his paternity. He never quite recognized it. *Bariona* thus counts among the bastards of the Sartrean *corpus*.

When questioned about his refusal to recognize it, Sartre most often justified his rejection on aesthetic grounds. I refused to take it up again, for performance or publication, because it is a botched play. Moreover, it was my first one: as yet, I hadn't had any experience. That judgment, plainly, could not be more debatable. It is, moreover, refuted by the extremely forceful impression which (according to the author himself) *Bariona* would have had on the audience attending (and participating in) its first and only performance. And on this score, the author's comments have been confirmed by those in the audience who could be contacted and questioned. *Bariona*, no doubt, is not a masterpiece. No doubt it is not Sartre's best play. But it is no worse than *Les Mouches* and undeniably better than, say, *Morts sans sépulture*, a play which the author himself would judge "*manquée*," but which he would nevertheless publish.

Curiously, in the several interviews during which he agreed to talk about *Bariona*, Sartre never failed to defend himself, if not exactly for having written the play, at least for having written what he feared would be read into it. It is a Christmas play, to be sure. But don't believe I believed in it. With remarkable obstinacy, he never evoked the subject of the play without resorting to the figure of speech which rhetoric and psychoanalysis call disavowal: don't think that . . . "If I took my subject from the mythology of Christianity, it does not mean that the orientation of my thought changed, even for an instant, during my captivity." "Some have been of the opinion that I was going through a spiritual crisis. Not at all!" And in a letter to Simone de Beauvoir written from the Stalag, and consequently contemporary with the composition of the play: "Don't be afraid," he tells her. "I won't become like Ghéon," evoking an author of pious plays that were the toast of many a parish celebration. Here we are no longer dealing with the aesthetic defects of *Bariona* but its subject, whose interpretation is the object of the author's repeated disavowals.

It is quite probable that that subject is also what motivated his reluctance, over a period of twenty-two years, to allow the distribution of the first of his plays.

Bariona takes place in Judea, under the Roman occupation. The play begins with what French allows us to call a problem of *perception*. Bariona, head of an obscure Jewish mountain village, decides that his people should no longer suffer the gaze of others, should become imperceptible and remove themselves from that costly mode of being perceived by others known as taxation. They should pay no more taxes. His depopulated village is already being pressured beyond the limits of toleration when a representative of the Roman occupation forces summons him to announce an anticipated rise in taxes. If he refuses, the soldiers will simply help themselves by pillaging the village.

In the next scene, Bariona commits himself to resist. He proposes to his compatriots a program of sterility. The only way not to pay is not to exist: let us take a vacation from existence and no longer have any children. "The village," he tells them, "has been in a state of agony ever since the Romans entered Palestine, and whoever begets is guilty since he prolongs that agony." But it soon emerges from his somber harangue that the fruitless politics to which he would like to commit his fellow citizens is only marginally and contingently related to the Roman occupation. Bariona wastes no time, in fact, in launching into a series of academic discourses whose existentialist amplitude has rather little to do with what Sartre would later call their situation. No doubt the Romans are intolerable, but even without them, existence is hardly any better. At the most, they have come to convert into a reality what was already unacceptable in existence itself. The political context is used as an allegory of an existence which was already not worth much before the occupation, even if they did not know it. If no more taxes should be paid to the Romans, it is because no more should be contributed to existence. "The world," continues Bariona, "is but an interminable and soft descent. The world is but a clump of earth that never stops falling. Men and things suddenly appear at a point in the fall and no sooner have they appeared than they are caught in the universal fall. They begin going under, disintegate, come undone. Life is a defeat." This is not a pretty picture, but one is hard put to see why the Romans should be held responsible. Then Bariona concludes: "My friends, we should not resign ourselves to the fall, for resignation is not worthy of a man. . . . We will not make any more babies. I have spoken."

No sooner are these words pronounced than Sarah, Bariona's wife, rushes forth to interrupt him with the news that she is pregnant.

Never mind that. Bariona, faithful to his resolution, delivers to her a short lecture on morality and manners. ("Do you understand what an enormous incongruity, what a monstrous lack of tact it would be to bring out new editions of this botched-up world?") He orders her to have the village sorcerer deliver her the herbs that will extricate her from her sorry pass.

It is here that the Christmas story begins. For the news has spread that in a neighboring village a child has allowed himself to be born. Rumor even has it that he is the Messiah and that he would like to render existence bearable. Bariona then goes to Bethlehem, intent on removing this refutation of his metaphysics, this resistance to his politics. But before the manger, he gives up: one does not kill a child. And he converts to paternity. Keep your child, he tells Sarah. As for me, I'll go off to wage war against the Romans so it will have a viable future.

Genophobia

"The world is a descent, a fall [*une chute*]," says Bariona. "Existence is a falling off [*un fléchissement*]," said Roquentin. Neither one of them had any inclinations toward descendants: reproduction provides no lifts. The enthusiasm that the Jewish leader in 1940 — at least during the first part of his play — manifests for sterility is nothing new. It can be situated at the center of a tradition established by *La Nausée*. Moreover, in many respects, the harangue with which Bariona turns his people away from procreation merely summarizes the long meditation to which Roquentin had been moved on 21 February, outside of any political context, by the spectacle of the Public Garden.

Among the first observations in Roquentin's diary we find the following, which we have no reason not to take literally: "I am afraid of what will be born." In other circumstances, Roquentin will mock those bourgeois who "make babies at random" or who are guilty of "the extreme foolishness of having children." And he does not lack in pride, before the family portraits in the Bouville Museum, at being able to introduce himself as a bachelor without children. On 21 February, the verb *to be born* [*naître*] recurs in his diary in order to characterize the revelation he has just undergone: "I was at last going to surprise existences in the process of being born." We know, moreover, that it is not a pretty sight. It was the publisher, who was skeptical about the commercial prospects of *Melancholia*, who suggested to Sartre that he entitle his novel *La Nausée*. But the word pops up often enough, with a capital letter, to justify its promotion to the first page. It is perhaps not irrelevant to recall in this context that in folk medicine it serves to designate the first symptom of pregnancy.

Simone de Beauvoir discusses it at length in the chapter on maternity in *Le Deuxième sexe*. She refuses, in particular, to see in its spasms a strictly physiological manifestation. It is rather a matter, she says, of the pregnant woman's visceral refusal of the physiological process taking hold of her. Nothing of the sort occurs, according to her, in the females of other mammals. Nausea would thus be a human reality, less an effect of the reproduction of the species than an expression of the revolt of the female individual against the species which, in order to reproduce itself, takes up quarters within her, occupies her, lives off her parasitically. That real inclusion of the species in the woman's body is at the origin of the curse condemning her to the immanence of the flesh and reserving for man the transcendence of the body. Maternity is a congenital defect which prohibits woman from individualizing herself by escaping from her sex, condemns her to allowing herself to be invaded by the species, to vegetating amid the physiological because sexual difference has mapped onto her body the mechanisms of reproduction. Simone de Beauvoir does indeed envisage, for the length of a paragraph, the possibility of a woman's being satisfied with such fulfillment. The name "egg layer" [*pondeuse*] that she applies to such a case gives some measure of the empathy she brings to that possibility. For a normal woman, to be pregnant is first of all to rebel against that enclave whose insinuation threatens the integrity of her body, to vomit up the stranger that has introduced himself inside her, and to experience nothing but repulsion for the "gratuitous proliferation" depriving her of herself. It begins, precisely, with bouts of nausea, continues with vomiting, only to end with deliverance, the final expulsion: a miscarriage if it comes on time; childbirth, for lack of anything better.

When *L'Etre et le néant* appeared in 1943, the volume was wrapped in a band on which was written: "What counts in a vase is the void inside." No need to insert any plant, flower, or vegetation: inside, the absence of any bouquet. If Sartre applied himself so methodically to tracking down and expelling outside the boundaries of consciousness every trace of an internal object, if he never overlooked an opportunity to refute the concept of the contents of consciousness, it was because — as feminine experience revealed — in allowing oneself to be filled, one automatically condemns oneself to being submerged by what one can no longer contain. And the misfortune of capitalism, as demonstrated in "Les Communistes et la paix," lies precisely in not being able to survive without accommodating within its economy a place for what will as a result sooner or later submerge it. The relationships of production that define it entail a proletariat; it needs, in order to survive, what condemns it to death. It has death in its soul because it has its undertakers under its skin. The "containment" of the working class is a contradictory objective. Contents are always prolific. "It is commonly said," writes Simone de Beauvoir, that women are "sick in their abdomen"; and it is true that they contain within themselves a hostile element: the species gnawing away at them. Who is it that "commonly" says such things? Several of Sartre's men might be suspected. No doubt no existent being is perfect, and even less so a woman, if we are to believe Aristotelian anatomy. But that is no reason to decide point blank, as does Roquentin, that the cashier of the Café Mably, Mme. Florent, "is gently rotting away under her skirts." In the last volume of *Les Chemins de la liberté*, Lola, Boris's mistress, has her turn. She has in her abdomen a tumor deemed to be the vocation of her sex. As for Ivich, her sister, she has just had a miscarriage and makes comments which elicit from Boris a joke that he modulates in every sense: "A woman has to talk of her interior or her interiors," as one of the three versions among which he hesitates has it.

The Garden of Delights

> He abhors — the word is not too strong — the seething life of insects and the swarming of plants.
>
> Simone de Beauvoir, "Jean-Paul Sartre: Strictly Personal"

Roquentin, in his diary, mentions only one consummation of an act of the flesh — on the evening of the 12th, just before Mardi Gras.

After paying with his person in the company of Françoise, he grows drowsy and soon crosses without realizing it the boundaries of the real. Even as he scrounges about [*grapiller*] distractedly (his words) amid the lady's pubic hair, he lets himself be won over by sleep and dreams: "I suddenly saw a small garden with low, thick trees from which were hanging immense leaves covered with hair." Those botanical images will be abandoned a few moments later for a dreamlike digression through some particularly repulsive regions of entomology (ants, centipedes, moths), after which the dream will rediscover the vegetal mode on which it began and evoke the garden of Bouville: "Behind cactuses and prickly pear trees, the garden's Velléda pointed at its genitals with its finger." At that moment, the dream transgresses the limits of the tolerable: Roquentin begins to scream ("This garden smells of vomit") and wakes up.

The principal interest of the dream is in its structure. It ends with a nested repetition of its starting point. Françoise's genitals (which he is touching) put Roquentin to sleep, those of the statue (which he is dreaming about) wake him up. Between those two instances of female genitals stretches the dream garden, metaphorically induced by the real pubic hair, the hirsute analogue on which the sleeper's fingers rest. This dream garden thus emerges only to lead us back to the genitals from which it came. An equivalence is effected, by way of that circularity, between the (soon to be interdependent) themes of the world of vegetation and the obscenity of female genitals. It is a sufficiently forceful equivalence for Roquentin, when the statue, at the end of the dream, designates its own genitals, to react by naming the garden. A pubic garden? A garden is born of genitals that return to it, reflect themselves in it, and fold back upon themselves therein.

But a second repetition frames the narration of this postcoital dream. "This garden smells of vomit," shouts Roquentin, within the dream, before the genitals indicated by the Velléda. Outside the dream, just before "screwing" the proprietress, he had already been victim of an analogous bout of naseau, a turning of his stomach that was also induced by an odor. His words will be recalled: "I had to screw her, but it was entirely out of politeness." He immediately explains his reticence: "She disgusts me a bit; she is too white, and then she smells like a newborn baby."

There is not a word telling us where this milky newborn — before whose odor Roquentin bridles upon approaching Francoise's genitals — comes from.

Nine days later, on the 21st, inaugurating a precocious spring, Roquentin — who has just passed an unclocked part of his afternoon seated on one of the benches of the Public Garden — abruptly leaves the premises in a gesture of breaking identical to the one through which he had torn himself (in the Rendezvous des Cheminots) from the dream taking place in that same garden. Once again, near the statue of the Velléda, he emits a cry of disgust: "What filth, what filth!" This time, he has just discovered the contingency theorem, whose formulation, it will be recalled, reads: "Every existent being is born without reason, is perpetuated out of weakness, and dies by chance."

The scene (a man by himself seated on a bench in the middle of a provincial public garden) in itself has nothing specifically sexual about it. And the simple fact that Roquentin satisfies his wish to know by raising the veil which, up to that day, had obscured the question of his origins may very well not constitute sufficient reason to authorize its sexualization. And yet the transcription that Roquentin, upon returning to the Hôtel Printania, makes, after the fact, of a scene that in itself had nothing specifically sexual about it resorts with suspicious self-indulgence to the register of the obscene ("There remained a disorderly array of soft, monstrous masses — naked, with a frightening and obscene nakedness") as well as to a whole metaphorics of engendering and birth that leads one to wonder if indeed it is a metaphorics and to what extent it remains one. "I was at last going to surprise existences in the process of being born," he notes.

He did not need anything else. ("My goal is achieved, I know what I wanted to know.") All that he desired was to be present at the engendering of the formula for engendering.

Conception of Conception

As far as the formula itself is concerned, that is, the philosophical content of Roquentin's discovery in the course of his apprenticeship in the Public Garden, it is not difficult to recognize in it, in philosophical garb, one of those infantile sexual theories by means of which, Freud has shown, children attempt to answer the question that a traumatic accident one day brings them to ask: "Where do children come from?" Its transcription, as proposed in his maturity by our loner in Bouville, is not particularly cheerful: "Every existent being," he says, "is born without reason." But it is precisely a question of forging a reason for oneself: if it is true that I did not ask to be born, it is equally true that there is no one to whom I can complain of the fact, because neither did anyone else ask me to be born. No existent being is the cause of any other existent being or, even less, his *raison d'être*. The contingency defining him, in fact, implies that an existent being can never be deduced or engendered from another existent being. Between two existent beings, there can be no other relation than that of contiguity, be it in space or in time.

The doctrinal statement of the theory of contingency, once envisaged as the rationalization of an infantile sexual theory, is thus not fundamentally different from the conception of freedom developed in *L'Etre et le néant*. Not having any cause (being born and existing without reason) is tantamount to being dependent only on oneself and assuming alone the entire responsibility for one's own existence. And yet there is a difference. The lesson of the Bouville Public Garden proposes the depressive version of what, in *Les Mots*, is presented as an almost manically happy orphanhood. For it was in vain that the diminutive Poulou had no cause; it was not he who would complain of it: I lack nothing. "I was orphaned of a father. The son of no one, I was my own cause." Without father and without cause. He thought, in fact, that his mother was his sister, and the results were a delight to behold. Poulou can imagine himself to be his own cause because, in the absence of his father, he is allowed to believe that he is the cause of his cause, the final cause of the existent beings that he needed in order to produce himself. On the other hand, translated in terms of an infantile sexual theory, what Roquentin discovered was that he had no cause, no longer because his father was not there, but because his mother was. In both situations, it will be observed that the mother, by implication, does not enter into account — as Aristotle had already said. He was no longer, like the little angel of the rue Le Goff, the child of a miracle, the darling of the Immaculate Conception, but the offspring of an indifferent propensity to fertility, an anonymous prolificacy, that of soft organisms unable to restrain themselves and allowing themselves to be submerged by their contents. To be without cause meant being necessary, doing without a father. Now it means being contingent, that is, rediscovering oneself beside a mother who lets you know that you are not the cause of her desire.

Sartre recounted that unpleasant experience more than once. When Orestes returns to the premises from which he sprung, he elicits the message that he is not welcome: there is nothing to be done about it. Clytemnestra was more woman than mother. Like Caroline Flaubert. Like the wife of General Aupick. That is why Baudelaire, a genophobe every bit the equal of Roquentin or Bariona, after the verdant paradise of a childhood in which, in his mother's shadow, he felt in his place and "justified," has to undergo, at age six, the traumatic experience known by Roquentin in the Public Garden. When one has a son like me, Sartre comments, one does not remarry. The primal scene is the one from which I am excluded. It signifies to me that I was never taken into account in my own engendering. Ceasing to be the cause of my cause, I lose my reason for being and discover myself as contingent. If it was not I that she wanted, I might well not have been and she, however, wouldn't have missed me. I would have been able not to be there without being missing. To be superfluous, strictly speaking, means not being able to be missed.

Botch-ups

It would be incongruous, Bariona explains to his wife, to reproduce in several reeditions a world so botched up. Why indeed reproduce what is no pleasure to behold? Roquentin turns into the mouthpiece of an analogous aesthetic just after having seen existences, as he says, being born. He is disappointed. "But why, I thought (his is the voice speaking), why so many existences, since they all resemble one another? To what end so many identical trees? So many existences spoiled and obstinately rebegun and spoiled anew?" Sartre's aesthetic would like to be able to ignore perpetually that the work of art has entered, in Walter Benjamin's phrase, the age of its mechanical reproducibility. It is and will remain an aesthetic of scarcity (*copia* in Latin bespeaks at once the abundance of what is copious and the imitation of what is merely a copy): beauty escapes reproduction. If existence is not a very beautiful sight, that is above all, no doubt, because to exist and to reproduce are synonymous.

Roquentin wonders why existence proliferates copies of what is in no way exemplary. At the Ecole Normale, Sartre and his pals had formed the Eugene gang. One might well be sensitive, in Roquentin's comments, to eugenically inspired presuppositions hostile to the reproduction of the deformed. But that is not the case. For the exemplary itself gets lost in its reproduction, and the origin is always in decline in its descendants: the only ones to reproduce themselves, as Roquentin notes, are "beings without origin." The serial multiplication of copies [*exemplaires*] sounds the knell of the exemplary, which was exemplary only because it was unique, and which stops being so as soon as it does not stand as the one and only. There can thus not be, properly speaking, any reproduction of the exemplary. The exemplary aborts in reproducing itself; it aborts from reproducing itself. A privilege of failures, there is no reason to dream that the Eugenes will take reproduction in hand. Existences do not reproduce despite the fact that they are failures but because of it. They reproduce for lack of being and reproduce only their lack of being, their reproducibility: You missed me, honey. At this point, the genetic code does not differ from its parasites: it has nothing to say. One does not leave trees, says Ponge, by treelike ways. Reproduction is but the never-ending return of the botch-up, the proliferation of the deformed, incomplete, unfinished; in reproducing, it does not stop missing what is being reproduced. Like a scratched record, like a stupid ontological stutter, existence repeats that it doesn't succeed in meaning anything. Which Proust, speaking of Flaubert, designated with a terrible expression: the eternal imperfect.

The Overproduction of By-products

In the profuse chaos that the spectacle of the Public Garden presented to a dazed Roquentin, it is not difficult to recognize a prefiguration of what Sartre would later call *series*, in a context in which the class struggle and the bourgeois would take the place of the burgeoning growths of spring. Insofar as it will characterize capitalist overproduction, the series, too, will be a copious horn of plenty spilling out its n + 1 supernumerary and deterritorialized members. We have recently seen Bariona depoliticize his condemnation of populationism. The *Critique de la raison dialectique* follows the same path in reverse: it repoliticizes contingency. It is no longer an eternal attribute of the human condition but a dated effect of the capitalist mode of production, governed by a competitive individualism which has every man feeling superfluous, not managing to consider his own a place others contest — a place constantly called into question by the gaze of others. Part and parcel of the fragmentation of assembly-line work (each doing what anyone could do), the abstract universality of the analytic democracies elicits in every individual the anguishing feeling of being perpetually replaceable or, as Roquentin puts it, superfluous. Interchangeable individuals live amid the risk of losing the place that they occupy, if it indeed be the case that institutionalized unemployment has not already prevented them from having one at all.

Vegetations

> He detests the countryside.
> Simone de Beauvoir, "Jean-Paul Sartre: Strictly Personal"

Gustave, a child of *ennui*, alongside a mother who did not desire him, has the feeling of being something of a mushroom. The Flaubert book also associates the experience of contingency with a thematics of vegetation. The site in which Roquentin receives it is part of the message; the botanical context has already programmed the answer he finds in it. Behind the shelter of its three walls, Bouville defends itself from vegetal insinuations. But in the Public Garden, the enemy has already been introduced within the fortress, contents ready to spill out like those of a Trojan horse.

It was very early that Sartre made of contingency his subject, his characteristic term. The end of *Mémoires d'une jeune fille rangée* and the first chapters of *La Force de l'âge* show how his interest in a concept borrowed from the lexicon of philosophy was gradually supported by an almost panicked obsession with vegetal growth. First there is a poem entitled "L'Arbre," which Sartre wrote when his deferment expired and he was to join his contingent and perform his military service. The existence of plants, recalls Simone de Beauvoir, "through its vain proliferation, indicated contingency" ("as in *La Nausée* later on," she stipulates). Then, the following year (1931), there is the "Factum sur la contingence," composed in Le Havre where Sartre was at the time teaching philosophy. Simone de Beauvoir was doing the same in Marseille. He tells her, in a letter intent on being perceived as a turning point, the circumstances that triggered the composition of the text, which is generally considered to be the germinal core of *La Nausée*: "I have been to see a tree," he writes her. "It was in Burgos that I understood what a cathedral is, and in Le Havre, what a tree is."

It will be recalled that in *L'Etre et le néant*, in order to contrast it with organs used to grip, Sartre said that a sexual organ could be only a manifestation of "vegetative" life. Aristotle had already defined vegetal life as the immobile proliferation of an existent entity pullulating without reason. The vegetal reproduces itself, and that's all it does. To vegetate and to reproduce oneself: strictly speaking, there is not the slightest difference. To reproduce oneself (a reflexive verb) is not to make a child (a transitive verb), but to proliferate (an intransitive verb). But even proliferating is too active; the Sartrean verb is to pullulate [*pulluler*]. And that is what sexual difference comes to put a stop to by allowing the male side to leave the bed and engage in politics. (Remember, comrade, that you are not dust: the P.C. System resists the molecular disorder of serial atomization.) But whereas man, by committing himself, is removed from the indifferent reproduction of copies of existent entities, woman, plugged into a matrix that proliferates even without seed, vegetates in a burgeoning more archaic than sexual difference. The Public Garden of Bouville, an indifferent matrix engendering without desire, out of lassitude, is the site of what might be defined as a femininity prior to sexual difference, a femininity that would be but the unleashing of material causation: it misses everything, but lacks nothing.

Primaveras

The importance of the vegetal context is reinforced, moreover, by the date of the Public Garden scene, which places it, too, under the auspices of Flora. Everything is arranged for us to know that we are being invited to the rite of spring. I shall not insist on the fact that Roquentin himself lives in the Hôtel Printania: he has lived there for more than a single day. But his diary notes insistently on that day that in the street, "faces are springlike," that women have taken out "their attire from last spring." Even the men, we learn, "smile at one another every spring." All these clues are released within a space of ten short lines. And a few pages later, it will be Roquentin's turn to smile and mock the "prodigious springtimes" described in books. Moreover, the author's statement on the back cover removes any uncertainty on the issue: "On the first day of spring," it reads, "Roquentin understands the meaning of his adventure: Nausea is Existence revealing itself — and it is not a pretty sight, Existence." The fact is significant, it goes without saying, only because a brief reconstruction of Roquentin's calendar elicits the gravest suspicions as to the verisimilitude of these unambiguous indications. It is, in fact, on 21 March that spring normally begins. And it is on 21 February that Roquentin discovers the key to his existence.

That slip, attributable to Sartre rather than Roquentin, is plainly a function of constraints linked to the thematics of birth which constitute the barely veiled content of the scene in its entirety. This might be confirmed, if need be, by the parallel with another singularly premature spring, which — by "miracle" and not "slip-up" — erupts in the middle of *Bariona* and disrupts the course of events. The play, as we have seen, takes place in winter, but it is a winter in the middle of which the birth of Christ insinuates an anachronistically springlike insertion. A traveler passing across the stage takes the trouble to inform a few shepherds and the audience of that fact: "There was cracking and murmuring and rustling all over, to my right, to my left, in front of me, behind me; it was as though nature had chosen these deserted and icy plains to accord herself, all alone, in the course of a winter's night, the magnificent feast of spring."

The same association between birth and spring will be found again in *L'âge de raison*. Marcelle is pregnant. At first it disgusted her that Mathieu should have thus "forgotten" himself inside her. But by now she is beginning to get used to it. "It was life," she told herself, "like the sticky blossomings of spring, it was no more repulsive than the thin gelatinous layer, reddish and fragrant, covering over buds." The spring: the season whose gelatinous thaw follows sterile winter.

1917

ORESTES: The seventeenth, I believe, was broken.

Sartre, *Les Mouches*

On the subject of sublimation, Laplanche recalls that the question "Where do children come from?" is not so much, on the part of the young subject whom it haunts, an inquiry concerning his own origin as the expression of a fear linked to the fact that — with another child threatening to appear — he must prepare himself for facing up to the traumatic necessity of sharing his mother's affection. The terms used by Laplanche are exactly the same as those to which Sartre resorts in describing serial production: "How could one manufacture others on the same model? Am I not unique?" In the same vein, Roquentin confronts the ungenerous matrix out of which his existential rivals endlessly swarm. If the loner by himself feels superfluous, it is because he might not be alone. Existences being born without reason, there is, in fact, no reason why still more would not be born.

Sartre bemused himself with fantasies of sister-incest. But he always depicted fraternity in colors of somber jealousy. At the beginning of *Le Diable et le bon dieu*, Goetz comes on stage by way of the death of Conrad, the brother whom he has had (or allowed to be) killed: "The glorious title of fratricide I owe only to my merits." In *Les Séquestrés d'Altona*, the relations of Frantz and Werner, von Gerlach's two sons, are also plainly worse than those between Frantz and his sister Leni, but also than those between Orestes and Electra in *Les Mouches* or Boris and Ivich in *Les Chemins de la liberté*. The rivalry begins when two men cohabit with a single woman. One might also recall the Flaubertological novelty claimed by Sartre for *L'Idiot de la famille*. He deemed himself the first to have "insisted on that aspect of the relation between the two brothers," Gustave's devouring jealousy of Achille. It should be mentioned, moreover, that during the first twelve years of his life, Sartre had — if we can accept literally the account in *Les Mots* — a sister with whom to share his dreams of chaste incest: his mother.

Where do children come from? Until age twelve — that is, until 1917, little Poulou had probably never asked the question. "In my bedroom, a girl's bed was installed. The girl slept by herself and awoke chastely; I was still asleep when she ran to take her 'tub' in the bathroom; she return completely dressed: how could I be born from her?" But it was precisely in 1917 that she began sleeping away from home, left her son's room for the bed of M. Mancy, the naval engineer whom she married and wasted no time in following to La Rochelle, where the little boy, heartbroken, joined them. He had lost his place. Felt superfluous. Lonely because he was no longer alone. And if another one were to show up? "Where do children come from?" The veil that once covered Anne-Marie when she emerged from the bathroom was brutally torn. "I understood. I *saw*." Existence is not a pretty sight. And neither am I, for that matter, I who am only its offspring. You missed me, mom. And all that remains for me is to be ugly in beauty.

It was in 1917, in fact, that Sartre discovered that since his mother loved another, he must be ugly. It is enough to count the years. "One day — I was seven years old — my grandfather couldn't take it anymore," he writes in *Les Mots*. There follows the scene at the barber's, who snips off the curls of the veil of hair through which the features of the little angel were filtered. Upon his return, Anne-Marie (who had not been forewarned) locked herself in her room to cry. She "was good enough," continues Sartre, "to conceal from me the cause of her chagrin. I learned it only later, brutally, when I was twelve." For five years, then, Sartre succeeded in not seeing his ugliness, since that is what was at stake in the image of himself reflected back to him by the maternal mirror. His was still the beauty that comes from being the only one. But that beauty does not survive the existential divide, the partition of the mother, the threats of parturition.

1917 bis

Another five years pass and Sartre (returned to Paris) publishes in a student journal the beginning of a novel in which he relates his season in hell. "Jésus la Chouette" can in effect be considered Sartre's *Aden-Arabie*, a kind of *La Rochelle-Charente-Maritime* by someone who went there and came back. This young man's narrative begins *in medias res*: "In 1917, as a result of circumstances not to be related here, my parents decided to send me to the lycée of La Rochelle." "The thought of living in the intimacy of persons unknown," the young narrator confesses a little further on, "caused me shame and provoked in me, when I thought of it, veritable nervous indispositions." His parents, in fact, not satisfied with sending him to the La Rochelle lycée, place him as a boarder with a professor whose house is named, melancholically, "Remember" [in English]. At the time I was twelve, specifies the narrator, who did not have the same age as his author (three years younger, he was only twelve), but already that of Roquentin.

The date 1917 appears twice in *La Nausée*. The first time is on 2 February, when Roquentin listens, in the Rendez-vous des cheminots, to the recording of his life, "Some of These Days." He has just missed the proprietress. And to compensate him for the pleasures he will not have (or for the melancholies he will not purge), he asks the ragtime song to let him suffer in rhythm. While listening he thinks back, and the memoir of the first time comes back to him.

There were American soldiers, and they whistled the melody in 1917 in the streets of La Rochelle. Perhaps the soldiers were each thinking of someone in particular who was not there to hear them. For they undoubtedly knew the words of the song even if they were not singing them. But Roquentin, who, moreover, may not have known English, did not hear them that first time. Before the Negress began to sing it, he didn't know what the song was saying. But then what was he doing in the streets of La Rochelle that year? Had he come to pay a visit to the boarder of the Villa "Remember''? Or to little Sartre, Mme. Mancy's son? Roquentin is not very talkative on the subject of his mother and whatever loves the woman she was may have entertained. But in the meanwhile, at the same place and date, we find Sartre moping melancholically at the prospect of no longer being the man in the life of the woman he regarded as his own.

One is not born ugly; one becomes it. I am thus no more ugly than I would be a Jew, a woman, or a café waiter. Ugliness, in fact, according to L'Etre et le néant, is a form of bad-faith behavior identical to any other. It is its sullen variety: since you don't love me, I won't be handsome. In 1917, in order to punish his mother for having allowed the gaze of an other to insinuate itself between them, Sartre decides to be a toad. He had just caught a glimpse of the fact, now that Anne-Marie was sleeping in a different room, that existence is not a very pretty sight. But it was at the same time, on precisely the same date, that he discovered avenging (or reparatory) beauty. At the very moment that his mother's absence is felt, after she abandons him, alone and ugly, in a provincial city, he hears ''Some of These Days,'' an occasional melody that announces to the missing person that one day someone might be missed by her. Perdita's song is Sartre's Siren Song, the equivalent for him of what "You are a thief" would be for Genet: he understands his vocation. One day it will be he who will be missed by his mother.

UGLINESS. Roquentin is harried by his own, of which he has heard others speak but which he does not manage to feel or perceive upon looking in a mirror. It is 2 February ("Friday"). He questions his face: "I can't even decide if it is handsome or ugly. I think it's ugly, because I've been told so. But it doesn't strike me." The previous day ("Thursday afternoon," the 1st), he had, for the first time, offered some information concerning the Marquis de Rollebon. The passage begins: "M. de Rollebon was quite ugly." As for Mathieu in L'Age de raison, if he takes Ivich to the Gauguin exhibition, it is because he wanted "to show her beautiful paintings, beautiful films, beautiful objects because he himself was without beauty." "And yet he would not have wanted to be handsome," we read immediately after. Johanna, in Les Séquestrés d'Altona, would know how difficult it is to be beautiful, above all in the vicinity of a director of shipyards.

Ugliness being the best-shared thing in the world, it appears every time something is shared. It was in 1917 that Sartre had to share his mother. Until then, they formed a single unit, united in the seamless unity of what the Baudelaire study would call "the unanimous life of the couple that he formed with his mother." And then, from one day to the next, they became two and even three and — who knows? — soon maybe even more. They were together and now found themselves side by side. He was with her; he is now beside her. From the day she was shared, he lost her (that second verb being perhaps more active than it seems).

Gestaltists regularly take melody as the example of what they understand by an indissoluble synthetic totality. Sartre himself does the same in *La Transcendance de l'Ego*. Melody, he writes, "actually and concretely unanalyzable," needs no support in order to sustain itself, no string to hold its notes together and ensure its unity. That is exactly the kind of reflection that "Some of These Days," in *La Nausée*, elicits from Roquentin. Every time he listens to or thinks about it, he cannot help marveling at the manner in which it frees itself from its support, the way in which it rests on nothing other than itself and is a function only of itself. It has nothing in common, more specifically, with the phonograph or the record which, as contingent modes of fragile substance, can very well suffer division (scratches, breaks, interruptions) without such accidents having the slightest effect on the resplendently indifferent entity which, above and behind them, does not exist, because it "is." Delivered of the sin of existing, a melody is not guilty; it literally escapes the spatiality of its score, just as, at the end of *L'Imaginaire*, the Seventh Symphony is situated "out of reach": Furtwängler's collapse in the course of its performance (on 17 November 1938) does not risk turning it into an unfinished symphony. Beauty, we have seen, does not tolerate reproduction(s). What is exemplary is a singular without plural. But that is, above all, because it cannot be divided. A beautiful woman would thus be a woman who is not shared (or divided) [*qui ne se partage pas*]. Such does not exist, says Sartre, but one can always imagine it.

Musical beauty is not alone in being indivisible. It is sculpture, Giacometti's in particular, that is described in identical terms in "La recherche de l'absolu." Sculpture proposes, in effect, to restore the "indissoluble unity" constituting man by means of "the infinite divisibility" of matter. A Giacometti sculpture is a piece of space that has escaped the Cartesian curse of divisibility, a victory won by space against its own divisibility. The previous year, 1946, Sartre had already congratulated for an analogous performance the American sculptor David Hare, who produced, he said, things "without parts." "There are no details. Hare makes indivisible sculptures."

1917 ter

The second occurrence in *La Nausée* of the fatal date, 1917, is the work of the Self-Taught Man, who refers to it on the 21st, in the course of a lunch with

Roquentin, to whom he explains the conditions under which he was converted to humanism. "At the end of 1917," he says, "I was taken prisoner." Prisoner of war, to be sure; it was a military experience. The Self-Taught Man was a soldier when it took place, just as it was soldiers who that same year were whistling "Some of These Days" in the streets of La Rochelle. I shall return to that.

In a certain sense, this episode in the life of the Self-Taught Man can be considered the exact antithesis of the contemporaneous episode of Roquentin's first hearing of "Some of These Days." The Self-Taught Man discovers (or rediscovers) what Roquentin has been mourning over ever since the day he heard his song. The prison camp affords him what the ragtime song takes away from Roquentin: a certain experience of communion, community, being together. Ever since his stay in captivity, he confesses to his guest, he no longer ever feels lonely. The situation is the opposite for Roquentin, who, ever since he has known the song, has decided to be a loner. With the same obstinacy that the Self-Taught Man dreams of communing and communicating, Roquentin resists contacts, refuses to share absolutely anything with anyone, is desirous of confiding nothing. Pitted against the social commitment of him who wants to be a man among men, we thus find the aesthetic commitment of him who has decided to cleanse himself of the sin of existing — to be together, or not to be. But those two options are perhaps not incompatible, and there is perhaps no reason to consider them opposites.

At the end of *Les Mots*, Sartre recounts the experience of being let out of the lycée at the end of the day. He was still in Paris, registered in the fifth form at Henri IV. When the bell was heard, he took off with his friends to play on the sidewalk of the place du Panthéon. "A man among men," he says, he freed himself amid the crowd of his fellow students of what he calls, once again, the "sin of existing." For the sin of existing being the morose pleasure of solitary bouts of sadness, there are but two ways of putting an end to it: renouncing (in beauty) existence or renouncing (in crowds) solitude. Evoking those group pleasures, Sartre writes: "Dry, hard, and happy, I felt myself made of steel." Those are the words Roquentin used to describe purifying melody: "thin and firm," he says, of "inflexible rigor," a "band of steel" like the little band of little men taking their time to return home.

Beyond their opposition, aesthetics and politics, beauty and commitment respond to a common inspiration that neutralizes a large part of their quarrel. Exactly as "Some of These Days" did for Roquentin, the experience of captivity would constitute for the Self-Taught Man the experience of a certain indivisibility. For like the melody, being-together also escaped fragmentation. "I felt myself," he says, "as no more than one with the men surrounding me." The unity of a group threatened by defeat and dispersion is restored: together they resist division. The melody's unity accrues to it from its uniqueness, the camp's, from its constitution as a group. But in each case, 1917 marks the appearance of an unanalyzable synthetic totality.

A supplementary element further augments the overdetermination of this date. For as every reader of Sartre knows, 1917 is not only the year of his mother's remarriage and his subsequent exile in La Rochelle; it is also that in which M. Serguine (Ivich and Boris's father) was obliged, on account of a revolution, to pack his bags and leave Moscow. The experience of solitude and serial dereliction (La Rochelle, 1917) thus turns out to be rigorously contemporaneous with its antithesis, the experience of being-together (Saint Petersburg, 1917). But Sartre did not realize it: the first concealed the second from him, and he remained until the following war (that of 1940) committed to the melancholic positions of Roquentin. He would have to have his turn, like the Self-Taught Man, in a prison camp in order to discover the communitarian solution. But at this point we can understand how deeply out of place he felt in 1917; for his place was in Moscow and he was in La Rochelle where he didn't know it.

Didn't he know it? Carried away by a somewhat hagiographical confession, Sartre would justify (in one of the interviews in *On a raison de se révolter*) the conflict that had pitted him against his stepfather by invoking his precocious Marxism-Leninism. "In 1917, I was twelve. . . . I was for the Russian Revolution." He seemed to have completely forgotten in 1972 that the target of his youthful insurrection, the director of the shipyards of La Rochelle, happened also to be his mother's husband.

When 1917 is mentioned in *L'Etre et le néant*, it is still under the aegis of Roquentin and "Some of These Days." Sartre evokes in that book ("Lafayette, here we come!") the entry of the United States into the First World War, an event thanks to which a few nostalgic sailors were able to whistle in the streets of La Rochelle a song from back home.

It was also in 1917 that Sartre, after moving, took up the piano. He told Contat that he played operetta scores. And sometimes played four-hand pieces with his mother. Might they have played "Some of These Days" together? But it may be wondered who, in that case, would have sung "You'll miss me, honey" to whom.

1940: From the Superfluous Man to the Man Among Men

> Around 1940, I still believed in Santa Claus.
> Sartre to Madeleine Chapsal, "Les Ecrivains en personne,"
> *Situations,* IX

In Shanghai (but perhaps it was in Hanoi or Saigon), Roquentin, in the office of Mercier, who had just asked him to accompany him to Bengal, gazed at a Khmer statue. Nothing seemed to be right. "All of a sudden, I woke up from a sleep that had lasted six years." He was, like Orestes, a man of rapid decisions.

The adventure was over, and two days later he would embark for Marseille, from which he would leave for Bouville, where the marquis's papers were awaiting him. It was around 1928. Four years later, the same scene is repeated. This time it is at Bouville, and Roquentin drops the marquis as abruptly as he had left Indochina. "Today," he notes, "I wake up in the presence of a pad of white paper." There is a lot of awakening in *La Nausee*. But it is not always euphoric.

On 12 February, Roquentin (who has dozed off beside the proprietress) dreams of a garden, shouts, "This garden smells of vomit," and wakes up. In the Public Garden where (as he digests the lunch to which he was treated by the Self-Taught Man) Roquentin's perception is atomized into pullulating sensations ("flickerings, filtered tremors, confetti of light"), he lets himself go so far as to imagine the breasts of a young woman, glimpsed in the restaurant, which caress each other in the lace of her bodice, and all of a sudden: "I cried out and found myself with my eyes wide open." Later on, in the café in Paris where he takes refuge after Anny's departure, he falls asleep, dreams of Bouville besieged by vegetation that has already established a beachhead in the city, inside the trellis of the Public Garden, and, once again: "What a horror! I wake up with a start."

One recalls the unfinished stories that little Poulou used to tell his mother before falling asleep. The narratives of his maturity would change both their destination and their addressee. I, who used to tell her everything that passed through my head, since she betrayed me, can't even tell her *that*. She has even taken away from me the possibility of telling her that I can't tell her everything. To be man, then, the first step is to sulk. Mother, I have nothing to tell you; let me speak to my comrades. Moreover, I don't even feel like sleeping or keeping myself suspended. What I want, as Husserl, Orestes, Goetz, and Sartre say, is to be a man from somewhere, "a man among men." To make for myself at their side the place I no longer have at yours. In 1940, Sartre undertood that if in order to sleep it is good to speak to his mother, in order to wake up it is preferable to address oneself to men. The war put an end to the clinical narratology of hypnagogic storytelling.

If we can believe the version that he himself broadcast rather generously, Sartre would have more or less continued to slumber and dream until 1940. That was the year in which the frontier that his philosophical works had traced between the real and the imaginary would finally traverse his life, which it cut in two. Before 1940, he was living in the unreal; starting in 1940, he began to perceive. "The war opened my eyes," he says in *On a raison de se révolter*. And to Jacqueline Piatier, who questioned him after the publication of *Les Mots*: "I had been dreaming my life for nearly forty years. What I was missing was a sense of reality." The narrative of *Les Mots*, in effect, retraces the genesis of a writer who does not survive the war of 1940. Like the celebrated self-denying pipe painted by Magritte, the self-critical portrait denies that it is that of its author:

this is not Jean-Paul Sartre. "I" is an Other [*Je est un autre*]. Without donning any gloves, the author of *Les Mots* beats the breast of that of *La Nausée*, with whom, he insists, he no longer has anything in common.

The cleric's perversion consists in a certain precession of signs, which take the place of the reality they announce. In the beginning he puts the Word, which he places before everything else and which he prefers to everything else. "I loved only words," says the author of *Les Mots*. The rest follows: "I was of the Church. I confused things with their names, which is to believe. I was blind to facts. For as long as it lasted, I considered myself set. At the age of thirty, I brought off the master coup of writing *La Nausée*, etc., etc." But at forty, I woke up. The force of things (that is, the war) returned signs, images, and literature to their place, which is second. History's lesson stipulates that *Les Mots* began poorly. It was a false start because it failed to separate words from things. In the beginning should have been action. *Qu'est-ce que la littérature?* would put everything in its proper place, calling language back to the realist's respect and to the humility appropriate to it. Sartre in that work defines the "verbal moment" as a "secondary structure" of our undertakings.

1. The statement of that sequence, we have already seen, is situated out of phase with the circumstances of its utterance. The affirmation of the primacy of the real is, in fact, presented as belated. In order to be brought about, it needs to say that it comes after the affirmation it corrects, the primacy of the secondary. In order to attain that first position, it was necessary that it not be the first position that the real occupied: in the beginning was the imaginary usurper.

2. But it is not clear that Sartre's guilt-laden biography should be accepted. It is not true, in particular, if we restrict ourselves to his published texts, that Sartre ever defended a position plainly implying the primacy of the imaginary and the derivation of the real. On the contrary: he always spoke in favor of perception. We have seen, for instance, how the arrangement of his first book, *L'Imagination*, implied that the real was primal: "I am looking at this blank sheet of paper," he began, and it was only subsequently that he turned his head away. Imagination, as the positional consciousness of absence, presupposes the presence of what it negates. And yet, starting in 1940 (which is the date he gives and which can be retained if only for its symbolic value), Sartre forgets it and begins regularly accusing himself of errors he did not commit: formerly, he says, I accorded a privilege to the imaginary. As though he did not see that the real was already occupying the place he wants to give it. He managed to conceive of the real in terms alternately Husserlian, Heideggerian, Hegelian, Marxist, or Maoist. But those shifts in opinion regarding it always left unchanged the unmoving position he accorded it right from the beginning. He thought he was dreaming but had simply failed to realize that he was not asleep. He imagined he was imagining, dreamed he was dreaming; his perception was not *index sui*. Like Roquentin awaking at Bouville from his awakening in Saigon, Sartre wakes up

at Trèves, a prisoner of war, from Roquentin awakening in Bouville. The break is but the repetition of what it is breaking with, a variation and not a change. The theme is never threatened. The war opened my eyes. But nobody had noticed that he was keeping them closed. The uncertainty that comes from Sartre's awakenings will always be dependent, as Caillois observed, on the fact that he does not realize that he is not asleep. He had forgotten to fall asleep. Imaginary dreams are, in fact, the most tenacious; one never stops not waking up from them.

3. Sartre's captivity brings us back to the vicinity of *Bariona*. At the beginning of *La Force des choses*, Simone de Beauvoir evokes the transformation her companion had undergone in his absence:

> His experience as a prisoner had marked him deeply: it taught him solidarity. Far from feeling oppressed, he participated in the gaiety of communal life. He detested privileges, his pride demanding of him that he conquer his place on earth through his own strengths. Lost in the mass, a number among others, he experienced an immense satisfaction in succeeding (having started from zero) in his undertakings. He made friendships, imposed his ideas, organized collective actions, mobilized the entire camp to produce and applaud at Christmas the play he had written against the Germans, *Bariona*. The rigors and warmth of comradeship loosened the contradictions of his antihumanism.

Sartre's first stay in Germany had been the occasion of a discovery of the real. His second stay would bring him an identical revelation, with the nuance that the real of 1940 was no longer, as in 1933, the correlate of perceptual intentionality (this cocktail, this tree). This time, it was an anthropological real, at once historical, social, and political. Along with the transcendence of the Husserlian real, there was now added, as in the Durkheimian definition of a social fact, its coercive character. The second section of *Les Mots* might have been called *Les Choses* in 1933; in 1940, it would have been called *Les Hommes*. "I have been to see a tree," Sartre had written to Simone de Beauvoir at the time of his "Factum sur la contingence." It was, in fact, entirely up to him. Seven years later, things were different. "One day in September 1939," he told Contat, "I received a mobilization call-up, and I was obliged to go to the Nancy barracks to join guys whom I didn't know and who were mobilized like myself." "I was even made a prisoner," he says elsewhere, "a fate which I nevertheless did my best to escape." Berlin and Trèves are two German cities. But between the French Institute and Stalag XII D, there is, all the same, a great difference: one is accepted to the latter without applying. Connections don't help. For Sartre could very well not have paid the chestnut tree in Le Havre the visit that was to decide so many things. He could also, without any risks, not have undertaken the initiatives necessary for his appointment to Berlin. But the reality of a war is a function of the fact that one cannot in any manner escape the risks it brings. Whether one wants to or not, one submits to it. "There is where," he continues,

"I passed from individualism and the prewar individual to the social, and to socialism. That is the true turning point in my life: before and after. Before, it led me to works like *La Nausée*, and after, it slowly brought me to *Critique de la raison dialectique.*"

Before and after. Blanchot, in *Le Livre à venir*, proposes this formula as a characterization of realist narration: "Something took place that was lived and subsequently retold." Sartre's conversion to realism (to perception), a conversion he attributed to his experience of the war, had among other consequences for him the project of recounting it, the project of saying in a novel what had happened and what he had lived — of describing, then, the realist conversion to which we owe the novel in which its story is told. *Les Chemins de la liberté* thus proposes to follow the war, in all senses of the word. Written — and modeled — after the war, it is intent on faithfully retracing what transpired, without either straying unduly from the facts or letting too much time elapse. The *Chemins* propose to retrace the circumstances under which their author came to understand where they were leading. And yet, despite these intentions and these resolutions, what happened and what Sartre lived, we know, would not be immediately recounted. The event that had consigned the narration to its secondary place ends up, within the narration, by being absent from its place. *Les Chemins de la liberté* stop short before having caught up with their source.

The pages of *La Dernière Chance* that were published by Sartre in *Les Temps modernes* under the title "Drôle d'amitié" do indeed take place in a prison camp, but nothing in its evocation recalls the virtual euphoria that would be the prime characteristic of the tales Sartre told of his own captivity. He talked a good deal of his friendship (his *drôle d'amitié?*) with the priests in the camp (those whom Brunet, at the end of *La Mort dans l'âme*, referred to mockingly as *curetons*); he also spoke of the debates he had with them about the Immaculate Conception. But we don't know whether there were also Communists among his companions in misfortune, nor whether he spoke with them of the problems caused them by the Hitler-Stalin pact. It is doubtful, moreover, that either Brunet or Vicarios (who was not a "young vicar") would have found within himself the resources to write a Christmas play.

Before, after. The novel does not tell subsequently what the author had first lived. But that is perhaps because the author, imagining what a realist conversion would be before living it, had in fact already recounted it. On 21 February 1932, in a restaurant in Bouville, the Self-Taught Man narrates for Roquentin the story of his captivity. "At the end of 1917," he says, "I was taken prisoner." The Self-Taught Man does not talk of either Santa Claus or the Immaculate Conception, but the end-of-the-year holidays, which were imminent, are not unrelated to the odor of religiosity with which his story seems impregnated. "When it rained," he continues, "they made us enter a huge wooden hangar, where about two hundred of us pressed against one another in almost total darkness." Something happened, says Blanchot, that someone has lived and subsequently recounted. Here, it is the opposite: one first recounts something which subsequently (three years after having been published, eight years after having been recounted, twenty-three years after the date on which it is said to have taken place) begins to take place. Before, after? The narrative announces the event which was to put it in its place, which is second. The priority of the real is prefaced by its own narration, broached by the anteriority of its fiction. The novel precedes the real that it was intent on following, and the real is, as a result, no longer anything but the copy of the novel with which it wanted to break. The break with *La Nausée* is inscribed within *La Nausée*. The real, which was to take precedence over its reproduction, is thus contained and programmed by that very reproduction. In the beginning, once again, was the word which said that in the beginning was action.

Together

> The best exemplification of the "we" may be furnished to us by a member of a theater audience.
>
> Sartre, *L'Etre et le néant*

Sartre often spoke of his stay in the Stalag. And he always did so in terms evocative of the rediscovery of a former love. "The duration of the war, and above all that of my captivity in Germany," he says in *On a raison de se révolter*, "were the occasion of a lasting immersion in the masses, from which I believed myself distanced, and which I had in fact never left." The most famous of these evocations (and the only one to figure in a work written by Sartre) concludes the passage in *Les Mots* in which he relates the quasi-clandestine escapades in moviegoing on which he dragged his still virginal young mother on rainy days. He has just described the screen with its disconnected shadows, its striped landscapes, and, all around him, the acid odor of invisible bodies clearing their throats. It was "in the egalitarian discomfort of neighborhood movie houses," he says in summary, that I learned to adore crowds, and he continues: "I have seen all kinds, but I never rediscovered that bareness, that obscure awareness of the danger of being a man except in 1940, in Stalag XII D."

It will be noted:

1. that in the Self-Taught Man's account, it was also when it rained that the camp authorities parked the prisoners in a hangar. Rain is, in fact, a good catalyst for sociability: there is humility in the air. And *La Nausée*'s last sentence, as Nizan had seen, thus opens the door to every communitarian hope: "Tomorrow rain will fall on Bouville."

2. that, furthermore, these two experiences of crowds — the one coming to

an end for Sartre in 1917 (since it was in Paris that he plunged into them, with his mother at his side; in La Rochelle, it is known, he would see operettas at the Municipal Theater) and the one beginning for the Self-Taught Man in 1917 — have in common the fact, which is undoubtedly also their enabling condition, that they occur in places which have been darkened in preparation.

3. that Sartre's experience in 1940, that of the Stalag, can be considered as the synthesis of what he had lost in 1917 and what the Self-Taught Man had discovered that same year. Like the latter, he was prisoner of war, a situation which undoubtedly led him to know an "egalitarian discomfort" utterly worthy of that of the neighborhood movie houses of yore. Moreover, for lack of movies, the most significant event of his captivity was to be the initiation of his career as a playwright: it was there, for the Christmas holiday of 1940, that he wrote *Bariona*, his first work for the theater.

The pages of *L'Etre et le néant* devoted to "being-with," *Mitsein*, the experience of the "we," come at the end of the most important section of the work, the one describing the different modalities of the relationship that a subject can experience with his fellow creature. That conclusion presents the singularity of providing an escape from the conflictual impasses described, for two hundred pages, throughout the section. Being-with has as its effective correlative a version of the Other with whom I enter into an experience of community and not rivalry. The competition between solitudes gives way to a kind of ontological solidarity. In being-together, for the first time, the presence of the Other is no longer that of a gaze.

The well-known descriptions of the Other's gaze (of the appearance of the Other as a gaze which dispossesses me) begin with a scene quite close to the no less well-known one during which Roquentin, on 21 February, had undergone the experience of the contingency of his existence: "I am in a public garden." There are, to begin with, myself and things (a lawn, chairs). Whereupon the Other appears. Immediately, through the mere fact of his presence, I cease being the center of the scene. His appearance has disintegrated the relations I had worked out between myself and things (the statue, the chestnut trees, he says this time). Up until now, I had seen those things from my point of view. But now that experience, which was entirely positive, takes a negative turn: I don't see them from the perspective of the Other. They offer to the Other a point of view that they refuse me, through which they escape me. They suddenly have something to conceal from me: the appearance of the Other (a stepfather, for instance) "has robbed me of the world." I discover at the same time that I am no longer in my place in a world no longer mine: I am superfluous, ugly, artificial, and contingent.

A few pages later, *L'Etre et le néant* proposes another example of the same phenomenon: that of the voyeur, his eye riveted to the keyhole. His gaze, solitary by vocation, is desirous of seeing without being seen, without being seen seeing.

Whence, precisely, his irritation when a creaking of the floor reminds him that he is visible and that, perhaps, behind another door another voyeur is spying on him. He, too, experiences himself as superfluous, ugly, contingent, and so on.

In both cases, the irruption of the Other does not culminate in his integration into a first-person plural: it merely elicits a conflictual multiplication of particulars. Several people want at the same time to be first. Several subjects all want to be unique. And if the theater constitutes the "best exemplification of the 'we,'" it is precisely because it puts an end to such situations. it is, in effect, an architectural and institutional apparatus that suspends the gaze of the Other. Instead of fighting to determine which of us will look at the Other, who will be seen and who will be the seer, we together look at the same thing. The voyeur is a loner. The spectator of a theatrical performance spontaneously becomes, on the contrary, a "cospectator." Sartre evokes in illustration the "unacknowledged discomfort that grips us in a half-empty theater." The texts reassembled in *Pour un théâtre de situations* deduce from that eidetic definition (the spectator "can look but will never be looked at") a certain number of practical recommendations regarding staging. The show must never move beyond the limits of the stage. Sartre considers — in order to condemn it — Gémier's aberration, in a production of *The Taming of the Shrew*, of introducing a walkway allowing the actors to move freely between the stage and the auditorium. More generally, he condemns all forms of "direct address to the public," for such a technique risks destroying in the audience the feeling of being-together by introducing the gaze of the Other. That, in fact, is why the lights must go out in order for the show to begin; I am with others as soon as I escape from their gaze. In putting an end to individualizing competition, the dark harbors the first experiences of the group in fusion. *Fiat nox: Huis clos*, precisely, would illustrate on stage the impossibility of being-together in a world in which, for lack of light switches, there would be no way to escape the Other's gaze. Lucifer's house rules forbid any blackouts: Hell is other people without interruption.

Sartre's feelings about the theater as such, however, have not always been so positive. Thus, for example, the passage in *Les Mots* containing the encomium on "darkened auditoriums," the one ending with the evocation of Stalag XII D, simultaneously issues an indictment, devoid of all sympathy, of the institution of the theater. In relation to *L'Etre et le néant*, in which the theater had been proposed as the primordial example of the experience of being-together, the switch is complete, since the theater is now accused of being the one place where the gaze of the Other triumphs: the spectators attend in order to offer themselves up as spectacle. The high point of that middle-class ceremony is no longer the turning off of the lights but, quite to the contrary, intermission, when the lights come back on and the tiered seating arrangement offers its beneficiaries an inverted view of the social ladder. "Egalitarian discomfort" is indeed one of the principal trump cards of the movies, "a commoners' art." For the same reason that its "inegalitarian comfort" constitutes a black mark (the blackest, an inexpiable blemish) retained against the theater.

Sartre manifested his disdain for the bourgeoisie by offering it, every three or four years, a play that the proletariat disdained to attend. The attack on the theater conducted in *Les Mots* and in several texts of *Pour un théâtre de situations* is strictly political: the theater should be a popular art form, but it is middle class. *L'Etre et le néant*, moreover, had already described in terms of class opposition the incompatible experiences of being-with and the gaze of the Other. Wherever he is, in a hotel or a public garden, in Paris or Bouville, a man on his own (a man depressed by the competition of others) is never in his place since an Other, he discovers, has always already been occupying it and taking it from him: he is everywhere a stranger. Solitude, Singularity, Strangeness: the life of the bourgeoisie. Victim of his competitive anarchism, which makes of his fellowman his enemy, the bourgeois by definition cannot accede to any form of the "we"-experience. Even class consciousness is refused him. He cannot escape the economy of scarcity induced by the Other's gaze. He lives under the rule of him-or-me. The proletarian, on the other hand, is alone in being able to say: he and I. For being-together means, above all, sharing objectives which exist only because they are common. As inevitably as members of the bourgeoisie face off in disputing the present (him or me), workers, side by side, share the expectation of a future that unites them (he and I). As long as there is hope, there is a proletariat. It faces the future united, as in the theater or a vehicle of mass transportation. Everyone in the same direction: forward.

In *L'Etre et le néant*, the theater was evoked as one of the modalities offered by the arts of spectacle. Because it was not yet set off against the movies, it constituted a rare enclave within which the bourgeoisie could periodically escape from its congenital curse (imposed on it by its class position), a place where it could experience for itself (aesthetically if not politically) a certain experience of being-together. One is never alone where one is in one's place, where one feels at home. It is consequently enough for the stranger or loner to enter into a theater for him to lose his singularity by becoming a co-spectator. But in *Les Mots*, precisely because it is contrasted with the movies, theater, instead of being the exception, becomes the exhibition par excellence of bourgeois sociability — no longer the place where one withdraws from it but, rather, where one renews one's subscription to it.

Men Without Women

Simone de Beauvoir has shown that there is no feminine society.

Sartre, *Saint Genet*

The antitheatrical indictment in *Les Mots* opens majestically with a masculine plural which, right up to the peroration, will maintain its hold over the incriminated spectacle. *"Bourgeois* males of the last century," it begins, "never forgot their first night out at the theater." The accusations soon become more specificity, but without undergoing the slightest change of gender in the process: "On both my late father and my grandfather, habitués of the second balcony, social hierarchy had bestowed a taste for ceremony." No doubt this is a metonymy: it is by no means excluded that they were accompanied by their ladies. And yet it nevertheless emerges that theater turns out to be, by right if not in fact, an expressly masculine institution. Since binarity is all-powerful in such circumstances, it will follow without a hitch that the movies, for their part, are described as the form of entertainment in which are found the *others* of sexual selection: it is the theater of non-men. "It was," as Sartre puts it more analytically, "the entertainment of women and children." There, too, the facts are not always in accord with principles. A pianist, soldiers, or an ossified old man can be part of the fun. But it nonetheless remains the case that, in the absolute, the seventh art is destined for those whom reasons of sex and age exclude from the virile caste. "I myself have never been there," declares the sententious M. Simonnot in the interim, "but my wife goes on occasion."

That strict separation of theater and the movies on either side of the line establishing sexual difference renders all the more surprising the reunion occasioned by Sartre's captivity of 1940.

One might already be astonished, as we have just seen, that the movie houses to which Anne-Marie, as long as she was named Sartre and there was no man in her life, was able to accompany her Poulou, those auditoriums whose nontheatrical, unceremonious character (the movies being a down-to-earth show: the kind you and I like) he cherished, should nonetheless evoke *in fine* the Stalag, that is, the episode in Sartre's life concerning which he seems to forget that it was there that he furbished his arms as a playwright, since it was there that he wrote and produced *Bariona*. There is still more.

Les Mots associates the movies with the unaffected sociability of an unmannered public. That is the aspect through which, above all, it is contrasted with the ritual of theater, the ritual, it will be recalled, which had given his late father and his grandfather "a taste for ceremony." In the neighborhood movie houses, on the contrary, what Sartre acquires is a disgust for it: "I grew disgusted with ceremonies," he writes. "I adored crowds." The rest is known ("I have seen all kinds," and so on): it leads back to the Stalag. But every movie house is not suburban. Like this tourism, Sartre's taste for movies is very carefully localized: in the movie houses of the Boulevards where he occasionally strays, the "incongruous ceremonial" of the movies trying to become bourgeois by imitating the ritual of theater irritates him. "I was annoyed," he writes. But there, too, he forgets that there was a time when it was precisely that ceremonial penchant for ritual which motivated his enthusiasm for the theater. One need only refer to his lecture ''Forger of Myths'' (New York, 1946), in which, after evoking his theatrical experience of the Stalag, he draws a lesson from it: "I understood what the theater should be — a great collective religious phenomenon." "Its greatness," he specifies a bit later, "is linked to its social and (in a sense) religious functions: it should remain a rite." It was thus the same experience, that of *Bariona* and the Stalag, which was described in 1946 as the fervent discovery of the ritual nature of being-together and in 1964 as the no-less-fervent rediscovery of its nonritual nature. In one case, rites are needed to to unify the public. In the other, "to separate men."

But the parallel is even more unexpected, the distance between the lost object (in 1917, the Parisian public of the movies) and the rediscovered object (in 1940, the fraternity of the prison camp) even more astonishing if it is envisioned no longer in terms of cultural codes (the theatre versus the movies) but of sexual difference. For even if, in reality, the masculine character of theater did not exclude, as we have seen, the circumstance that gentlemen were escorted by their feminine halves, that division between principle and actuality disappears in the case of theater in the army. Since war remains, in effect, the last institutional refuge of intransigent sexual difference, if not because of the theatrical nature of the event at least because it occurred in a camp of prisoners of war, the performance of *Bariona* should and could have taken place in the absence of any feminine presence. The appearance of a man (M. Mancy) had provoked a disappearance of the crowd, the object of his first loves. In 1940, the disappearance of women provokes its reappearance.

It may all the same be regretted (in passing) that no one has deemed it worthwhile to tell by whom and how, a man among men, the role of Sarah, Bariona's (finally) fertile wife, was played during the premier of that Nativity which was to see Jean-Paul Sartre, more than thirty-five years old, already the author of *La Nausée* and several works that, all the same, cannot be classified as children's literature, give up his belief in Santa Claus.

Before, after. It was Simone de Beauvoir who first noted, as soon as he returned to Paris, the transformations that had occurred in Sartre's political sentiments during his absence. Camp comradeship had elicited from him something that their morganatic concubinage could not: in order to stop being a man alone, a man on his own, all he had needed was for women to depart. His kingdom would have been of this world only after women were no longer part of it. Politics are in gear, linked to an eclipse of the feminine.

What Simone de Beauvoir noted in Sartre was a change, not a variation: he had gone off as Roquentin and come back as the Self-Taught Man. "A man among men," his "antihumanism" had finally yielded, and there he was, ready to write "Existentialism is a humanism" as well as *Qu'est-ce que la littérature?* He had understood that one always writes for someone — whether one wants to or not, whether one wants to know it or not.

I was of the Church, but I am no longer. Even though he never cultivated eternal verities in an official manner, Sartre for a long while had only an indifferent tolerance toward the miseries of his time. There were, as we saw, two paths for whoever would escape existential solitude. The first, which is clerical, consists in renouncing existence and pursuing Beauty, which does not exist. That is the one chosen by Roquentin. The other, chosen by the Self-Taught Man, consists in renouncing solitude — no longer cleansing oneself of the sin of existing, but cleansing what exists of the lonely man's sin, or, in more concrete political terms, liquidating the peccadillo-laden dividends of liberalism. The camp would thus have marked for Sartre what Benda has called the end of the eternal: thereafter, he would no longer want to hear of any kingdom that might not be of this world. That, at least, is what he said. For he, too, thought, like Simone de Beauvoir, that it was not a simple variation. I changed. The war finally opened my eyes.

And yet, as usual, the break is condemned in advance to repetition because it fails to perceive that it repeats what it claims to break with. Seven years earlier, for example, Sartre (who happened to be in Germany) had already concluded his first philosophical essay with a call to what was called at the time the betrayal of the clerics, a call of which there was not a word to which he would not have continued to subscribe, had he remembered it, in 1940 and after. "So long as the "I" remains a structure of absolute consciousness," he wrote in "La Transcendance de l'ego," "phenomenology can still be reproached with being a "refuge-doctrine,' with still drawing a fragment of man outside of the world and thereby distracting attention from true problems." The true problems were thus already in 1933 (the date of the essay's composition) those born in the world: moral and political problems, the anguishes, sufferings, and revolts which give man his weight. For nothing in man escapes the earth's gravity: there is not an anthropological fragment that can be withdrawn from the world's attraction. I have embarked, and there is no refuge. It is no doubt true that when Sartre, in that essay, takes apart the Husserlian concept of the transcendental ego, it is not clear which of the two final entities he prefers. He does indeed campaign in favor of the transcendence of the ego and its anthropological weight, but transcendental consciousness, with its imponderable inexistence, nonetheless elicits from him moments of exaltation, which although more concealed, are perhaps for that reason all the more profound. But that reservation itself does not characterize "La Transcendance de l'ego" exclusively; it might be reformulated and applied in the case of all the texts that followed, from *Qu'est-ce que la littérature?* to *Les Mots*.

It nonetheless remains the case that as of 1933 the atopia of consciousness did not at all imply the extraterritoriality of the subject.

Essay on the Regime of the Chaste

I think, moreover, that had I been married, I would never have written
La Trahison des clercs.

Julien Benda, *Un régulier dans le siècle*

In *Qu'est-ce que la littérature?* in order to sketch the portrait of the committed
writer, Sartre uses as a foil the figure of the cleric. The first reproach he lodges
against the medieval intellectual is, as has been noted, that he addresses only
his peers: he writes only for those who know how to read or, worse yet, for
those who know how to write. In the twelfth century, a sad time for intentionality,
those two functions were but one: whoever wrote, read and vice versa. As for
the second accusation in the indictment, it merely recycles without great original-
ity (and with its seductive simplicity) the central argument of Nizan's *Les Chiens
de garde*. Like Mme. de Cambremer, who, "as she came less and less to believe
in external reality, brought all the more passion to securing a prominent position
within it," the propagandists of the eternal are always quite adept, whatever they
may say, in profiting from the transitory. In addition, a handful of fanatics
chanting that their kingdom is not of this world is in no way offensive to those
trading in the properties of the republic. The perspective of Sirius is not without
interest for those who prefer that nothing move here below. That a cleric is a
reactionary is perfectly normal. The problem begins when Benda claims to be
a left-wing cleric. That rationalizing clown, says Sartre, would not be dangerous
if he didn't make us waste our time. Running off at the mouth is hardly any
better than barking. He may not be a watchdog, but he is nonetheless deserving
of a dunce cap. We don't want to miss a thing of our time.

But the portrait of the cleric popularized by Benda's jeremiads offers too
sweetened an image of the role for us to accept it as valid currency. Nothing is
more debatable, for instance, than the opposition between clerisy and commitment
which it sets up. And yet it is on that basis that Benda rejects the century. On
that basis as well that Sartre, arguing against Benda, launches his anticlerical
campaign. Now the institution of the clerisy — to which was entrusted, amid the
power conflicts racking Christian Europe around the twelfth century, the (su-
premely political) task of defending the hierarchical superiority of the spiritual
over the temporal — may indeed offer one of the most explicit instances of what
can be termed a committed intellectual: a cleric is not a monk. "For a long time,
I took my pen for a sword," Sartre will say at the end of *Les Mots*. But he does
not see that in that, precisely, he was a cleric. For the theory of the two swords
excludes the first from making sentences: the words it traces baptize, excommuni-
cate, or pardon. It is not a matter of effecting one's own salvation, but deciding
on that of others. The clerisy is thus far more than an instance of knowledge,
one of power. No doubt the second sword, although second, remains independent

of the first: the emperor, like the pope, need account only to God. But that is precisely because clerical power substitutes an exemplary causality for an imperative one. The Church does not give orders to the Empire; it gives it an example. The cleric's power can thus be defined, in the strict sense of the term, as an exemplary power. It is the power engendered by an exception.

Moreover, whatever the importance of the political aspects of the betrayal denounced by Benda, it remains secondary — and his novels, particularly *L'Ordination*, as well as his autobiography, show it clearly — in relation to an infinitely more decisive perversion of the modern clerical institution. From book to book, the same refrain traverses his work: he deplores a decadence of the mind's mores resulting in the situation that philosophers today have quite simply installed themselves, as he puts it, "*within* life": they take jobs, marry, have children. Sartre would say: just like you and me. The betrayal of the clerics begins with married priests (what Benda calls the "Judeo-Protestant" heresy). And it is true that in distinguishing themselves from the monks of primitive Christianity, who practiced chastity as a method of individual *askesis*, the cleric was defined historically by the institutional consecration of celibacy. Alongside marriage, which is the sacrament of secular life, celibacy was promulgated as the sacrament of the clerisy, an institution which generates its power through the genetic exception of male individuals removing themselves in exemplary fashion from the commerce of reproduction.

"A part of mankind, devoted to higher things, is not destined to engender," wrote Gerson in the fifteenth century. In the twentieth, a licensed cleric, Troisfontaines, reproached Sartre for frequenting cafés. In his defense, the accused demonstrated that he was no longer a novice: "The anonymous consumers arguing noisily at the next table," Sartre in effect responds, "bother me less than a wife and children who would walk on tiptoe in order not to disturb me." The conditional should be appreciated: he escapes from a noise that does not exist by plunging into an actual racket; he withdraws to the Café Flore (to each his own cell) in order to escape from the wife and children he doesn't have. But if the cleric does not enter a household, it is to ensure not only calm and peace of mind but also the concentration assuring his power and efficiency. His celibacy is militant. Thus it was that Caillois, at the time of the Collège de Sociologie, could contrast the benign image spread by Benda with a more virulent version of the clerisy: "The pleasures he abdicates," he recalls in "Sociologie du clerc," "and the satisfactions he rejects are what confer on the cleric an essential right over those who take their happiness in what he disdains."

These remarks will not seem completely out of place if one recalls the context in which Sartre claims to have broken with the positions that had led him to write *La Nausée*, the context in which he claims to have emerged from his clerical period. A concentration camp is, to be sure, not a monastery. And all those who were united in Stalag XII D were not necessarily single by vocation (like Sartre himself) or by sacrament (like his priest friends). But at the very least they were so de facto, since the army, even when democratized, is constituted as a body only after the prior exclusion of women.

The symbiosis between mother and son, "the unanimous and religious life" of the couple they form, constitutes, according to Sartre, the prototype of being-to-gether. In the shadow of a woman who, at once Anne and Marie, combined in her first names the complete genealogy of generation without division (Anny, the woman he loved, was named Anne-Marie), Poulou, until 1917, was able to enjoy it in the darkness of movie houses. And then the film was over. It was *The Immaculate Conception* with Jean-Baptiste in the role of Daddy: he announces the son of no one, and then withdraws. But nausea was waiting at the exit. "What an uneasiness when the lights went on again." His stepfather, beside whom he decided to feel ugly, was there. We were surprised awhile ago to see Sartre rediscovering in 1940, amidst a group composed exclusively of men, an experience he had known through those crowds of his childhood which he had just characterized as feminine. But the reason is precisely that in the Stalag, he discovered (along with war and a life that was also "unanimous and religious") the Immaculate Conception that he had lost twenty-three years earlier with the obligation to share his mother. "My everyday company," writes Sartre from his camp to Simone de Beauvoir, "is priests. Above all a young vicar and a Jesuit novice, who, moreover, detest each other, are at each other's throat over theological questions relating to Mary, and have me resolve their arguments. I decide. Yesterday I found myself accusing Pope Pius IX of being wrong about the Immaculate Conception." Those clerical discussions are probably not unrelated to the subject of *Bariona*, the play Sartre wrote to celebrate, among men, the Nativity of the child of the miracle.

Politics, according to Clausewitz, is but the prolongation of war through peaceful means. The structure of the speech-act through which Sartrean discourse turns political belongs to the most orthodox clerical tradition. And there are grounds for wondering to what extent Sartre's politics would remain, once peace had returned, indebted to the wartime structure that presided over its elaboration. Maurice, the proletarian of *Les Chemins de la liberté* (who appears in *Le Sursis*), also loves crowds. He is happy, during those days of general mobilization (the week of Munich), to feel himself surrounded by "men standing erect, men without women." At his side there is still Zézette, his wife, who would like to tempt him: they might still be but one, close in on each other, be a couple by themselves. But it no longer works. "He chuckled in the broad daylight, and women were superfluous."

In peacetime it was man. Now it is women. Collaborators as well, it is true, but Sartre is categorical concerning them: collaboration "has a sexual aspect."

It was not for nothing that it recruited so heavily in the homosexual bourgeoisie. But when one is a man, it is enough for war to break out for one no longer to feel alone. With the women gone, one rediscovers one's place, one finds oneself again in one's place. Alone, like a man; but not alone in being alone. Alone and together at the same time, whereas with a woman one is neither one nor the other. Alone in being together because together in being alone. As soon as there is no woman to be shared, fraternal rivalry turns into fraternity. For a man is never alone in being without a woman. He is never superfluous in the absence of a woman. From superfluous man to a man among men: he is a man only by being one among men. And if man is the measure of man, he loses that measure as soon as he agreess to measure himself against a woman. The story called *Les Chemins de la liberté* thus ends in a camp where the first sex takes up winter lodging in the absence of half of heaven. It is the best of endings: they did not marry and did not have any children. For lack of female combatants.

Sartre, once liberated, returned to Paris in March 1941, by then resolved not to miss anything of an age he was committed to making his own. "We almost lost our language abroad," wrote Hölderlin upon returning from France. Sartre, on the contrary, found his in Germany and tried it out as soon as he arrived in Paris. Back in what he had decided to call his country, he makes his first literary act a play: *Les Mouches*, in which he presents his compatriots with the *vaterländische Umkehr* of a young man who, upon returning to the land of his birth after an extraterritorial sojourn, also voices the firm resolve to make of it his city, his country, his homeland. The manner in which he executes that project is not lacking in interest. Upon returning from the Stalag, the author had in fact managed to ascertain that around the aforementioned M. Mancy (who since 1917 found himself in something of the role of Aegisthus to the widowed former Mme. Sartre) the absence of the legitimate heir had been exploited to consolidate the usurpation. "Most of his stepfather's friends collaborated," notes Simone de Beauvoir, "even though he himself was a Gaullist." Sartre would reduce Baudelaire's revolutionary enthusiasm in 1848 to the insurgent's desire to get at General Aupick. There can be no question of interpreting *Les Mouches* as no more than so private and idiotic an act of resistance. But there is no reason, either, to forget the play's contents: it is, in fact, rigorously attuned to the political lesson of the Stalag. Inspired by a hatred of the gynecocracy, Aeschylus' Orestes returned to Argos in order to avenge his father's death. Sartre's was unconcerned with such piety, unworthy of his vocation as an orphan. He quite simply wanted to purge the political powers of anything smacking of women. For there was something rotten in the kingdom of Argos: the *odor di femina* at the helm. After Clytemnestra's execution, the elimination of Electra at the play's end confirms that the fundamental axiom of its politics is misogynistic.

A Winter's Tale

Winter is for prose.

Mallarmé, "Crayonné au théâtre"

The political revelation of the Stalag is also not unrelated to the season in which it occurred. At least if we agree to refer, despite Sartre's oft repeated resistance to them, to the models of Durkheimian rather than Marxian sociology.

From Mauss to Granet and Dumézil, the French school of sociology has, in fact, rarely deprived itself of the pleasure of a bravura description, in the four corners of the earth, of those preferentially hibernal institutions in which men secede in order to ensure a renewal of the social order.

1. It will be recalled, to begin, that *La Nausée*, with the exception of a few days in January, covers the exact duration of a February, the month which — in conformity with the author's narrative slip, which would make of it the month of spring's return — was, in the Roman calendar, the last of the year. It was, that is, the month in which the new, in order to surface, had to expel the old and the forces of creation take priority over the forces of conservation so as to ensure a renewal of time. It was the month of purification (*februatio*), the one in which what was old was cleansed of the sin of having existed. That opposition is represented in Sartre's novel by the hatred that Roquentin, who is young, focuses on the *salauds* — the old bastards. Dumézil made of the great feast of the month, the *februatio* of the Lupercales (15 February), one of the major moments of his *Mitra-Varuna*. In a ceremony he compares to the carnivals of our Mardi Gras, the brotherhood of the Luperques — a society of men comparable to the Germanic *Männerbund*, a brotherhood which intervenes at no other moment of the year — "storms" through the city. The young men composing it do indeed run riot through the streets, striking passing women to impregnate them: February is also the month of the fertilization of the Sabine women. It will be noted that it is the exceptional outburst of an exclusively male brotherhood that allows society to reconstitute itself after a year's wear and tear. The unfettered Luperques *bind*; they bind because they are unfettered.

DEDICATION: *La Nausée* was dedicated "*au castor*," to Simone de Beauvoir. But the beaver was already there. In the pages where he proposes a phonetic analysis of the word serving to designate the month and the ceremony around which it is defined, Dumézil links *februus* to the Latin *fiber*, the Cornish *befer*, and the French *bièvre*, that is, "*castor*," known elsewhere as *beaver*, an animal whose name (according to some early etymologies) would be a function of the fact that when it was in danger, it cut off with its teeth its own genitals, which it knew the other to be after: *castor a castrando*.

2. That Roman ritual is not without analogies to the year-end celebrations, described by Granet, around which archaic Chinese society pivoted. (a) These

are solstice celebrations and are thus linked with darkness (they are frequently referred to as "feasts of the longest night"). For that very reason, they are socially more important than their summertime equivalent: the anguish of short days tightens the social bond. (b) The feasts occur, moreover, during twelve days that the Chinese calendar does not attribute to any month, each of which simultaneously represents one of the twelve months of the calendar. They thus exist in a kind of internal-external zone in temporality, a time which counts the months of the year even as it excepts itself from them, a time valid for the whole of the year of which it is nevertheless only a part. (c) That temporal condensation is accompanied by a social condensation. According to the alternating movement of dissemination (*yin*) and concentration (*yang*), the return of these holidays marks the moment in which a society dispersed in the fields by summer's labors rediscovers itself once again within the confines of the village. Given this material concentration of a large number of individuals in a small portion of social space, the celebrations help produce a self-consciousness of the group present unto itself. Through their mediation, says Granet, "a human group managed to conceive of itself as a permanent and *total* unit." (d) But that totalization, to come about, presupposes a contrary movement of separation. At the same time that the society reassembles on the village territory, the men withdraw into their communalhouse. Each is impossible without the other: the totalization would not have taken place if the men had not withdrawn. Further still: the totalization is produced by the fact of their separation. "Gathered in the communalhouse, the men were intent on offering themselves as a massive counterweight to the powers of dispersion assailing the world in winter: in those forces, philosophers in every age have recognized a feminine nature (*yin*)."

3. The source of this sociological model is to be found in Mauss's *Essai sur les variations saisonnières des sociétés eskimos,* a study which Lucien Febvre has quite properly proposed to treat as the manifesto of the French school of sociology. There, too, everything begins with the winter, which concentrates (after the summer dissemination) the totality of the population under a single roof, that of the communalhouse, which is no longer in this case, as in China, one of men (in contrast to the individual houses of couples) but one of the entirety of the group, men and women together. And there, too, there emerges from the morphological concentration of individuals a kind of sociological self-consciousness: holidays are "not only celebrated there in common, but the feeling that the community has of itself, of its unity, emerges there in all forms." But once again, it is only on the basis of a masculine secession that society (as a collectivity of men and women) is engendered: "All the families of the same station, or at least," Mauss corrects himself, "the entire masculine population, experiences the need to gather in the same spot and live there a common life."

Secerno: to separate, withdraw, reserve. Politics is the reserve of men. Behind the first communalhouse, one common to men and women, there is its secret, the *kashim*, the house for men alone, whose secret society reserves for itself, exclusively, the secret of society. Men are on both sides: within and without, with and without women, inside a collectivity which attains closure only because they withdraw from it, which they totalize through their very secession. Society is born at the moment its men separate from that of women, which otherwise — as Simone de Beauvoir said — would not exist. The social collectivity is generated over the severe crypt from which women are excluded: politics is the sheaf of forces which resist a feminine dissipation of energy.

All other things being equal, moreover, Stalag XII D, the womanless crypt in which Sartre, as a good cleric, discovered that the secret is political, is comparable to those masculine houses, sites of the cohesive secessions of the cold season. Near Trèves, where Marx had been born more than a century before, his discourse joined easily with the most archaic structures of enunciation of political discourse, the very ones that have always allowed the cleric, medieval or not, to base his power on the sacrament of celibacy.

The New-Born

"Whoever among us engenders is guilty," said Bariona to his people. The antinatal policy that the Jewish chieftain asks his men to adopt in order to spare their pride the fiscal humiliations imposed by the Roman occupant is nothing new: it associates guilt and reproduction as intimately as Roquentin's esthetic had. The seniority of the genophobic motif in Sartre's work, the misogynistic tradition already well established in 1940, render all the more surprising the ultimate conversion of this militant for sterility. We had left him at Bethlehem, intent on suppressing with his own hands the bad example who, by being born, had taken the liberty, against his orders, of restoring hope to man. But there he himself realizes, not exactly before the manger but before the hope men feel in its presence, that a child just born may be the Messiah — that is, the future restored to humanity — that a birth can thus escape "the swarming of wood lice and bedbugs" and elicit the sunrise of "the first morning in the world." A birth, on the world's first Christmas, ceases for the first time to mutter the tired refrain of all that vegetates in the repetition of the deficient. It divides the future from the past (before, after), and produces a future which, instead of repeating it, detaches itself and takes off from the past; it constitutes the event which divides and makes the difference between a break and repetition.

This turn is all the more surprising in that it would have no future within Sartre's work. After the return from the Stalag, Orestes kills his mother in order to become a man. But the "roads of freedom" never cross the precincts of paternity. As soon as he rejoins the mixed realities of civilian life, Sartre forgets almost everything of the tender emotions that a harsh winter had momentarily revealed to him in the presence of a cradle. He even goes so far as to try to forget that he wrote a play entitled *Bariona*. Not that his thinking had changed, even for a moment, during his captivity; the play, quite simply, was bad. As if to bring into relief the exceptional character of Bariona's conversion, the composition of the play happened to interrupt that of *L'âge de raison*, the first volume of *Les Chemins de la liberté*, on which Sartre had been working for two years. Mathieu, the novel's protagonist, goes to great extremes in order to arrange an abortion for the mistress in whom he is furious at having forgotten himself. Those preparations, it is true, will in the end be useless, since Marcelle will keep the child. But that melodramatic surprise *in extremis* has nothing to do with the messianic revelation of *Bariona*. After the most grotesque of happy endings, Daniel, the homosexual, in order to punish himself for not having had the courage to do what beavers [*castors*] do, casually proposes marriage to her. The affair does not bode well. This is not the first morning in the world.

It will be noted, nevertheless, that the final conversion to paternity, which distinguishes Bariona from Mathieu, remains quite abstract. It is still excluded, for example — should the child be a male — for two men to coexist beneath the same roof. Men are not co-possible in the vicinity of a woman, and Bariona's paternity does not escape the schema of fraternal rivalry. It's either he or I. And since it is not he, my dear Sarah, I shall forthwith go and kill myself. The best of fathers is always the one who dies so his son can survive. Bariona converts to paternity only at the moment he realizes that there is no father except a dead one.

It nonetheless remains the case that Sartre will have never been closer to a populationist line of discourse than in a discursive context bereft of fertile organisms. I am not speaking for myself, says the cleric, who seeks authority in his vow of chastity to commit the rest of the species to the path of procreation. Grow and multiply: that second person plural authorized Joseph de Maistre to decorate the cleric with an unexpected medal. "There is nothing so fertile," he said, "as the sterility of a priest." Which is to be understood, of course, with the requisite degree of mediation.

"The sight of a pregnant woman, a baby in diapers, a mother nursing repels me," wrote Benda. "I venerate the Cathars, with their anathema on the act of reproduction." One realizes that the pertinence of the ecclesiastical models with which Benda supports his arguments is but approximate. It was thus that Caillois correctly reproached him with minimizing the effects of power accruing to the cleric through his indifference to the world's course. The reference to the Cathars in this case is perhaps even less pertinent to his intentions. The anathema which that heresy pronounced concerning procreation, in fact, has nothing in common in its inspiration with the institution of clerical celibacy in whose support Benda invokes it. For the condemnation of the reproductive act by the Cathars extended to the entirety of the human species. It is thus an anathema which takes no account of the hierarchical context outside of which the distinction between cleric and layman loses its meaning. Rather than being an exceptional vow, sterility is the norm to which humanity as a whole is invited to submit in order to cleanse itself, like a single man, of the sin of existing. For that reason it has nothing to do with what is at stake in the practice of celibacy for the clerisy.

It is with a single self-same stroke, in fact, that the Catholic hierarchy makes of marriage (that is, fertile marriage) the share allotted to the human species and celibacy the duty of those who guide it. The sin of existing, this time, is expiated by procreation (*proles*). In a world in which sterility remains a curse as long as it is not sanctified by chastity, in which virginity is suspect of heresy as long as it has not received the sacrament of an order, the clerisy is constituted as an exemplary enclave in which a creature can without sinning fall short of the imperative of procreation. Further still: reproduction is instituted as a law by the very individuals who cut themselves off from it, and it is that removal which gives it force of law. There can be no question of desecrating chastity by imposing it on the common run of mortals, for on it, in fact, rests the ecclesiastical hierarchy.

Anti-Malthus

> What I like in my madness is that it has protected me, from the very first day, against the illusions of the elite.
>
> Sartre, *Les Mots*

On 17 February ("Saturday," "the afternoon"), Roquentin visits the Bouville Museum. Upon entering the exhibition hall, he notes, almost as an epigraph, a new acquisition entitled for his edification "The Death of the Bachelor." It's not a masterpiece, but the message is clear. Man on his own dies without anyone missing him. Some of these days, nobody will miss you, honey. Roquentin is now able to grasp the theme that gives a measure of unity to the collection of portraits before which he has once again come to meditate: "None of those who were represented had died a bachelor; none had died without children or intestate."

That well-known passage from *La Nausée* is based on a demographic presupposition that would reserve to the elite — of Bouville or elsewhere — the (almost exclusive) privilege of reproduction. One has children in a family, and the family is an invention of the bourgeoisie of the nineteenth century. That demography, it goes without saying, is entirely imaginary: a whole literature is devoted to the conflicts of various orders provoked in the French bourgeoisie by its decision to reproduce itself as little as possible. Contrary to the familialist implications of Bouville's iconography, power belonged above all to men living alone. Most of the political figures of the Third Republic died without children. Zeldin gives a list. It includes Thiers, Ferry, Gambetta, Spuller, Challemel-Lacour, Goblet, Floquet, Waldeck-Rousseau. Etymology is not always sufficient to cause the proletariat to proliferate, but it sustains our doubts that the bourgeoisie might do so in its place.

Moreover, Sartre himself, twenty years after Roquentin's last visit to the Bouville Museum, would abandon that untenable demography. "Les Communistes et la paix" and "Réponse à Claude Lefort" concentrate the heart of their arguments on a critique of the Malthusian practices of the French bourgeoisie. The conclusion of the *Critique de la raison dialectique* would deal, in turn, with the simultaneously economic and demographic Malthusianism through which neo-capitalism manages to serialize its proletariat: "Malthusianism as an economic practice is seriality." At the time of *La Nausée*, the bourgeoisie was the butt of numerous sarcasms because it had children, but in 1953, the fact that the proletariat wasn't having any more was the sign of its *embourgeoisement* or, more exactly, its contamination by bourgeois discouragement. A proletariat faithful to its mission should begin by reproducing itself: now that the bourgeoisie no longer has the courage to endure, the future of man reverts to the workers.

For the bourgeoisie, in fact, it is sterility that is now the norm. Nothing could be more comprehensible, moreover. As the victim of an implacable Oedipal mechanism dilated to the dimensions of a civilization, it does not have a choice: its slightest move unwittingly foments a future which condemns it. It is trapped. No available perspective is encouraging: the *status quo* still remains the best that it can hope for, given the fact that survival entails undertaking the task of supporting its own undertakers.

Before that impasse, the bourgeoisie of the nineteenth century adopted two attitudes:

The first, which is virile and combative, channels whatever remains of energy and a will to live among the most resolute members of the class. It is an aggressive stance, going right to the problem and attacking it: one stands up to the class enemy, finger on the trigger, and every time the proletariat commits an excess, one fires.

The second solution is more subjectively oriented. It might be described, in metapsychological terms, as the brushing back toward its source of the aggressive impulse at work in the preceding one. It is opposed to it, says Sartre, as "the feminine is to the masculine," or as "depression" is to "repression." While their men massacred in the streets the economically superfluous portion of the toiling masses, the ladies of the bourgeoisie, for their own internal use, perfected, with death in their soul, the technology of sterility. Since the future was threatening, was it not best not to think about it? By virtue of not considering it, they would end up forgetting it. Sartre rediscovers the vocabulary of the *Esquisse d'une théorie des émotions*: "Bourgeois sterility," he says, "bears a strong resemblance to behavior intended to fail."

It will be immediately perceived, however, that those two reactions to the proliferation of the proletariat, because they are contemporary, are mutually contradictory. They duplicate each other. One renders the other useless. For in strict logic, a carnage of the others should allow one to dispense with an abortion of oneself. If, on the other hand, it is the bourgeoisie which renounces, of itself, its ambitions concerning the future, one is hard put to see why it persists in massacring workers to whom its retreat has left the field open. The aggressive Malthusianism which, according to Sartre, would define the neo-capitalism specific to the French bourgeoisie of the twentieth century puts things back in their proper place. England and, even more, Germany and Italy would let their proletariat multiply with complete freedom, reserving the option of later starving and massacring it when needed, as during the heroic phases of the Industrial Revolution. More delicately, the French bourgeoisie was intent on not sullying its hands. It donned gloves to do the job. And that is how it proceeded, through an insidiously depressive propaganda campaign (which Sartre calls its analytic propaganda), to sadistically turn against the proletariat the masochistic Malthusianism which had first been a failure-oriented pattern of behavior intended for internal use and which now, projected onto the enemy class, serves as an outwardly acceptable substitute for the massacres of yesteryear. The abortive practices which proletarian proliferation had elicited from a disheartened bourgeoisie are now exported to the proletariat itself, in order to contain it. The worker, for example, will be convinced that it is in his every interest to want to get out of the working class rather than ameliorate it. If numerous children put him in a good position for the conquest of the future, they are, on the other hand, an obstacle to the enjoyment of the present. "Formerly criminal," says Sartre, "our bourgeoisie has become abortionist." It arranges things to prevent the birth of those proletarians whom current taste no longer permits it to massacre in the streets.

Abortion is a first quarter of the bourgeoisie. The question remains how the proletariat allowed itself to be aborted by the bourgeoisie — or *embourgeoisé* by abortion. Those articles were written by Sartre in the course of the personal and international crisis of the years 1953–54. It was the deepest of those he traversed, probably, among other reasons, because the breaks it implied, and first of all Sartre's break with himself, were clearly articulated in the form of a repetition. And Sartre undoubtedly never thought more clearly against himself than in that anti-Malthusian crusade launched for the benefit of the Communist party. The general theme of "Les Communistes et la paix," in fact, is an exoneration of the Party for the very little revolutionary nerve the working class was showing during those cold war years. As for the "Réponse à Claude Lefort," it essentially attacks the spontaneist ideology of its addressee: You maintain that the proletariat is revolutionary in its essence, in its nature, and that it is so independently of the P.C. "But will you also say that its abortive practices are revolutionary?" Sartre hints at the response, which is negative: "One has no more social duties, be they toward one's comrades or toward future generations: this genocide is a refusal of the future." From which it plainly follows, since the future belongs to the proletariat, that the genocide is also a suicide. The essay on Baudelaire had already articulated the cult of sterility and the refusal to subscribe to the primacy of the future. But if it is now the proletariat that settles into the back seat, moves in reverse, and stares at the road disappearing behind it, where indeed might one be heading? Pregnant women must be reminded that they have the future in front of themselves.

The positions taken in the Stalag were to know no further development after *Bariona*. They did, however, have something of a brief afterlife in 1953. Foucault has recently interpreted those demographic techniques centered on birth control in relation to the emergence of a new form of control and biological regulation (a "bio-power") which would have taken the place of the archaic, repressive, and spectacular (exemplary) forms of the right of life and death. It would be indifferent, from this point of view, whether the effects of the power were positive or negative, whether they provoked or prevented a birth: Malthusian technology is not sensitive to the Romantic opposition between life and death. For Sartre, on the contrary, population control is proof that, despite appearances, the old power is still at work: one no longer kills men, but one causes women to have abortions. He regards birth control as a survival of the tortures and executions of the Old Regime: an abortion executes a sentence, being, says Sartre in the *Critique*, "the oppressive exercise of the right of life and death." Whence comes, apparently, a heroic reading of fertility. Every proletarian born is a Cartouche spitting in the hangman's eye. That move joins up with the numerous aspects, in Sartre, taken on by the romanticism of humility. A revolutionary ought to be hungry, according to *Les Mains sales*. But in order to be hungry, one has to be born. To paraphrase Corneille: what would you have had him do against them all? Answer: live!

For the worker is the man of praxis. Let him make children. Nothing better, as Sartre has said. It was having them which condemned the bourgeois. The proletarian will thus make children, who will themselves be had by the iniquitous bourgeois. As for the writer, once again, any plan to stop him will be given up. One does not ask such people for their papers. And no more their family register than their passport or driver's license.

What difference would it have made, moreover, if he had engendered some that he did not have — or even if he had had some that he did not engender?

Kindertotenlieder

What counts in a vase is the void inside.
Sartre, on the band around *L'Etre et le néant*

Sartre claims always to have thought against himself. It may indeed be that behind the theses of "Les Communistes et la paix" there is something of a self-criticism. Not so much concerning his prewar errors in demography: he surely forgot that he had accused of having children the class that no longer produces any. It is not out of the question, on the other hand, to imagine him repenting for having yielded, as recently as in responding to Lefort, to a kind of mellowness or decadent enthusiasm which more than ever, during those years of crisis, he would have liked to escape definitively: The bourgeois is a man alone; to be a worker is to be together. From which it follows that working women, even while forgetting their duties toward their class and the future by undergoing abortions, nevertheless, by dint of the mere fact that they are workers, succeed in giving the character of a "collective practice" to that nonrevolutionary act. It must be condemned because it is suicidal, to be sure. But it will be condemned with the jury's congratulations, because, all the same, it is a "suicide in common."

The tone of "Les Communistes et la paix," whose third section was written a year later, is more severe, harsh, and pessimistic. Proletarian sterility is acknowledged without any esthetic compensation. Sartre corrects himself: there can no more be a a suicidal mode of being-together than a working-class abortion. We should consequently not attempt to see a specifically working-class response to serialization in the Malthusian practices of the contemporary proletariat, but quite simply and to the contrary, alas, a logical consequence of that serialization, which they prolong without offering any resistance to it.

Even as he was campaigning against Malthusianism, Sartre had thus allowed himself to be seduced still again by the beauty of *Kindertotenlieder*. Is there anything more beautiful than a dead child? To the extent that thinking against himself will always have been for him thinking in the direction of politics — resisting the aesthetic temptation — nothing could be more normal than seeing Sartre, in 1953, during the crisis in which he cursed himself for being in literature, do all he possibly could to remove the problematic of the dead child from any aesthetic indulgences and put an end to the romanticism of abortion.

He does so explicitly in the preface written for an album of photographs by Cartier-Bresson, *D'une Chine à l'autre*, in a series of pages stripped of all ambiguity, although — unfortunately for them — not lacking in either beauty or poetry. Unfortunately for them, since that is precisely what he says should not be done. *D'une Chine à l'autre* proposes a fable: "Imagine Barrès in Peking." It will involve the corpse of a child, wrapped in a red cloth and awaiting the morning street cleaners. As well as the poetic associations which — by contrast, contiguity, or similitude — the sight might have inspired in the author of *Du sang, de la volupté et de la mort*. All that, of course, is a story invented by Sartre. But there will subsequently be a consideration of a child's corpse and this time it is not a story. There is no longer any need to imagine Barrès: Sartre saw it, with his own eyes, through a half-opened stable door in Naples. And it is precisely because he saw it that he can no longer say what Barrès would have said in Peking.

Those pages were written in the U.S.S.R., where Sartre was traveling for the first time — in the U.S.S.R., where man, instead of writing pages *à la Barrès* about lives that were not, has chosen that they be and acts in a manner to allow them to last. Sartre does not specify whether he is thinking solely of children who have been born or if he is also including those who have not yet been, but whatever the case, against the gamy exoticism of *fin de siècle* imperialists, he chooses Soviet prose, which has decided that everything necessary must be done to prevent children from dying.

Before the dead Neapolitan child, "the idea does not occur to us," says Sartre, "to evoke the silk shawl or the silken flesh of the beautiful Ts'eu-hi." This is not a denial, as Magritte might have said. Other evocations, however, which Sartre does not attribute to Barrès, are well worth that of Ts'eu-hi. There is, for instance, the "ninety-year-old cardinal who had performed mass the preceding Sunday," with whom the six-month-old baby is compared. And is not the "immense nuptial bed" on which the baby is lying, whatever he says, more or less in the manner of Barrès? But Sartre nonetheless thinks that this is no time for metaphor. "We will limit ouselves to thinking that children must be prevented from dying." The intention is perfectly clear: if it is necessary, for beautiful books to be, that children die, then may books and literatures perish this very day.

Although *Qu'est-ce que la littérature?* did not broach the question, Sartre was probably not wrong. Between heaven and hell, the twelfth century introduced limbo, a border zone for those who would not have known either sin or pardon, those whom (guilty as they were of remaining innocent) no baptismal water would ever cleanse of the sin of existing. Need we refer to Dante's first circle, with which everything begins? to the stillborn children, whose number Montaigne no longer keeps? to Plutarch's letter of consolation, which he forwarded to his wife and which put Bardamu in a frenzy? to Baudelaire, who wanted to call his anthology *Les Limbes*? Scansion and spasmic implosion. One bar for nothing. On the frontispiece, a premature announcement. *Qu'est-ce que la littérature?*: *Libri aut liberi*. Whereupon it rests, leans, is propped and sustained. It profits from the children it doesn't have, fails to produce, and buries. Writing is commited to nothing but the death of a child, the only thing it is absolutely concerned with signing. "For the true dead a child," said Mallarmé, inspired by that of his own. What counts in a vase is the void inside. Literature celebrates those whose first hour it will have prevented: what Malraux calls limbo's mirror.

And that is its defect.

In 1964, after the publication of *Les Mots*, Sartre was interviewed by Jacqueline Piatier, to whom he explained that ten years earlier (at the time he was writing "Les Communistes et la paix," "Réponse à Claude Lefort," and "D'une Chine à l'autre," the period in which he was denouncing the politics and aesthetics of antinatalism), he had almost renounced that work. At the least he regretted having wasted all that time writing. He had wanted to achieve his salvation, but now he knew that literature does not save. He also knew that nothing saves: no salvations, only victories. Let us not sing. Let us change — first ourselves, then the world. "I have changed," he says. "I have served a slow apprenticeship to the real. I have seen children starving to death. In the face of a dying child, *La Nausée* is singularly lacking in weight." He thus discovered literature's defect. He could now weigh it, now know how little it weighed. The book is no longer by Barrès, but by Sartre himself. But ten years after "D'une Chine à l'autre," he repeats the same assessment of relative weight: a book, a dead child. For a dying child no longer falls under the category of literature, but perception: it is reality's lesson. It is what one opens one's eyes to upon awakening; it is that, in fact, which opens the eyes. The germ, birth, or first step of perception. He says he has seen several, without giving place or date. Was it recently, since he published *Les Mots*? Was it at the time it was first projected, precisely ten years before? Was it in Naples, once again? in a Parisian hospital? in South America? It was of starvation that they died, but concerning the child in Naples, Sartre did not list a cause of death. Perhaps he didn't know it. Does one die of hunger in the city of "Nourritures"? In 1964, in the singular as in the plural, death had not yet taken place: it took place before his eyes (before the eyes that it opened up). But he does not say what it did to him; he simply says that he simply saw it. He speaks of it a bit in the manner of Roquentin, once back in his hotel, speaking about the revelation in the park: "I understood; I *saw*." But what did he feel? Did he do anything? call a doctor? curse heaven? accuse imperialism? cry? throw up? or simply assess the relative weight of *La Nausée*? Nor does he say the age of the children. (Is a child that is not born a child that is dying?) In Naples, it was a baby of six months. Certain children die at twelve years. Are there any who don't die? And would *La Nausée* have taken on more weight if it had been an adult? Ten years before (in 1953, once again), the Rosenbergs died in an electric chair. They were not children, but Sartre did not retain his calm for all that. But it was not the same thing: there are two weights, two measures. Starting with what age would *La Nausée* have the requisite weight? What does it weigh today in the face of its author's death? One surmises correctly that with adults, there is less of a risk of making literature, be it by Barrès or by Sartre. The specific weight of their death, in fact, seems easier to determine. And if, in the face of that of children, *La Nausée* does not have the requisite weight, it is perhaps not because literature is not sufficiently grave, but because those ethereal and premature deaths remain forever imponderable. In 1953 (once again), Sartre wrote *Kean*, the story of a child "who died at a young age" and who performed scenes "in order to drink and eat," in the hope of succeeding, one day, in having the requisite weight: "Do you understand that I want to weigh on the world with my true weight?"

A few months before the interview given to Jacqueline Piatier, Sartre had sent to *L'Unità* a long letter in which he intervened in the debates provoked among Communists by the recent Soviet film *L'Enfance d' Ivan*. I recall that ten years earlier, he had denounced (in "Les Communistes et la paix") the Malthusianism of an abortion-prone bourgeoisie, after which (in "D'une Chine à l'autre") he had decided to definitively renounce the secondary esthetic benefits of overly young corpses: a dead child would never again be a poetic event; it was now a political crime. Russia, where Sartre wrote those words, is not as picturesque as Naples or Africa, but at least the children born there have some chance of surviving. That was in 1953. But in 1963, from the land where children don't die, came a film on which Sartre delivered an aesthetic judgment: it is, he said, "one of the most beautiful I have been privileged to see in the course of the last few years."

Sartre wrote that letter because *L'Enfance d'Ivan* had been used by the left-wing press to accuse its director, Tarkovski, of being a petit bourgeois. I have not seen the film. But Sartre's letter, reprinted at the end of *Situations* VII, gives the main lines of its scenario: Caught up in the violence of the Second World War, a Russian child dies, killed by the Nazis. The Soviets have entered Berlin. An officer searches in the archives and comes upon the photo af an adolescent, who has been hanged: Ivan. A petit bourgeois film? That bitterly false note amid the optimism of victory was decidedly not good for the health of the proletariat. Instead of dreaming of the future that Ivan would not have had, the general line, on the artistic front, required comrades to think of the future we *would* have. Moreover, what did Tarkovski want to prove? Was it the Party's fault if the Nazis executed children? Sartre, evidently, did not accuse the Party, or even communism. But he thought that communism should and could not contribute to forgetting Ivan: "Amidst the joy of a nation that paid severely for the right to pursue the construction of socialism, there is — among so many others — this black hole, an irremediable pin prick: the death of a child amid hatred and despair."

Is *L'Enfance d'Ivan* a Barrèsian film? It is, at the least, a beautiful one, which recalls that children die, at the heart of socialism, without any more reason than anywhere else. That there are, despite everything, despite politics and the direction of history, existential black holes. Sartre thus reaffirms through his references to it, against the theses of 1953, the absolute irredentism of the dead child. Nothing, he says, not even the socialism of the future, will "redeem" that death. That thorn in communism's flesh does not allow of resorption. It is, he says again, "radical Evil amid Good," that Evil of which "Portrait de l'aventurier" had said that "it should not be eliminated, but preserved within the Good." "Those dead of anguish, of hunger, and of exhaustion and those vanquished by arms are gaps in our knowledge," Sartre explained during the same period in a discussion of Kierkegaard. Successes are relative, because they can be explained, but the unredeemed loss of failure, because it eludes knowledge, is the only existential absolute.

Before a child dying, *La Nausée* may not have the requisite weight. But a few months earlier, Sartre had said that socialism didn't either. His rapprochement with the Soviet Union stemmed from a desire to escape the charms of *Kindertoten- lieder*, to construct a space from which the temptation of the dead child might be exorcised. But it was from the heart of that country where it was no longer to be that it resurfaced on the screen with *L'Enfance d'Ivan*. Ivan was twelve years old — the age at which one learns that existence is not a pretty sight; at which one discovers one's own ugliness and violence; at which one hears, for the first time, "Some of these days, you'll miss me, honey," which, to be sure, does not have the requisite weight, either.

To prevent a child from being born, Sartre told Lefort, is genocide. But he immediately added: such genocide is simultaneously a suicide. It might be seen, by following in detail *Les Mots* (which Sartre wrote between 1953 and 1963, between "D'une Chine à l'autre" and "A propos de *L'Enfance d'Ivan*") to what extent the motif of the dead child, which is omnipresent in the autobiography, becomes narcissistic, an identificatory motif in which the author laments over his own absence. The murder of the father unravels amidst the dualist impasses of the murder of a peer. Mine died "at a young age," says the author, but if I had let him grow up, he would have crushed me. In addition, Uncle Emile ("he intrigues me: I know that he stayed a bachelor") died because of his own, the terrible Charles, whose voracity, happily, stopped at the first generation: Poulou (already intuiting the charms of "Some of These Days" in English?) knew what he was doing when he stuffed his ears as Anne-Marie sang *Der Erlkönig* in French. But soon it was literature in its entirety which was sounding the melody of infanticide: "Brutus kills his son, and that's also what Mateo Falcone does." Later would come, "prematurely taken away," the fragile Bénard, whose death would engender Nizan. In that slaughter, the place of honor goes to Poulou. However relentlessly he might proceed, Sartre does not manage to kill him: the imaginary child was dead from the beginning. *Les Mots* is a suicide. *L'Enfance d'Ivan*, Sartre explains, ought to be seen as the death of its author: "A child dies. And it's almost a happy ending, given the fact that he could not survive. In a certain sense, I think that the author, this very young man, wanted to speak of himself and his generation. Not that those proud and austere pioneers died (quite to the contrary!), but their childhood was shattered by the war and its consequences." A child dies. And that child is its author. He is the author of a dead child. He has a dead child as an author. What is a great writer? Sartre had already asked in his preface to *Le Traître*. The answer is the same: Pascal, Racine, or Saint-Simon, every classic author, is "a deceased child who prefers himself to everything else." The author of *Le Traître*, he explains, is not classic: if he didn't die, it is because he has not yet been born. Which is not the case for the author of *Les Mots*, but he, after all, is a great writer. Rest assured, he says, that I would have been quite beautiful had I not existed. All children are mirrors of death, because life has not sullied them. If, according to Mallarmé, the only real dead are children, it is because the only real children are dead. From Sartre to Tarkovski, that is what those who have chosen not to eliminate, but to preserve, Beauty in the Good, kill themselves saying.

Less even than that between the cocoon and the butterfly is the transition from the child to the man continuous. A man is never a child who grows up: children do not grow up. He is a child who has been killed. The silent world is our only country. He would not have been a child if he had survived.

In *L'Age de raison*, Marcelle ends up not having an abortion. Abortion is, in fact, but the anecdotal metaphor for a far more ample and fundamental motif, an infinitely more pregnant motif, in Sartre's work. We are living in an era of impossible revolutions: it is thus a sign of the times. *Time is out of joint.* "They have us die," said Nizan, "before we are even born." Before, after. It is too early to be born and too late to die. The precipitousness of the future robs us of the present. It was to be. We awaited it. But it didn't come. We are left lamenting over the memories we will not have had. Mathieu has just learned that Marcelle is pregnant. For his own future, it is a harsh blow: it had to happen just when he decided to be a man. He withdraws to consider the situation in the local public garden, the Jardin du Luxembourg, since we are not in Bouville, and meditates, in a state of prostration, on the contingencies of the world. He recalls his distant childhood, the day on which "he had said to himself: 'I will be free.'" The principal clause is in the past perfect, followed by a future in quotation marks. It comes back to him again a few days later before another congealed future, Lola's (false) corpse: what remains of our dreams? And he thinks, once again, of the day on which "he had said: I will be free.'"

What Marcelle awaits, she will have: the child will be born. But man's future is not the same as woman's: the latter is already present; the former will never be. In the following volume, *Le Sursis*, Mathieu has not advanced a single step. He was preparing for peace, and it was war that was approaching. Carried away by the general mobilization, he engages in some paradoxical conjugations: "I had a peaceful future," he thinks. And he lowers his eyes. "Now that future is there, at my feet, dead." Such is, in effect, the virile future: it dies at birth; presence is fatal to it. A dead child, a dead future: two futures that will never have been present, both dead before having seen the day, past before having been present, past without ever having been present.

"We want the writer to hold his era in tight embrace." "We do not want to miss anything of our time." "We do not want to look at our world with future eyes." "We write for our contemporaries." The "Présentation des *Temps modernes*" repeats it in every key: Sartre has chosen the present. Things, however, grow complicated as soon as he defines that present: "An era, like a man," he says, "is first of all a future." He comes back to this point in "Ecrire pour son époque": Every age, when it was alive, "was a perpetual movement of going beyond its limits toward a future that was *its* future and that died with it." *Emile* and *Les Lettres persanes*, for example, "sketched out a future; and if it is true that that future never became a present, it at least remains the case that in order to decipher them, one has to return to them *by way of* that future." Things get complicated, we see, because the present that Sartre chooses in preference to the future is at the same time defined in terms of its future, a future, he specifies, that has never been a present and will never be one because it dies with its present. The future thus never survives the present which it begets — and presents. The analyses of temporality in *L'Etre et le néant* had already defined the future as "what does not allow itself to be joined up with." The Sartrean future, that through which an era presents, produces, and introduces itself, thus turns out to be simultaneously that which will never be and will never have been a present.

At the end of *La Nausée*, Roquentin decides to write a novel that would have his life as its subject. He thinks of it in the conditional tense, a conditional that would have the value of a future perfect. There would indeed come a moment, he thinks, when the book would be finished. That is when "I would succeed — in the past, only in the past — in accepting myself." The difference between the novel Roquentin is writing and the novel he dreams of writing is but a difference in tense. In the first, he writes what he is; in the other one, he will write what he will have been. Subsequently, Sartre would frequently criticize the illusion of retrospection: "We do not want to look at our time with future eyes." And yet, if the future perfect must be condemned, it is not so much because it kills the present by making of it a past future, but more fundamentally because it authorizes the belief that the future is a present future. Tomorrow rain will fall on Bouville. The day after tomorrow, consequently, rain will have fallen on Bouville. But the Sartrean definition of the future excludes precisely the case that it might ever be transformed into a future perfect. Or, more exactly, the transformation of a future into a future perfect always implies the simultaneous transformation of an affirmative proposition into a negative proposition: what today will be, tomorrow will not have been. The future of *Les Lettres persanes* died along with the book, without ever having been present. When a present passes and becomes a former present, the future that it contained, instead of taking its place as the new present, is also called off: it is no more than a former future, the memory of a hope. The future is thus the unrealizable co-present of a present that it will not survive, which it accompanies without ever rejoining. "A blocked future," Sartre had told Faulkner, "is still a future." Rigorously speaking, it is even the only future there is. The marriage of the future with the present is in no way for today. It was to be for tomorrow. That is why, relative in his successes, man is absolute only through his failures, according to the lesson learned from Kierkegaard, the ex-future husband of Regina.

Chapter 10
Silence: An Angel Passes

> There's somebody missing here; it's Sartre.
>
> Sartre, *Les Mots*

On two occasions in the course of *La Nausée*, Roquentin has "Some of These Days," the ragtime song of lost steps, played for him. The first time is on 2 February, just after missing the proprietress of the Rendez-vous des cheminots. But the second time, the situation is reversed. It is on 29 February, his last day in Bouville. His trunks have been shipped off, and before going to the station, he passes by the café to announce his departure to the proprietress, who, for a change, has not gone out. "I am coming to say farewell to you," he tells her. "You will be missed, Monsieur Antoine." As the song had said: You'll miss me. To each his turn: the first time, it's me; the second, you. Since you're dropping me, I'm leaving you. So long, I'm going. "I'll miss you, Tony."

A change of scene — and of books. We leave the novel for the autobiography. Rue le Goff, about 1910. We are at the Institute for Modern Languages, the pedagogical institution founded by the author's grandfather, which he directs in collaboration with his associate, M. Simonnot. The party is at its height when suddenly, amid the disorder of conversations, Karl's voice thunders: "There is somebody missing here; it's Simonnot."

Les Mots connects that exclamation with an experience of jealousy described by the author as knowing no limits.

What exorbitant privilege authorizes the self-sufficient M. Simonnot to be missing, to be missing "here", that is, to be present where he is not, by virtue of an absence infinitely more present than any presence, being present not in spite of his absence, but precisely thanks to and through it?

The diminutive Poulou, an only child, an orphan spoiled by the absence of a father he does not miss, the object of attention on all sides, to whom his mother and grandfather outvie each other in repeating that he is, the little darling, their sole reason for living, the final and at long last revealed cause of their existence, little Poulou had played the monkey in vain at the party: a single unfortunate phrase, uttered by his grandfather, has just dethroned him. M. Simonnot weighs more in his absence than he himself will ever succeed in weighing in his presence. An unimaginable — real — absence has just surfaced: before it, he feels brutally excessive, supernumerary, superfluous. "Emptiness had just cut into that packed room like a knife": the absence is a column, its emptiness a blade; its nothingness has the pure hardness of a diamond. To evoke it, *Les Mots* makes use of the vocabulary to which *La Nausée* had resorted for listening to "Some of These Days."

The hour of the fundamental choice has come. Sartre has received his vocation, his mandate: *Anch'io son mancante.* You won't lose anything by waiting. I, too, will end up cleansing myself of the sin of being present. And then you'll see who's missing the most. "Some of these days, you'll miss me, guys." Or at least such is the decision concluding the story: "I wanted to be missed," says Sartre, "like water, bread, or air, by everybody else in every other place." He who wanted to miss nothing of his time had in effect begun by wanting to be missed by it.

The first daydreams he mentions after that crucial party show that he was not long in discovering the true path. Their infallible weave seems to be constituted by what might be called, after Pirandello, a tragic version of characters in search of an author. A few female creations, moving in their weakness, are each time reduced to the most anguishing extremities. Their life, however, is not in danger; it was simply a matter of frightening them. The all-powerful *metteur en scène* of such tribulations, in fact, has but one wish: to obtain at the last minute from his desperate creations the redemptive cry "There's somebody missing here; it's Sartre!" One should imagine Julien Sorel in his prison cell shouting "Stendhal, Stendhal, why have you forsaken me?"

The second step in the conquest of absence obeys a less childish scenario. Sartre, still the author, but this time by identification, no longer plays the role of hidden god. And it is no longer his creations, but his clients, his readers, whom he now asks to name him to the order of the missing. It will be recalled in this context that *Qu'est-ce que la littérature?* defines the public as a "passive, female expectation" whom the writer must fulfill with his absence. One fine day, then, an etching comes into his hands: the famous British novelist Dickens (his future colleague) is expected in New York. The ship has not yet arrived, but already the docks have been invaded by a dense and impatient crowd. Overwhelmed by the spectacle of that human mass assembled by an absence, Sartre sighs what will become the scene's caption: "'There's somebody missing here; it's Dickens!' and tears came to my eyes."

What counts in a vase is the void inside. Thus did Sartre commit himself, in writing, to be missed. Like the little girl who turned around to see what things were like when she wasn't looking at them, he wrote to see what his absence would do to us. And now that the ablative absolute has him speaking in an offscreen voice, perhaps the moment has come, without counting ourselves among his creations, to say what he always wanted to make us say: there's somebody missing here; it's Sartre. Which, since 15 April of last year, is no longer quite a quotation. He finally succeeded in depriving us of himself.

Index

Index

Denis Hollier is professor of French at the University of California, Berkeley. Among his books are *Panorama des Sciences Humaines; La prise de la Concorde: Essais sur Georges Bataille*; and *Le College de Sociologie* (forthcoming in translation from Minnesota). His articles regularly appear in *Raritan, Representations, Enclitic,* and *October.*

Jeffrey Mehlman, an associate professor of French at Boston University, is the author of *A Structural Study of Autobiography: Proust, Leiris, Sartre, Lévi-Strauss; Revolution and Repetition; Cataract: A Study in Diderot;* and *Legacies: Of Anti-Semitism in France* (Minnesota, 1983). His most recent translation is *The Affair: The Case of Alfred Dreyfus* by Jean-Denis Bredin.

Jean-François Lyotard is professor of philosophy at the University of Paris at Vincennes. Best known for his studies of aesthetics and the psychopolitical dimensions of discourse, he is the author of eleven books, including *The Postmodern Condition* (1984) and *Just Gaming* (1985), both from Minnesota.